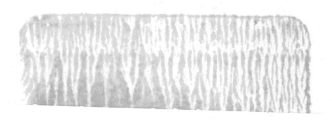

RAINER MARIA RILKE
NEW POEMS

Rainer Maria Rilke
NEW POEMS

*The German Text, with a
Translation, Introduction, and Notes
by*
J.B. LEISHMAN

1964
THE HOGARTH PRESS
LONDON

Published by
The Hogarth Press Ltd
42 William IV Street
London WC2

*

Clarke, Irwin and Co. Ltd
Toronto

Printed in Great Britain by
Robert Cunningham & Sons Ltd
Alva, Scotland

To The Memory of
PAUL OBERMÜLLER
29 June 1899 - 17 August 1961

CONTENTS

vii

CONTENTS

viii

CONTENTS

NEW POEMS: SECOND PART

CONTENTS

CONTENTS

xi

CONTENTS

PREFACE

WHEN I published in 1960 *Selected Works: Volume II, Poetry*, I
believed that, except for revisions of earlier work, my long task
as a translator of Rilke was over. However, during the summer
of that year my German friends insisted that there still remained
something which I ought not to leave undone, namely, a complete translation of the *Neue Gedichte*, Rilke's most generally
accessible, most various, and perhaps not least wonderful
achievement, of which rather less than half the contents (85
poems out of 189) had been included in the volume I have mentioned. I therefore addressed myself to this task without delay.

After some hesitation, I decided to give both the dates of
composition and the, for the most part, very brief occasional
notes at the foot of each poem. Not only is it inconvenient to
turn to notes at the end of a book; few readers make a point of
looking to see whether there is a note on the poem they have
just read, or are just going to read, and with several of these
poems they might easily, for want of so doing, begin, and even
end, on a completely wrong track, or miss the point of some
allusion which, had they recognised it, would have increased
their understanding and enjoyment.

For the many quotations from Rilke's letters in my Introduction I have given the dates and the names of the recipients, but
not, except in certain special cases, page references to particular
editions. There are now, in addition to several complete correspondences, no less than three chronologically arranged collections of Rilke's letters: a six-volume edition published between
1929 and 1937 and a five-volume edition published between
1939 and 1940, both (though no more than selections) described
by the publishers as *Gesammelte Briefe* (Collected Letters), and
a two-volume edition published in 1950, which, though not so
described by the publishers, is now commonly referred to as
Ausgewählte Briefe (Selected Letters). Readers, therefore, who
wish to consult the originals from which I have quoted may
turn first to whichever collection they happen to possess.

PREFACE

I have dedicated this book to the memory of my dear friend Paul Obermüller, of Heidelberg, who died suddenly and unexpectedly a few weeks after our last meeting in the summer of 1961. Owner of what was probably the finest private collection of Rilkiana in the world, he was tireless, despite exacting professional duties, in assisting all students of the poet who consulted him. We had been intimate friends for more than thirty years, and he had encouraged and helped me in my work from the beginning. Any enquiry of mine would bring a letter, often of several pages, almost by return of post – a letter which he had probably risen an hour earlier in the morning in order to write. Did I, did others, tend to accept the selfless devotion of this most generous man too much as a matter of course? We know now that we shall never experience anything like it again. It was at his house, nearly thirty years ago, that I first met our mutual friend Ernst Zinn, whom I have so often had occasion to thank, and whom I here thank yet again: this time, for the hours during which, last summer in Tübingen, he went through with me all passages in the *Neue Gedichte* which he had noted as difficult. But, on this occasion, my chief indebtedness has been to Dr George Hill, proprietor of the firm of Bruno Cassirer, who read through the whole of my translation in typescript and spent many evenings with me discussing passages which seemed to him either inadequate or simply wrong. To his exceptional taste, judgment, and linguistic sense I have owned more than I can say. My old friends Dr Werner von Matthey and his wife, with whom I usually spend part of my summers, were often consulted and always with profit, and Professor Eudo Mason of Edinburgh has often made me wish that we did not live so far apart.

J. B. L.

Oxford, December 1962

INTRODUCTION

I

THE two parts of Rilke's *Neue Gedichte* (New Poems) were published in December 1907 and August 1908. The first was originally entitled *Neue Gedichte* and the second *Der Neuen Gedichte anderer Teil* (New Poems: Second Part); since, however, the two parts form a single whole, it is now legitimate to refer to the first volume, despite its original title, as the First Part of *New Poems*. The earliest poem in the First Part, the famous *Panther*, was written not later than 1903 and perhaps as early as 1902, shortly after Rilke's first arrival in Paris; all the poems in the Second Part were written between the end of July 1907 and the middle of August 1908; and most of the poems in both Parts were written in Paris. Rilke had come there with a commission from a German publisher to write a book on Rodin, whom he got to know well, for whom he had a boundless admiration, and under whose influence he deliberately tried to put behind him his earlier 'romantic', or neo-romantic, way of experiencing and of writing and to achieve something altogether more objective and workmanlike. How could he find some means of practising that precept which Rodin kept on repeating, *Il faut toujours travailler*? Would it be possible to introduce into his own art of poetry, or to discover there, something corresponding to that practical and manual element he so envied in the plastic and visual arts, something that would enable him to exercise his creative gift continuously and almost as a matter of course, without waiting for 'inspiration'? There is a story that one day Rilke was trying to explain his problems and difficulties to Rodin, and that Rodin said to him: 'Why don't you just go and look at something—for example, at an animal in the Jardin des Plantes, and keep on looking at it till you're able to make a poem of it?'; that Rilke took this advice, and that the result was *The Panther*. *The Panther* was certainly the earliest of *New Poems*, and Rilke always regarded it as a kind of standard. Its concentration, the continuity of its movement, the absolute subordination of the parts to the whole, so that, one might almost say, no line or phrase has any independent significance, or would be worth quoting out of its context—this is characteristic of all the best of *New Poems*, several of which compose a single complex sentence.

The Austrian novelist Robert Musil, in an address delivered early in 1927,[1] a few weeks after Rilke's death, declared that his significance in the history of German literature could best be described by saying that it was he who first brought the German short poem to perfection. Goethe, despite his wonderful genius and wonderful achievement, had written a lot of trivial and occasional verse, and had often been content to fill out poems containing a few magnificent lines or stanzas with very inferior material; and most of the (in Musil's opinion) insignificantly small German lyric poets since Goethe, poets whom, as he said, literary history preserved with the impartiality of a stamp-collector, would seem to have regarded Goethe's too frequent easy-goingness as a precedent and justification for their own undistinguished loquacity. It was not, he declared, until the end of the nineteenth century that the Germans learnt once again, from the example of foreign poets, what a poem was. Here, despite his not unjustified contempt for literary historians, Musil displayed some ignorance of literary history, for, in addition to the names of Verlaine and Baudelaire, he mentioned those of Poe and Whitman, from whom Rilke learnt, and could have learnt, nothing; he omitted the names of many other French poets—Mallarmé, Francis Jammes, Maeterlinck, Verhaeren, to name but a few—whom, although it may be hard to say exactly what he 'learnt' from them, Rilke admired; and he failed to give due credit to Stefan George and Hofmannsthal, as well as to Rilke, for their part in this rejuvenation of the German shorter poem.[2]

New Poems, then, were new for Rilke himself (*i.e.*, unlike what he had written before), new, in Musil's sense, for German

---

[1] Reprinted in *Tagebücher, Aphorismen, Essays und Reden*, 1955, pp. 885ff.

[2] For a similar criticism of Musil, whom he quotes with approval, see J. R. von Salis's Introduction to *Rilkes Leben und Werk im Bild*, Insel-Verlag, 1956, p. 18.

poetry, and also, I would add, despite the lessons in form, elegance, and concentration which Rilke had learnt from various modern French poets and also, perhaps, from the early poems of Stefan George,[1] new for European poetry. But, although he wrote the first of them, *The Panther*, in 1902 or 1903, it was not until 1906 that he began to write these new kinds of poem continuously and systematically. He compiled a list of more than a hundred titles, or subjects, for poems, and, as he completed each prescribed poem, he drew a line through the listed title and appended a date. He seemed to have found a recipe for continuous 'work', 'making', as distinct from intermittent rhapsodising (of which, for a time, he was inclined to look back upon his *Book of Hours* as an example); and, as he paced to and from the indispensable lectern in his Paris room, he no doubt felt that he had at last found a kind of 'work' no longer so desolatingly different from that which Rodin pursued in his studio. 'It's a *book*,' he wrote on 9 August 1907 to his wife, who had been looking through his manuscript of the First Part before transmitting it for him to the publisher: '*Work*, the transition from inspiration that comes to that which is summoned and seized.' And on 18 August 1908 he wrote to his publisher, Anton Kippenberg, to whom he had sent the manuscript of the Second Part the day before:

> As I arranged the poems, I had the impression that the new volume could very suitably keep company with the earlier one: the course is almost parallel – only, it seems to me, somewhat higher and at a greater depth and with more distance. If a third volume is to join these two, a similar intensification will still have to be achieved in that ever more objective mastering of reality, out of which emerges, quite spontaneously, the wider significance and clearer validity of all things.[2]

No doubt some of the shorter and (by Rilke himself) uncollected poems written during the next year or two, as well, perhaps, as some which had been written earlier, were originally

---

[1] On this subject, see an important article by Professor Eudo C. Mason, 'Rilke und Stefan George', in *Gestaltung und Umgestaltung: Festschrift zum 75. Geburtstag von Hermann August Korff*, Leipzig, 1957, pp. 249ff.

[2] *Briefe an seinen Verleger*, 1934, pp. 39-40; 1949, Bd. I, p. 47.

3

intended for a Third Part of *New Poems*[1]; however, this eternal beginner soon became dissatisfied with the prospect of repeating himself and of continuing, even 'at a greater depth and with more distance', this particular kind of 'mastering of reality'.[2] In the same letter Rilke also told Kippenberg that for a moment he had thought of entitling the Second Part, after one of the poems it contained, *The Pink Hydrangea*, and changing the title of the earlier volume to that of the companion poem, there included, *The Blue Hydrangea*. He fortunately decided not to proceed with this idea (what a present it would have been to the philistines!), on the ground that no one would believe that it had occurred to him as spontaneously as it actually had done.

Every poem has a title, and nearly every poem is the record of something either intensely seen or intensely visualised. We sometimes encounter difficulties arising from grammar or syntax (which 'which' is which?), or from very concentrated, or elliptical, or, occasionally, too idiosyncratic expression, but we almost never have to ask what any poem, as a whole, is *about*. The poems are indeed re-creations, not just objective or naturalistic descriptions, but the starting-point of almost every one of them is something that has (or had) a particular individual existence outside the poet, however much it may also have become something within him: a scene or incident from classical legend or the Bible; a representative figure from some period of

---

[1] A translation of all the surviving uncollected poems which Rilke wrote from 1906 onwards will be found in *Poems 1906 to 1926*, Hogarth Press, 1959. The letter to his wife of 9 August 1907, quoted above, reveals that the poem *Marionette Theatre* (*op. cit.*, p. 88) was in the original manuscript of the First Part, for he told her that when he got the proofs he might decide to replace not only, as he did, that poem, but also the exquisite *Gazelle*, which he wisely retained, 'by other less questionable things' (*weniger anzuzweifelnde Sachen*). Three poems written in 1909, of which translations will be found in *Poems 1906 to 1926*, namely, *Prayer for the Idiots and Convicts* (p. 109), *Urban Summer Night* (p. 109), and *Endymion* (p. 111), were unjustifiably included by the editor, F. A. Hünich, in the Second Part of *New Poems* in the 1927 collected edition of Rilke's works; and in Walter Ritzer's *Rilke Bibliographie*, 1951, p. 32, it is erroneously stated that these three poems had been added in the Second Impression of the Second Part of *New Poems*, 1913.

[2] Why Rilke did not continue to write in the manner of *New Poems* and the nature of his 'new beginning' is discussed in the Introduction to *Poems 1906 to 1926*, pp. 15-45.

European history or from modern life; a painting, a piece of sculpture, a building; a landscape or garden or street-scene; an animal or a flower. When Rilke came to arrange the poems for publication he adopted a roughly chronological sequence of subjects. The first poem in the First Part is entitled *Early Apollo* and the first in the Second Part *Archaic Torso of Apollo*, and in each Part there is something like an historical panorama of what to Rilke seemed most striking or significant in human civilisation and achievement: evocations of early Greek antiquity are followed by scenes and incidents from the Old and New Testaments, and from these we proceed through the Middle Ages, the Renaissance, and the so-called 'Baroque' until we reach the modern world, which provides subjects for the majority of poems in each Part. This 'historical' procession is often interrupted by various evocations of landscapes, animals, and flowers, and by occasional presentations of more or less timeless human situations and predicaments; and, although each Part begins with a more or less consistently chronological progress through the centuries, when Rilke has once reached modern times he does not entirely remain there, but often evokes scenes and incidents from earlier periods.

Many years ago, in a stimulating and perceptive essay on *New Poems*, Sir Maurice Bowra suggested that the poetic ideal which Rilke was there trying to realise might be regarded as an attempt to reconcile two views of poetry, that of the Romantics, with their eager quest for sensations and their belief in the uniqueness of the poet's calling, and that of Mallarmé and, to some extent, of the Parnassians, for whom the ideal poem was something absolute in itself and free from anything that might be called the private tastes of its maker.[1] This was well said, although it should perhaps be regarded rather as a description of what Rilke has actually achieved in these poems than as an attempt to infer what he was consciously trying to do; for, except in the most general terms, it is impossible to demonstrate what he actually learnt from the example of other poets, or even to distinguish with any confidence between what he learnt from modern poets and what he learnt from Rodin (not only from

---

[1] 'The *Neue Gedichte*', in *Rainer Maria Rilke: Aspects of his Mind and Poetry*, edited by William Rose and G. Craig Houston, 1938.

Rodin's works, but from all the things he tried to look at with Rodin's eyes) and, later, from Cézanne.[1] The important question, perhaps, a question that can be answered with some approach to certainty, is, what did he learn from France, or, more specifically, from Paris? Rudolf Kassner once remarked that Rilke, despite all his foreign preferences, remained an essentially German poet, and that the only un-German thing about him was his unbourgeoisness. In how many even of the best nineteenth-century German poets there sounds what Matthew Arnold used to call 'a note of provinciality'!–a certain smugness and cosiness, a certain amiable garrulity, a certain inartistic self-indulgence. Whereas, from Baudelaire and Flaubert onwards, how many great French poets, writers, and painters seem to be engaged in a common crusade against the bourgeois and all his values, and to be trying to realise in their work a kind and degree of perfection which they perhaps expect only a few fellow-craftsmen and a few lay brands plucked from the burning to appreciate or understand! Among the many French writers whom Rilke came to know during his intermittent, though often prolonged, residences in Paris between 1902 and 1914 was André Gide. Gide, who had at least a fair knowledge of German, was greatly impressed by Rilke's remarkable prose work, *The Note-Book of Malte Laurids Brigge*, which he read immediately after its publication in 1910. He communicated his enthusiasm to his friend Madame Mayrisch-Saint Hubert, the wife of a wealthy Luxembourg industrialist and a very cultivated woman, famous for her hospitality to writers and artists of all nations, and with her assistance he translated some portions of *Malte*, which, together with an article by Madame Mayrisch on Rilke

[1] Contrary to what is commonly asserted and supposed, only a tiny handful of *New Poems* were demonstrably inspired by particular works of art. There is only one poem, *The Poet's Death* (p. 73), which seems definitely indebted to a work of Rodin's, and there is not one that can be convincingly related to any single painting of Cézanne's. Many confident identifications have proved to be quite illusory, and more than once I have found myself trying to recall a painting which I believed I had seen somewhere, but which I was finally compelled to recognise as a painting which Rilke had led me to imagine. He has many painterly poems, but they were not inspired by particular paintings. As the result of much looking at paintings he had come to look at things in a painterly way.

and his book, were published in the *Nouvelle Revue Française* in July 1911. This was Rilke's first introduction to the French intellectual public. At the beginning of their collaboration Gide had written to Madame Mayrisch (14 January 1911) *N'est ce pas que par ce dernier livre Rilke prend place près de nous?*,[1] and there is abundant evidence[2] that from then onwards Rilke, at any rate as the author of *Malte* (of which a complete and beautiful translation was published by Maurice Betz in 1926), has increasingly remained for many French readers and writers *près de nous*. *Malte* is indeed full of evocations of Paris and could, as Rilke himself acknowledged, have been written nowhere else; nevertheless, the full depth of his indebtedness to French culture is apparent only in *New Poems*, of which the Second Part was so appropriately dedicated *A mon grand Ami Auguste Rodin*. Mr H. W. Belmore, in the most thorough and illuminating study of Rilke's specifically poetic achievement (as distinct from his ideas, 'philsophy', 'religion', etc.) that has yet appeared, has remarked that what French culture gave him was a certain taste and assurance which, with all his virtuosity, he had previously lacked, and that what he learnt from Baudelaire and other French poets was not any particular manner or device, but simply the possibility and desirability of achieving in every poem a certain precision and elegance. Elegance Mr Belmore defines as a conscious will to perfection of style and a real or apparent ease in attaining it, and he justly observes that what distinguishes *New Poems* from almost all other collections of German poetry is their astonishing consistency of achievement, and that 'two qualities come together in these poems that seem to exclude each other, intensity (*Innerlichkeit*) and elegance of form, a synthesis almost unique in German lyrical poetry'.[3] Elegance and *Innerlichkeit*; yes, these poems may be regarded as one of the most remarkable examples of Franco-German co-operation that the world has yet seen.

In the already quoted letter to Kippenberg we have heard

---

[1] *Rainer Maria Rilke-André Gide: Correspondance*, Paris (Cornea), 1952, p. 53.

[2] For example: *Reconnaissance à Rilke*, Les Cahiers du Mois 23/4, (Emile-Paul Frères), 1926; *Rilke et la France* (Plon), 1942; *Rainer Maria Rilke*, Les Lettres Nos. 14-15-16, 1952.

[3] *Rilke's Craftsmanship*, Blackwell, 1954, pp. 194-6.

Rilke speaking of an 'ever more objective mastering of reality' (*immer sachlicheren Bewältigen der Realität*), and, from the moment of his first real discovery[1] of what seemed to him the real greatness of Cézanne in the autumn of 1907, he several times uses the words 'objective' (*sachlich*) and 'objectivity' (*Sachlichkeit*), words which friends or art-critics had perhaps taught him to apply to Cézanne, in order to describe what he believed that he himself had been, and still was, striving for in *New Poems*. When, stimulated, it would seem, by the impulse given and sustained by the steady publication of his letters, the major industry of writing books on Rilke began, these words, as was to be expected, were seized and clapped as thought-saving labels upon *New Poems*. The result was the gradual establishment of various greatly over-simplified and, as commonly stated, thoroughly false antitheses between the kinds of poetry which Rilke wrote at different periods of his career. *New Poems*, it was generally agreed (had those who said these things ever really read them, ever tried to look at them, as it were, for the first time?), were hard, objective, external, a kind of *tour de force*, and the really important Rilke was to be found only in the inwardness of the *Duino Elegies*, the *Sonnets to Orpheus*, and the poems written during the last years of his life. The author of one of the earliest of these general studies of Rilke[2] entitled his chapter on *New Poems* 'The City of Stone' (*Die steinerne Stadt*), a title which suggests a cold, petrified objectivity which is present, if at all, in only a very few of them; and partly, perhaps, by way of reaction, a reaction into an equally extravagant extreme, against this long-prevailing view, the author of a recent learned, lengthy and

[1] In a letter of 8 November 1900, from Berlin, he told his future wife that, among many beautiful things he had seen during the last few days, had been 'the paintings of a singular (*eigentümlichen*) Frenchman, Cézanne'. On 26 February 1924 he wrote to Alfred Schaer, a teacher at the University of Zürich, who had asked what had been some of the chief influences upon him, that, since 1906, there had stood before him as 'the most potent example' (*stärkste Vorbild*) the work of Cézanne. If his memory was not at fault, and if he had really begun to make a careful study of Cézanne in 1906, it must almost certainly have been under the influence of his friend Paula Modersohn-Becker, who had taken a studio in Paris from February until the end of that year, and who saw much of Rilke.

[2] Fritz Dehn, *Rainer Maria Rilke und sein Werk*, 1934.

elaborate study[1] devoted entirely to *New Poems* attempts, so far as I can make out, to present the whole collection as a systematic and progressive exposition of Rilke's views about God, poetic inspiration, and other deep matters.

New Poems, in fact, are both objective and subjective, are concerned both with outwardness and with inwardness, although the predominance of one or other of these two nearly always co-existent elements varies considerably from poem to poem. In many of them (to employ that useful phrase which, whether or no he actually invented it, Mr Eliot has made generally current) he has found 'objective correlatives' for various feelings, convictions, and intuitions; nevertheless, it would be unwise to try to interpret either the collection as a whole, or Rilke's whole 'effort' during these years, or what he has written about the 'objectivity' of Cézanne, entirely in terms of a search for the 'objective correlative'. For during these years Rilke was trying to do, not just one thing, but two things: he was indeed trying to find some means of expressing his subjectivity objectively, as distinct from confessionally, ecstatically, or rhetorically, but, at the same time, he was also trying, as he put it, to 'master reality', to extend, that is to say, as widely as possible the range of his sensibility, sympathy, and experience. What might be called an essentially expounding poet, a poet who had made up his mind on all subjects he considered important as finally and unalterably as, let us say, Dr Johnson, might still be continuously engaged in a search for ever new 'objective correlatives' for old and unchanged convictions. Rilke, though, was an essentially experiencing, or discovering, poet, trying not merely to find in things outside him a means of expression for things inside him, but also trying to appropriate, trying to get more and more inside him, more and more of what he found outside him. It is therefore not unnatural that, in his letters, his emphasis should be now more upon one of these elements, or 'moments', in his 'effort', and now more upon the other, and

[1] Hans Berendt, *Rainer Maria Rilkes Neue Gedichte: Versuch einer Deutung*, 1957. The book contains much valuable material and its more purely grammatical interpretations are often excellent; nevertheless, its whole method and intention seems to me wrong-headed and incongruous with its subject.

also, perhaps, that his interpreters should have concentrated their attention upon whichever one of these two emphases best supported whatever thesis they were trying to maintain.

Let us begin with some of his letters about Cézanne, where his emphasis is mainly upon objectivity and 'mastering of reality', for this will also enable us to devote a little more attention to the so important subject of *Rilke et la France*. After spending six months with friends in Capri, Rilke had returned to Paris at the end of May 1907 and had been devoting himself with tremendous concentration to his 'work'. He had sent off the manuscript of the First Part of *New Poems*, had written many of the poems he included in the Second Part, and had continued *Malte Laurids Brigge*. By the beginning of October he was feeling very tired, and, as he wrote to his wife on the second of that month, it looked as though the time had come when he would have to pay for having 'held out' for a whole summer at his lectern. Then came the exhibition of Cézanne's paintings at the Salon d'Automne. Greatly influenced, no doubt, by his reading of the recently published *Souvenirs* of Emile Bernard and other personal recollections of the painter, who had died two years before, Rilke seemed to find in Cézanne's life and achievement the fullest, the final, confirmation of that conception of the artist as an incessant and dedicated 'worker', striving to realise an ideal of almost unattainable perfection, perpetually dissatisfied with his achievements, which he had first learnt from Rodin, and which had been held in some degree by so many modern French poets, writers, and painters: by Mallarmé, for example, whom Stefan George described as 'bleeding for his concept'; by Dégas, who declared that, if he were a wealthy man, he would buy back all his paintings and put his foot through them; and by Rodin, who, as Rilke has recorded,[1] used to greet his friends with the question, not 'How are your books (or pictures) selling?', but 'Avez-vous vien travaillé?' For the next few weeks Rilke wrote long and almost daily letters to his wife (herself a sculptress and pupil of Rodin) about these paintings and about Cézanne as a 'worker' and 'masterer of reality'. Years later, while reciting and lecturing upon his poems at

[1] In his 1907 lecture on Rodin, *Gesammelte Werke*, IV, p. 398; *Selected Works: Vol. I, Prose*, p. 149.

Winterthur in 1919, Rilke found occasion to mention Cézanne, and exclaimed: 'Only a saint can be so united with his God as Cézanne was with his work!'; and, indeed, in a letter of 9 October, describing and commenting upon some of the facts of Cézanne's life, there is something of the accent and ardour of a dedicated young priest describing the life of one whom he has suddenly come to recognise as, above all, *his* saint. Rilke recalls how Cézanne, after having led a bohemian sort of life until the age of forty, suddenly acquired from Pissarro a taste for work, and thereafter did nothing else; how, although he was a 'believer' and dearly loved his mother, he did not attend her funeral, because on that day he happened to be *sur le motif*; and how in the end he just

sits in his garden like an old dog, the dog of this work, that calls him in and beats him and lets him go hungry. And yet clings in spite of all to this incomprehensible master, who only on Sundays lets him return for a while to le bon Dieu, as to his first owner. – And outside the people are saying 'Cézanne', and the gentlemen in Paris are writing his name with emphasis and with pride in being well-informed.

He was delighted when his wife mentioned certain affinities she had noticed between what he had written to her about Cézanne and the poems she had been reading in manuscript, and on 18 October he wrote to her that, although he had been to some extent aware of it, he could not have positively stated how far a development corresponding to 'the immense progress in Cézanne's paintings' had already proceeded in him.

It's not the actual painting that I'm studying (for, in spite of all, I remain uncertain in front of pictures, and learn only slowly to distinguish good from less good, and continually mistake earlier for later). The turning-point in this painting is what I recognised, because I myself had just reached it in my work, or at least had somehow got near to it, probably long prepared for this particular experience on which so much depends.

That what Rilke meant was the turning from a kind of self-indulgent self-surrender, which might be called either romantic or subjective or impressionistic, to an objective and workman-like wrestling with reality is revealed in a letter of 13 October,

recalling the autumn of six years ago when, at Westerwede,
where his wife was now living, he had written the Second Part
of his *Book of Hours*:

> If I came up to you I should certainly see the pomp of moor and
> heath, the hoveringly bright green of the meadows, and the birches
> newly and differently; it's true that this transformation, as I once
> fully experienced and shared it, called forth a Part of the Book of
> Hours; but at that time Nature for me was still a general occasion,
> an evocation, an instrument in whose strings my hands rediscovered
> themselves; I didn't yet sit before her; I let myself be rapt away by
> the soul that went out from me: she came over me with her spacious-
> ness, with her vast excessive existence, as the prophesying came over
> Saul; precisely so. I strode along and saw, not Nature, but the
> visions she inspired in me. How little I should have been able to
> learn at that time in front of Cézanne, in front of Van Gogh. Through
> the fact that Cézanne now gives me so much to do I can see how
> very different I've become. I'm on the way to becoming a worker . . .
> To-day I've again been with his pictures . . . One notices, better
> every time, how necessary it was to get beyond even love[1]; it is
> indeed natural for one to love each of these things, when one makes
> it; but, if one shows this, one makes it less well; one judges it instead
> of *saying* it. One stops being impartial, and the best, love, remains
> outside the work, doesn't enter it, remains untransmuted beside it:
> this was how impressionist painting arose (which is in no way better
> than naturalistic). One painted: I love this; instead of painting:
> here it is. Whereby everyone is forced to see for himself whether I've
> loved it. . . In the poems there are instinctive approaches towards
> a similar objectivity.

In *The Note-Book of Malte Laurids Brigge*, which he had begun in
1904, at which he was still working, and of which his wife had
seen portions in manuscript, Rilke had made his young Dane,
trying to describe in a letter something of the transformation in
his whole attitude to life that was taking place in him under the
too potent influence of the grandeurs and miseries of Paris,

[1] Here, in 1907, we find Rilke declaring that one must get *beyond* love;
in 1914, in the poem *Turning*, we find him reproaching himself that he has
not yet got *to* it: *Poems 1906 to 1926*, pp. 183-4, and Introduction thereto,
pp. 43-44. The doubleness, the polarities and apparent contradictions, in
his experiencing of life and art and of the relationship between them are
endless, and it may well be that the tension they generated was one of the
chief sources of his poetic power.

mention Baudelaire's poem *Une Charogne* ('A Carrion') and remark: 'It may be that I now understand it'; and in a letter of
19 October he told his wife how excited he had been by the
discovery that this poem had been a favourite with Cézanne,
who knew it by heart and could repeat it until the end of his
life. The poem is indeed such a landmark in the history of
modern artistic sensibility that, before quoting Rilke's reflexions
upon it, I will translate it for the benefit of any readers to whom
a translation, however inadequate, may be useful.

> Can you recall, my dear, that lovely day,
>   To what our footpath led?
> How, as it turned, a hideous carrion lay
>   On a dry torrent's bed:
>
> Legs, like some lecherous woman's, in the air,
>   Burning and sweating pest,
> With cynical indifference it laid bare
>   Its pullulating breast.
>
> The sun was blazing down as though it meant
>   To cook exactly right
> And give great Nature back at cent per cent
>   All she had made unite.
>
> And the sky watched that carcass uncompeer'd
>   Like a great flower expand.
> The stench was so terrific that you feared
>   You'd faint there out of hand.
>
> Flies buzzed above that belly's putridness,
>   Whence issued from their beds
> Black grubs that flowed like some thick liquidness
>   Along those living shreds.
>
> And all this, like a wave, advanced, retired,
>   Or darted sparklingly;
> It seemed the body, by some breath inspired,
>   Lived reproductively.
>
> The whole emitted a strange harmony
>   Like wind's or water's sound,
> Or like the grain a winnower rhythmically
>   Keeps shaking round and round.

INTRODUCTION

Into a shadowy dream all shape retreated,
    A sketch come gradually
On some forgotten canvas, and completed
    Only from memory.

Behind the rocks a restless bitch stayed on,
    With aggravated look,
Bent on retrieving from the skeleton
    The morsel it forsook.

One day, though, you'll be like that loathsomeness,
    That thing without a name,
You, the bright centre of my consciousness,
    My angel and my flame.

That's what you'll be, whom all the graces tend,
    When, the last rites conferred,
Under the grass and rank growths you descend
    To rot with the interred.

Then, O my beauty, tell the worm, which thence-
    forth eats you with its kiss,
I've kept the form and heavenly quintessence
    Of my corrupted bliss.

You surely remember [Rilke wrote to his wife] that passage from the Note-Book of Malte Laurids Brigge about Baudelaire and his poem 'The Carrion'. I couldn't help thinking that without that poem the whole development towards objective saying which we now seem to recognise in Cézanne could never have begun; that poem, in its inexorability, had to be there first. Artistic contemplation had first to get that far in overcoming its reluctance to see even in the horrible and apparently only repulsive that existence which, together with all other existence, *counts*. Aversion from any kind of existence is as little permitted to the creator as selection: a single withdrawal at any time thrusts him from the state of grace, makes him wholly and entirely sinful. . . Behind this devotion, in a small way at first, begins holiness: the simple life of a love that has stood the test, that, without ever pluming itself on so doing, goes up to everything, unaccompanied, inconspicuously, wordlessly. Proper work, plenitude of tasks, all first begin behind this endurance, and anyone who has been unable to progress that far will indeed get a sight of the Virgin Mary in Heaven, of a few saints and minor prophets, of King Saul and Charles the Bold: – but of Hokusai and Leonardo, of Li Tai Pe and Villon, of Verhaeren, Rodin, Cézanne – and even of God, what he learns even there will only be hearsay.

INTRODUCTION

In all these passages from Rilke's letters about Cézanne his whole emphasis is upon self-suppression, objectivity, 'mastering of reality', enlargement of the capacity to experience and in-see. Nevertheless, on 24 September 1908, a month after the publication of the Second Part of *New Poems*, we find him writing to Frau Rosa Schobloch, a German friend living in Paris, of his own life and activity in terms of what, to most readers, might seem the most extreme subjectivism: thanking her for her understanding of his need for solitude, he remarked how everything conspired to hinder the artist in his attempt to get inside himself, and condemned him for wanting to cultivate and perfect his inner world so that one day it might be able 'to counterbalance the whole of externality, everything, right up to the stars, and become, so to speak, the equivalent of all that'. This, admittedly, is an extreme expression of what may be called the other side of Rilke's complex attitude to the relation between the creative artist and external reality; nevertheless, there are many passages, both early and late, in his letters where his main emphasis is upon the search for 'objective correlatives', or (to use his own phrase) 'external equivalents', for something within him. On 7 June (Russian style, 27 May) 1899, during his first visit to Russia, he wrote to Frieda von Bülow:

At bottom, one seeks in everything new (country or person or thing) only an expression that helps some personal confession to greater power and maturity. In fact, all things are there in order that they may in some sort become images for us. And they do not suffer thereby, for, while they express us ever more clearly, our soul broods in the same measure over them. And I feel during these days that *Russian* things will give me the names for those most terrible pieties of my being which, ever since childhood, have been yearning to enter my art.

This, it is true, was written by the Rilke of the *Book of Hours*; nevertheless, however 'different' the fascination Cézanne's paintings were able to exercise upon him made him feel that he had since become, on 17 March 1907, at the end of a letter to his and his wife's friend the painter Paula Modersohn-Becker, he had written something not so very different from what he had written from Russia in 1899. His wife's letters from Egypt, where she was then travelling, were, he said, like the travel-letters of their grandparents, that took so long to arrive and were full of strangeness and foreignness—except, he added, that to 'us' (to us, he meant, as artists) 'all foreignness is akin, because we seize it and require it as expression for something within'. Nine days earlier, on 8 March, he had written to his wife herself that the 'thing' out of which a poem is made was the only possible name for an inner event, which was only able to take place in us while we were looking at something else—an hermetic utterance, perhaps, which may be illuminated by a passage from a letter of many years later, where we find the author of the *Duino Elegies* and the *Sonnets to Orpheus* looking back upon the period of *New Poems*, and where those so apparently opposite and irreconcilable emphases on subjectivity and objectivity, inwardness and outwardness, to which we have been listening, seem suddenly to combine into a mysterious and paradoxical unity. Writing (in French) on 3 February 1923, 'A une Amie', after describing the happiness he used to find as a complete stranger in various foreign towns, where he had been able to correct the accident of having been born in a particular place by experiencing a whole series of new births and new existences, Rilke continued:

Now that you know some of these enjoyments of my nomadic life, do the 'Neue Gedichte' still seem to you so impersonal? Look, in order to be able to say what happened to me, what I needed was not so much an instrument of feeling, but clay; I involuntarily presumed to make use of what is called lyrical poetry in order to *form*, not feelings, but *things I had felt*; every one of life's events had to find a place in this formation, independently of the pain or pleasure it had brought me at first. This formation would have been worthless unless it had gone as far as the *trans*-formation of every accidental detail, it had to reach the essential.[1]

Is there not a subtle but tremendously important difference between what Rilke wrote from Russia in 1899, about finding in outwardness a means of expression for personal confessions, and this notion of an 'inner event', first expressed in 1907, and later, in 1923, associated with the distinction between feelings and 'things felt'; and may not this difference be regarded as the

---

[1] *Ausgewählte Briefe*, 1950, II, p. 389 (not in other collections).

measure of what he owed to that long immersion in French 'workmanliness' and objectivity which had begun in 1902? The poet of the *Book of Hours* had been a poet of confessions and feelings; the poet of *New Poems* had become a poet of 'things felt'; a poet still, indeed, of feelings, but of feelings which, as the result of sudden and unforeseen co-operations between inner and outer, had achieved the dignity of 'inner events'. The poet of the *Book of Hours* knew what he was looking for; the poet of *New Poems* often did not know what he was looking *for* until he found himself looking *at*.

Presumably because Rilke, especially in his first enthusiastic letters about Rodin, had spoken so often and so emphatically of 'things', critics who do not really seem to have understood what he meant have often affixed to *New Poems* the thought-saving label *Dinggedichte*, 'thing-poems',[1] usually intending to convey thereby, like the writer who entitled his chapter on these poems 'The City of Stone', an impression of cold, inhuman impersonality. When, though, Rilke spoke of 'things' he did not mean what we do when we speak of inanimate objects; he meant rather animate objects, things made by man, from the Parthenon and the Gothic cathedrals down to the humblest implements of daily life, in and through which, both by their first makers and by generations of beholders, worshippers, and users, a kind of quintessential humanity had been rescued from transience and transmitted from age to age. It was of 'things' in this sense, so rapidly being supplanted and even destroyed by the products of modern technology and mass-production, that he wrote in the famous letter to his Polish translator on 13 November 1925:

Even for our grandparents a 'House', a 'Well', a familiar tower, their very dress, their cloak, was infinitely more, infinitely more intimate: almost everything a receptacle in which they both found and enlarged a store of humanness. . . The animated, experienced things that *share our lives* are running out and cannot be replaced. *We are perhaps the last to have still known such things.* On us rests the responsibility of preserving, not merely their memory (that would be

---

[1] The term seems first to have been used by Kurt Oppert in an article entitled 'Das Dinggedicht', *Deutsche Vierteljahrschrift für Literaturwissenschaft und Geistesgeschichte*, 1926, Heft 4.

little and unreliable), but their human and laral worth. ('Laral' in the sense of household-gods).

Only a comparatively small number of *New Poems* (of which the great majority are about human figures, legendary, historical, or contemporary) are about 'things' even in this special, Rilkean sense, and in by far the greater number even of these the 'things' are closely associated with human lives and human feelings: in, for example, *The Cathedral* (p. 77), *The Porch* (p. 79), *Roman Sarcophagi* (p. 95), *The Lace* (p. 99), *Tanagra* (p. 103), *In a foreign Park* (p. 105), *Before Summer Rain* (p. 111), *In the Drawing Room* (p. 111), *The Steps of the Orangery* (p. 121), *The Reliquary* (p. 197), *The Parks* (p. 235), *The Lute* (p. 249), *The Pavilion* (p. 279), *The Coat-of-Arms* (p. 283), *The Ball* (p. 291). In a few poems, it is true, humanity is present only in the almost human personality with which these 'things' are endowed (*The Capital*, p. 83, *Roman Fountain*, p. 123, *The Tower*, p. 127, *Quai du Rosaire*, p. 131, *The Beetle-Stone*, p. 295); and there is a similar distinction and a similar numerical relationship between the various evocations of townscapes and landscapes: in *Venetian Morning* (p. 243) the city (like the Appian Way in *Roman Campagna*, p. 231) is almost an independent personality, while in the immediately following *Late Autumn in Venice* (p. 245) it is closely associated with the splendour of its human past.

While, though, *New Poems* are far from being, as has too often been suggested, a collection of coldly impersonal descriptions of inanimate objects, neither are they to be regarded as anything like the deliberate and systematic presentation of a 'philosophy', or as a series of attempts to find symbolic expression for more or less definite ideas, ideals, or convictions. Rilke, who once defined what he understood by 'being' as 'the experiencing of the completest possible inner intensity',[1] had a rich and active interior life, but he also had a passion both for gazing at things in, as it were, delighted astonishment at their being there, and for what he called 'inseeing'. On 17 February 1914 he wrote to Magda von Hattingberg ('Benvenuta'):

I love inseeing (*Einsehen*). Can you imagine with me how glorious

[1] Letter to Rudolf Bodländer, 23 March 1922.

it is to insee, for example, a dog as one passes by – *insee* (I don't mean in-spect, which is only a kind of human gymnastic, by means of which one immediately comes out again on the other side of the dog, regarding it merely, so to speak, as a window upon the humanity lying behind it, not that) – but to let oneself precisely into the dog's very centre, the point from where it begins to be dog, the place in it where God, as it were, would have sat down for a moment when the dog was finished, in order to watch it under the influence of its first embarrassments and inspirations and to know that it was good, that nothing was lacking, that it could not have been better made. . . Laugh though you may, dear confidant, if I am to tell you *where* my all-greatest feeling, my world-feeling, my earthly bliss was to be found, I must confess to you: it was to be found time and again, here and there, in such inseeing, in the indescribably swift, deep, timeless moments of this divine inseeing.[1]

Readers incapable of sharing in some degree this passion for gazing and 'inseeing', and who cannot but suppose that a great poet, though he may *seem* to be primarily concerned with such, for them, rather trivial and unserious activities, must 'really' be concerned with something far more serious and important, which it is our business to ferret out – such readers will never be able to see *New Poems* 'as in themselves they really are', and will derive little pleasure from them – except, perhaps, the dubious pleasure of writing misunderstanding theses upon them as candidates for academic promotion or 'higher degrees'. For although, in a sense which I shall proceed to define, some of the poems are more 'symbolic', more doubly or multiply descriptive, than others, almost every one of them is primarily the record of something (sight or story) 'inseen', or, as Rilke himself expressed it, is the transformation into words of what was essential in that 'inner event' which took place in him while he was gazing at something, or reading something, or remembering something he had read. What we are invited to share is better described as a way, or ways, of looking at things than as a philosophy of life. Indeed, Rilke's philosophy of life, in so far as he can be said to have had one, was something like the sum of his ways of looking at things, a web of infinitely subtle and complex relationships between innumerable intensely remembered experiences. Here there is a great difference between him and two English poets

[1] *Briefwechsel mit Benvenuta*, 1954, p. 94.

with whom, especially in the claims he made for art and imagination, he has certain affinities, Blake and Yeats. He has something of Blake's preoccupation with inwardness and something of Blake's intense visionary power; yet, in comparison with Blake, who expressed contempt for what he called 'this Vegetable Universe' and declared that 'natural objects always did, and now do, weaken, deaden, and obliterate Imagination in me', Rilke is almost earth-bound and materialistic, for he could imagine only in terms of what he had actually seen, his similes and metaphors are nearly always drawn from what we call (rather question-beggingly, perhaps) the 'real' world, and he has none of those shadowy figures–Urizen, Los, Enitharmon, and the rest–which 'stand *for*' something which generations of students have been, and will long continue to be, engaged in trying to 'explain'. In his continuous development, his progress from a kind of romanticism to a kind of realism, his concern with craftsmanship, and his ability to introduce into strict metrical forms, and thereby to transfigure into the finest poetry, the rhythms, sentences, and words of the spoken language, he has perhaps more affinity with Yeats than with any other contemporary poet; but he has none of that fixed or invented symbolism with which so many of Yeats's poems are cluttered, and which makes them such a godsend to the research student. Yeats often seems to begin with an idea and then, as it were, to sensationalise it; Rilke more often begins with a sensation and then, as it were, intellectualises it, and much of his poetry might be described as the intellectual interpenetrating, or sublimating, of sensation. He was, I suppose, in some sense an 'intellectual', and in his letters we find him ready to speculate about almost anything in the most fascinating way; nevertheless, unlike Yeats, he had a contempt for systems, and he seems to have felt little need for any kind of external or metaphysical guarantee to bolster up his conviction of the importance of art and artists, poetry and poets. Yeats, as Edmund Wilson convincingly argued, seems to have found it necessary to build up his gimcrack system of correspondences in order to be and to remain a poet in a world hostile to poetry as he understood it; Rilke was content to point to a long line of great 'workers', from Rodin and Cézanne in the present to Leonardo and

Michelangelo in the past, whose superiority to ordinary humanity he was seldom tempted to doubt.[1]

There is only one poem in *New Poems* which I find almost
totally incomprehensible, and that is *The Bed* (p. 271), a poem
in which there is an unhappy combination, and even confusion,
of allegory, symbolism, and personification, and where Rilke
seems to be trying (perhaps not hard enough) to say something
about the act of love. It is the only one of *New Poems* where
what is said, or shown, seems to have no independently significant meaning, and to 'stand *for*' something else, some idea,
which, if one has the patience, one is being invited to worry out.
It is the only poem which definitely requires some sort of key to
unlock it, which there would be any sense in trying to interpret
equationally ($A = X$, $B = Y$, etc.), and which, if not profitably,
at least not wholly nonsensically, might be endlessly 'explicated'
and argued about in theses or in letters to the *Times Literary
Supplement*. It is not only perhaps the most un-Rilkean poem that
Rilke ever wrote; it is also the only really bad poem in *New
Poems*, and I mention it in order to indicate what all the other
poems in this collection are essentially *not*.

I will now briefly attempt to indicate some of the very different ways in which inner and outer, objectivity and subjectivity,
realism and symbolism, are related in these poems. In the first
place, every poem was intended to be, and usually is, as independent and self-sufficient as any painting, statue, building, or
other 'thing made' (the original meaning of Greek *poiema*), and
as far removed as possible from anything like a mere fragment
of some vast, vague, and endless confession. It is always primarily and essentially concerned with the subject of its title, and
is never the mere occasion for reflections which might equally
well have been suggested by something else. Nevertheless, while
every poem is continuously concerned with what Hopkins

[1] A letter to Lou Andreas-Salomé, 28 December 1911, reveals that he
had been greatly shaken by the way in which Rodin, in his seventieth year,
had been making a fool of himself for the sake of what seemed to Rilke a
thoroughly contemptible woman, 'as though all his infinite work had never
been'; but, although his gratitude to Rodin, and much of his old admiration
for him, remained, Rodin as *Vorbild* (example) had now definitely been
replaced by Cézanne.

would have called the 'thisness' of some particular 'thing felt',
the 'thisness' that emerges, even from the most apparently
'objective' poem, is a 'thisness' that was apprehended by Rilke,
and there is therefore in every poem more or less of the 'thisness' of Rilke himself as well as of the 'thing felt'. Every poem,
then, is in a sense both objective and subjective. Nevertheless,
further distinctions remain, which, to avoid prolixity and an
excessive multiplication of bemusing subtleties, I must be content to formulate with a certain crudeness, employing the
words 'description' and 'descriptive', which Rilke himself would
probably have rejected as inappropriate. All the poems are
more or less descriptive; while, though, some are purely descriptive and suggest nothing beyond themselves, others are in
various ways representative or symbolic. Sometimes we just feel
that they are in some way symbolic, although we cannot say
precisely how, or of what; in others we can clearly feel that
Rilke has found 'objective correlatives' for some of his own
characteristic values and convictions. As an example of what,
for present purposes, may be called pure description, or pure
evocation, I will mention *The Group* (p. 221), that wonderful
tour de force, where, in a single sentence and by means of a single
elaborately and continuously worked out comparison with someone gathering a bunch of flowers, Rilke has described the assem-
bling of a group of spectators in a Paris street to watch a professional weight-lifter perform his act. It is unlike any poem by
any other poet, but it is without a trace of anything that can
properly be called either symbolism or subjectivity. All that can
be inferred from it about Rilke himself is that he had the power
to write it and that (to quote a famous line of Thomas Hardy's)

He was a man who used to notice such things.

Or consider *The Gazelle* (p. 89), where, in and through a suc-
cession of similes, he evokes the 'thisness' of that creature. 'Like',
'as if', 'as when': has any other great poet used these words and
phrases quite so often as Rilke? Of all poetic devices the most
indispensable to him was the simile, and it might almost be said
of him, as Mr Eliot said of the critic, that his two chief tools are
analysis and comparison. He told his wife in a letter that he had
spent a morning looking at the gazelles in the Jardin des Plantes.

INTRODUCTION

First, one may suppose, he was just fascinated; then he began to analyse what it was that so fascinated him: the way the creatures held their heads, the way they moved their limbs – what was it *like*? These so frequent similes are usually both beautiful and surprising, but, at the same time, there is often an almost scientific precision about them, and this, together with the careful analysis from which they arose and which is often present in the poem, perhaps partly explains the foolish talk about 'coldness', 'Cities of Stone', 'thing-poems', and so on; for it is the very opposite of that rhetorical and over-emphatic expression of emotions and convictions, that working oneself up in order to work one's hearers or readers up, which the Germans call *pathos* and which Rilke was now trying to leave as far as possible behind him. Such a poem as *The Gazelle* (and many of *New Poems* are essentially of this kind) cannot properly be called symbolic, since, although it relates one particular 'thing felt' to many other 'things felt', there is not even incidentally present in it any general reflections upon, or intuition into, the human situation in general, or Rilke's situation in particular, or the mystery of life, and so on. *The Swan* (p. 95), on the other hand, may properly be called a symbolic poem, for here, although the contrast between the bird's 'unshaped' walking and the kingly swimming into which it at first so unconfidently subsides, is accurately seen and evoked, it is seen primarily as a symbol, or emblem, of something else, namely, of Rilke's very personal intuitions into the relation between life and death. There is a similar contrast between *Roman Fountain* (p. 123), where, although the three basins of the baroque fountain in the Villa Borghese are evoked not as inanimate but as animate objects (for, if Rilke often describes persons as though they were things, he often describes things as though they were persons), they are evoked purely for their own sakes, and *Roman Sarcophagi* (p. 95), where the transformation of the sarcophagi and their original contents into troughs of sparkling water is explicitly offered as a symbol of what death may ultimately do with us.

The many fine poems inspired by Old Testament scenes and stories are symbolic only in the sense that they give concentrated expression to that representativeness which every sensitive child to whom these stories were read must have unconsciously felt in them: the contrast between apparent and actual invincibility in the Lord's enemies and in the Lord's chosen servants, whom his enemies oppose or seek to destroy; the contrast between towering splendour and total downfall and humiliation. Again and again a glance at his Old Testament sources will reveal how Rilke has exploited all their possibilities of pictorial and dramatic contrast, and how, now and then, certain details have particularly fired his imagination: how, for example, in *Absalom's Rebellion* (p. 183) the young man's hair, the most pictorial of his physical attractions and the immediate cause of his death, flashes throughout the poem. It is true that for Rilke, who once spoke contemptuously in a letter of 'that red violence which most people understand by reality', the contrast between the whirlwind and the earthquake, wherein the Lord was not, and the still, small, voice with which he spoke, provided, as did so many of these Old Testament contrasts, an 'objective correlative' for much that was fundamental in his whole attitude to life: his sense of the essential superficiality and insignificance of most human activity; his contempt for conventional distinctions between important and unimportant, great and small; his conception of the artist as the lonely servant of some higher power, as a dedicated spirit, a chosen vessel.[1]

Here, I think, one becomes aware of a certain deep difference between the dedicatedness of Rilke and that of many of those French poets and artists from whom he learnt so much, a difference, too, that can be only superficially explained as a reflection of his characteristically German *Innerlichkeit*: his dedicatedness is interpenetrated by a spirit of what, however it may differ from true religion, can only be called religiousness. The subject is far too complex and difficult to receive here the kind of treatment it deserves, but I cannot leave it unmentioned. The violent anti-Christianity, or anti-ecclesiasticism, which Rilke has often expressed in his letters was perhaps largely a reaction against the piety of his rather shallow and foolish mother, who had filled

---

[1] In one of these Old Testament poems, *David sings before Saul* (p. 61), it is hard not to feel that Rilke has found an 'objective correlative', not merely for certain values and convictions, but for a particular relationship, that between himself and Rodin, with whom he was living at Meudon at the time when he wrote the poem.

her home with tawdry images and taught her son to speak of 'Heavenly Papa' and 'Heavenly Mamma'. He turned from this, as did so many of his contemporaries, to a kind of Nietzschean life-worship, 'this-worldliness', and contempt for 'other-worldliness', and to various liberating speculations, such as that God was a progressive creation of man's, which had been expressed again and again by various French and German, especially German, thinkers since the end of the eighteenth century. Many of these by no means original ideas he continued to express from time to time, though more often in his letters than in his poems, until the end of his life, often with such freshness and power that he has been able to persuade many of his readers (as he had perhaps been able to persuade himself) that he was announcing them for the first time. While, though, with various passages in his letters and in certain of his prose writings it would be possible to produce parallels from numerous modern life-worshippers, in his poetry, which seems to have been written from far deeper levels than his prose, we find again and again, as distinct from the confident and aggressive 'humanism' and Prometheanism of Nietzsche and other life-worshippers, something far closer to what Nietzsche regarded as the slave-morality and slave-values of Socrates and Christ: an exaltation of the saint, of the child, of the woman (as Rilke habitually imagined her) over 'worldliness', over 'humanist' man and 'humanist' values. No doubt there was some element of aestheticism in this religiousness; no doubt Nietzschean man, humanist man, 'progressive' man seemed to Rilke a rather vulgar and bourgeois figure, and in the saint, the child, and the woman, the Rilkean woman, he found 'objective correlatives' for his conception of the poet and artist. Nevertheless, the significant fact remains that the poet who, in his letters, is so often found 'humanistically' and 'progressively' insisting on 'this-worldliness' and 'this-sidedness', cannot in his poetry, especially in his later poetry, imaginatively apprehend either humanity or himself, cannot imaginatively assess their achievements, misachievements, and possibilities, except against a perpetual background of 'other-worldliness' and 'other-sidedness', a background of angels, constellations, and even gods. This is not the place to discuss Rilke's later poetry, but, as an example of what I mean by his 'religiousness', I will quote a

short poem he wrote in February 1924, which has always seemed
to me one of his most powerful and unforgettable expressions of
what, deep, perhaps deepest, within him, was ultimately irreconcilable with any kind of Nietzscheanism or 'humanism':

> Gods, for all we can tell,   stride as richly bestowing
>   now as in former years;
> gently their wind as well   reaches our harvests, blowing
>   over more loaded ears.
>
> Quite to forget it will fail   quite to elude the relation;
>   they will perform their share.
> Suddenly, silently there,   prizing your proudest creation,
>   ponders their different scale.
>
> Schweigsam, einfach und heil   legt sich an seine Errichtung
>   plötzlich ihr anderes Maß.

However passionately Rilke might insist to his Polish translator
that the Angel of the *Duino Elegies* had *nothing* in common with
the angels of the Christian heaven, the fact remains that it is to
this non-human arbiter with the *anderes Maß*, the different scale,
that he appeals again and again to judge the achievements of
humanity. I sometimes think that the ten years which he required to complete the *Duino Elegies*, and his many unsuccessful
attempts to re-achieve that mood of intense concentration in
and out of which the first two had been written, should be regarded as a measure of the distance between what was deepest
in him and what could always find ready expression in his letters.
If, though, at what may be called his prose level, any mention
of organised religion, which for him, I think, was always in some
way associated with the foolish piety of his mother and the
stifling conventionality of the family circle in Prague, could
provoke defiant affirmations of 'this-worldliness', it is also true
that expressions of a superficial 'humanism' could sometimes
provoke him into affirming their direct opposite. Shortly after
his first arrival in Paris he wrote in his pocket book:

> Ernest Renan: Tout est possible, même Dieu!
> Everything is chance, one thing alone is necessary: God.
> Nothing is certain but God.   R.M.R.[1]

[1] Quoted by Eva Cassirer-Solmitz, *Rainer Maria Rilke*, 1957, II, p. 2.

INTRODUCTION

Almost all the attitudes and responses I have been trying to indicate, from the superficial to the profound, appear in those of *New Poems* inspired by the New Testament, by the Lives of the Saints, and by Christian art and architecture. One or two of them, in perhaps rather questionable taste (*Crucifixion*, p. 203, *Pietà*, p. 71), seem almost deliberately intended to shock, and even hurt, the believing Christian, and in *The Arisen* (p. 203) Christ appears to Mary Magdalene solely in order to proclaim the characteristically Rilkean doctrine of love without the beloved. In the concluding lines of that almost purely descriptive and unideological poem *The Capital* (p. 83) there is some suggestion of what is more explicitly stated in the third and last poem of the little cycle *The Porch* (p. 79), where, recalling (at Chartres and in or on other cathedrals) sculptured bishops with their staffs planted upon the brows of monsters or men-monsters writhing at their feet, he speaks of

> that wildering world they have not trodden out,
> where shape and beast, as though imperilling,
> writhe and upsurge and yet uphold them all:
>
> because, like acrobats, that monstrous rout
> only indulge in such wild gesturing
> so that the brow-supported staff shan't fall.

The suggestion here, which could scarcely have seemed other than heretical to the medieval mind, that saintliness could not exist without 'beastliness', may perhaps be regarded as a less aggressive presentation of that savage anti-asceticism which Rilke later attributed to the imaginary author of his *Young Workman's Letter*, written in February 1922: there, after having tried to represent St. Francis of Assisi (as Rilke himself had done, nearly twenty years before, at the end of the Third Part of the *Book of Hours*) as one of many who had disregardedly attempted to reconcile Christian renunciation with 'the obvious friendliness and cheerfulness of the Earth', the young workman satirically asks why the Church does not boast of having been vigorous enough not to collapse under the living-weight of certain Popes, whose throne was burdened with their bastards, their courtesans, and those they had murdered; recalls the thoughts that occurred to him when he discovered that the Palace of the Popes at Avignon had been erected above the antique torso of a Hercules, and declares:

> Even the cathedrals are not the embodiment of that spirit which we are now asked to believe is the actual Christian spirit. I could imagine the fallen image of a Grecian goddess to be lying under some of them; so much florescence, so much life has blossomed in them, in spite of the fact that they soared away from that hidden body, as with a fear characteristic of their age, into heavens which the sound of their great bells was to keep continually open.[1]

The two companion poems *Adam* and *Eve* (pp. 206-7), suggested by the sculptured figures by Viollet-le-Duc on the façade of Notre-Dame, are characteristic examples of the coolness, the 'remarkably little fuss'[2] (to quote a phrase it always gives me pleasure to repeat), with which Rilke will objectify, as though they were self-evident and incontrovertible, the most heterodox interpretations of traditional figures and stories. While, though, in the first poem Adam is presented as a Promethean and God-defying character, in the second he is reduced to something more like the proportions which man in Rilke's poetry normally assumes when he is contrasted with woman, and looms there in the background as an energetic and insensitive busybody, dragging poor Eve away from her communing with the non-human inhabitants of Eden and from the God she has as yet scarcely got to know. The reduction of the apple ('with the apple in the apple-pose') to the status of a kind of identifying property may perhaps be regarded as one of Rilke's 'potent asides'. Several of *New Poems* are concerned with the lives of saints, which Rilke was continually reading and re-reading. Especially characteristic are *The Temptation* (p. 193), *The Stylite* (p. 199), and *From the Life of a Saint* (p. 211), to which, because of an essential similarity in spirit and interpretation, may be added *The Donor* (p. 93). How these lives presented themselves to him as 'objec-

---

[1] *Selected Works, Vol. I: Prose*, pp. 70-72.

[2] 'Milton's dislodgment, in the past decade, after his two centuries of predominance, was effected with remarkably little fuss. The irresistible argument was, of course, Mr Eliot's creative achievement; it gave his few critical asides – potent, it is true, by context – their finality, and made it unnecessary to elaborate a case' – F. R. Leavis, *Revaluation*, 1936, p. 42.

tive correlatives', what it was in them that seemed to him un-
superseded and still relevant, emerges very clearly from a passage in *The Note-Book of Malte Laurids Brigge*, where Malte, after
describing pictures representing the temptation of St. Anthony
and other saints, continues:

> There was a time when I regarded these pictures as antiquated.
> Not that I doubted their reality. I could imagine that such things
> might have happened to the saints, at that time, to those zealous
> and over-hasty souls who wanted to begin straight away with God,
> at any price. We no longer make such demands upon ourselves. We
> suspect that He is too difficult for us, that we must postpone Him in
> order slowly to perform the long labour that separates us from Him.
> Now, though, I know that this labour is just as combative as saint-
> hood: that such things rise up around all those who are solitary for
> that labour's sake as took shape around those solitaries of God in
> their caves and empty shelters, long ago.[1]

For Rilke, it would seem, any disinterested, unselfregarding
ardour and intensity, undirected to the satisfaction of any particular desire or to the achievement of any particular object, all
infinite and insatiable longing, was ultimately directed to what
he continued to call God, and was the only kind of religion, or
religiousness, he was able to accept. In comparison with this,
the religion of churches and of creeds seemed to him impure and
mingled with all manner of irrelevancies. He was, in fact, an
intense individualist and anti-institutionalist, and although he
lived much of his life according to rules of almost monastic
strictness, they were rules which had been imposed upon him
only by himself. How easily, for him, the ardour of the saints
could be associated, almost identified, with the ardour of certain
great unsatisfied women-lovers, such as the 'Portuguese Nun',
Marianna Alcoforado, who wrote to her now 'irrelevant' lover,
'My love no longer depends on the way you treat me', is revealed in a letter of 9 January 1913 to Annette Kolb, about a
short novel of hers he had been enthusiastically reading in a
periodical. 'In considering humanity,' he began, 'I can't do
otherwise than think straight on to the saint (in whom at last
everything becomes comprehensible and necessary to me).' He
then proceeded to declare that Mariclée, the heroine of this

---

[1] *Gesammelte Werke*, V, p. 218.

novel, had once more suggested to him that the saint was perhaps no longer quite so exemplary and relevant as he had once been, and that it more concerned us to trace what such 'expenditure on God' could achieve when it was dispersed, less noticeably and conspicuously, within relationships here on earth.

In their intensity, their self-surrender, their fervent absoluteness (*innigen Unbedingtheit*) these two months of Mariclée's existence are the life of a saint; when the book arrives, and I once more have my books around me somewhere, I shall insert it in that region: close beside the Portuguese Nun and Angela da Foligno.

The figure, shocking to the believer, presented in *The Olive Garden* (p. 69) objectifies Rilke's total rejection of the idea of Christ as a mediator and of a God who has been once and for all revealed. This Christ is a symbol of those who will have to begin again and again the long search for God; a symbol, too, of the essential loneliness of those (among whom Rilke assigned a high place to poets and artists) who have made that search the chief purpose of their lives. This conception of the most 'real', the most 'significant', kind of living as a lonely pilgrimage, a continual arriving and departing, finding and losing, is unforgettably expressed in those two very personal poems *The Departure of the Prodigal Son* (p. 67) and *The Stranger* (p. 271).

Besides these unorthodoxly 'religious' poems, the only others of *New Poems* behind which there is anything approaching an expoundable ideology are some in which Rilke's very personal notions of the contrast between typical manhood and typical womanhood appears. I have already mentioned those women whom he called 'the great lovers', whose unsatisfied and unsatisfiable ardours and longings he associated with those of the saints. These women had in a sense re-achieved their original intangibility and independence, for again and again in Rilke's poetry and prose appears the figure of a young girl or young woman startled out of the self-sufficiency, lonely without feeling lonely, of her own interior life and interior world by the impact of love, by the sudden and disturbing recognition of a reality outside her, by which her own inner world is threatened, and by which it may be overwhelmed (*Girl's Lament*, p. 47, *Woman in Love*, p. 265). In that splendid poem *Orpheus. Eurydice. Hermes*

(p. 143) Eurydice has, as it were, re-attained her original in-
tactness and intangibility, and the poem may well have been
written for the sake of that culminating moment when, hearing
Hermes exclaim 'He has turned round!', she asks uncompre-
hendingly 'Who?'; and that no less splendid poem *Alcestis* (p.
147) culminates in the speech where Alcestis says, in so many
words: 'You want a ransom, do you? Then take me. Aren't I as
good as dead already, torn out of the world of my girlhood and
married to that man?' Similarly, *The Abduction* (p. 281), a poem
which, like several others, recalls a poet whom Rilke had certainly never read and with whom few would think of comparing
him, Thomas Hardy, might almost have been written for the
sake of the point, or sting, in its last two lines:

> And heard estrangedly a stranger say:
> I'mherewithyou.

This woman whose appearance so often concludes with some
explicit or implicit satire on man as the eternal outsider (outside what Rilke understood by 'reality'), this woman whose
representatives in *Song of Women to the Poet* (p. 71) hail the poet
as 'you us-expresser', is of a type which many modern critics
would describe, contemptuously and in inverted commas, as
'sensitive', and has almost nothing in common with such memor-
able and un-Rilkean extraverts as (to name but a few) the Wife
of Bath, Mrs Quickly, Juliet's Nurse, Lady Macbeth, Emma, or
Mrs Proudie. Nevertheless, this Rilkean woman, as one may
call her, exists and has existed, and how her image came to take
shape in Rilke's mind and imagination may be suggested by
two prose quotations. On 7 September 1906 he wrote to Countess Mary Gneisenau, thinking of their friend Countess Luise
Schwerin, who had died at the beginning of the year:

It's strange (and in front of all portraits of women I saw here in the
neighbouring castles I felt it again and again), how very imperish-
able are the histories of women: perhaps because, even while they
are occurring, they already contain something unreachable, no-
longer-visible, in deepest misery blessed; because everything that
happens to women is already so detached, so yonderly distant: that,
perhaps, is why it can appear as though death did not carry a
woman any further off than she had always been, in her lonely
experiencing and longing, from everything already.

INTRODUCTION

In *The Note-Book of Malte Laurids Brigge* there are some more elaborate reflections on this detachment and intangibility of women:

> We know about her and her, because letters exist, which have been miraculously preserved, or books with reproachful or mournful poems, or pictures that look at us in a gallery through a mist of tears, with which the painter has succeeded because he did not know what it was. But there have been innumerably more of them; some who burnt their letters, and others who had no more strength to write them. Grey-haired women, who had grown hard, with a kernel of deliciousness in them, which they concealed. Shapeless, corpulent women, who, having grown stout from exhaustion, allowed themselves to become similar to their husbands and yet within were utterly different, there, where their love had laboured, in the dark. Bearers of children who never wanted to bear, and who, when they finally died in the eighth birth, had the gestures and the lightness of girls looking forward to love. And those who remained beside brawlers and topers because they had found the means of being in their own selves more distant from them than anywhere else; and when they came into company were unable to repress it, and shone as though they always consorted with the blest.[1]

I have described this woman as being lonely without feeling lonely; nevertheless, she is still a 'lonely figure', and it may be that in her, as in other lonely figures (the child, the shepherd, the prophet, the saint, even Christ himself) Rilke found some kind of objective correlative for his own situation as a poet, engaged in the lonely struggle to find what he once called 'my ownest expression' for so much that others had expressed differently.

Besides these ideologically symbolic poems (as they may be roughly described) and such poems as *The Swan* and *Roman Sarcophagi*, in which explicit comparisons are developed, there are several where, without saying that something outward is 'like' something inward, Rilke has described something outward, something seen, in such a way that we feel, or even know, that it is also, and equally, the description of something thought, or of some insight fleetingly apprehended. A beautiful example is *In a foreign Park* (p. 105), where we cannot but feel that the scene

---

[1] *Gesammelte Werke,* V, p. 161.

and situation so vividly evoked is a kind of objective correlative for certain deep and subtle intuitions into the relationship between brightness and darkness, life and death. So too in *The Apple Orchard* (p. 289), also inspired by recollections of Borgeby-Gård, we cannot but feel that, in describing the ingathering and outgiving of the orchard trees, Rilke is also describing the life-long activity of the poet and of all who in some ways resemble him. That he was probably thinking chiefly of the poet is suggested by a passage in that letter of 3 February 1923, 'A une Amie', from which I have already quoted.[1] Recalling some of his solitary experiences in foreign towns, he declared that he had not travelled in search of what are commonly called 'adventures', since he lacked the necessary quickness and decision and presence of mind: 'Myself, I am inwardly slow, I have that intrinsic slowness of the tree which is composing its growth and its florescence – Yes, I have a little of its admirable patience.' Nevertheless, even though in this and in some other poems Rilke may have been thinking chiefly of the poet, or of himself as a poet, we must resist the temptation, to which many have succumbed, of trying, on the one hand, to discover in every more or less representative figure in *New Poems* a symbol of the poet, and, on the other hand, of underestimating the wider relevance and validity of those qualities which Rilke regarded as most indispensable to the poet. In *Falconry* (p. 253), for example, one of my own great favourites, it was no doubt Rilke's 'admirable patience', a quality which he regarded as a most important part of his specifically poetic equipment, that enabled him to sympathise to a quite exceptional degree with the patience which at last enabled Frederick II to become a co-ascender with the falcon he had tamed; it would, though, be perverse to maintain either that the Emperor in this poem is primarily a symbol of the poet, or that the poem is in any sense a superficial presentation of that amazing man (*stupor mundi* to his contemporaries), who wrote a treatise on falconry, who regarded skill in it as one of the most important qualifications for offices of trust, and who lost the city of Parma while absent on a hawking expedition with one of his sons.

In the course of this attempt to suggest some of the ways in

[1] See p. 16.

which objectivity and subjectivity, 'pure' description and sym-
bolical description, are present in *New Poems*, several examples
have emerged of that ambiguity, or doubleness of attitude,
which makes it so difficult to see Rilke and his poetry as in
themselves they really were and are. A reader opening this book
for the first time and noticing the many poems in which castles,
parks, and various old-fashioned elegancies and graces appear,
might be inclined to suppose that Rilke was not only a tradi-
tionalist and a conservative, but also something of a snob; a
closer reading, though, might suggest to him that Rilke was
also something of a revolutionary, or, at any rate, a not very
dependable kind of conservative or establishment-defender, in
his attitude to life no less than in his style. In his attitude to the
world of elegance and great houses he has this in common with
Proust,[1] that he was fascinated by these things without being
taken in by them. There is nearly always some touch of irony
or light satire in his handling of them. He was more exclusively
concerned with their poetry than was Proust, and perhaps it
would not be unfair to Proust to say that Rilke's attitude towards
them was less worldly. His old friend Rudolf Kassner has recorded that, when he was a guest in houses where one dressed
for dinner, he used to wear, instead of a waistcoat, a high satin
or silk vest, similar to those worn by ecclesiastics, with a Russian
Cross suspended over it, in order to take away some of the
worldliness of the 'smoking', or even to disparage it a little.[2] He
had persuaded himself (see *Self-Portrait from the Year 1906*, p. 115),
groundlessly, as later research has revealed, that he was descended from an ancient aristocratic family in Carinthia, but even
about this there was perhaps something of make-believe, some
attempt to give himself roots in a world where he felt so rootless.
From a superficial reading of *New Poems* there might emerge the
image of an idle and elegant, though supremely gifted, *flâneur*,
leaning upon a silver-headed cane as he contemplates buildings,
sundials, fountains, animals, or flowers, an image quite incom-
patible with the *travailleur acharné* who achieved what he once
called 'the gigantic concentration' in which these poems were

[1] On other affinities between Rilke and Proust, see Introduction to *Poems
1906 to 1926*, 1959, p. 41.

[2] *Buch der Erinnerung*, 1938, p. 163.

written; and the similar image which, except when writing to very intimate friends, he sometimes presents in his letters, that of a homeless and rather helpless cosmopolitan aristocrat of great sensibility but almost exhausted energies, was largely, perhaps, a defiant protest against the bustling efficiency of the modern world. Indeed, all this side of him should probably be regarded as the Rilkean equivalent of Yeats's *A Vision* and all connected therewith, in which Edmund Wilson has seen an elaborate self-defensive mechanism to protect the poet from a world hostile to poetry. During and after the 1914 war he often expressed in letters his conviction that the old order was doomed. He detested Austria, and in modern Germany he detested everything except what he called 'the hidden roots'. He at first hailed the German revolution as a new beginning, and, while admitting that his own roots were in a world that had gone, continually exhorted his younger friends and acquaintances to welcome the opportunity of building a new one. In almost no matter of importance is it possible to give a plain answer to such questions as 'What did he really believe?', 'What was his real attitude?', 'Where did he really stand?' Perhaps he always stood, as it were, on the frontier, between two worlds, or between several worlds.

II

So far I have spoken chiefly of the content of *New Poems*, and I have left myself little space to consider what, as a translator, I have had mainly to concern myself with, their style. Mr H. M. Belmore, in that admirable study which I have already mentioned,[1] and which I recommend to all readers who desire a fuller treatment of this subject than I can offer them here, has well said that the language Rilke uses is that of German poetry, 'yet modified in such a subtle manner that we feel the variation more than the continuity'.[2] Here the operative word is 'subtle'; for although, as I have suggested in another context, there was something revolutionary about Rilke, he was no dogmatic or programmatic revolutionary. Unlike Hopkins, with whom Mr Belmore has compared him,[3] he never presents himself as a

---

[1] *Rilke's Craftsmanship* (Blackwell, Oxford), 1954.
[2] *Op. cit.*, p. 224.   [3] *Op. cit.*, p. 192.

conscious innovator or proclaimer of a new style, and he carried out his stylistic revolution 'with remarkably little fuss'.

I have already said that for Rilke perhaps the most indispensable of all poetic devices was the simile; nevertheless, important as is the part played by imagery in his poetry, I will venture to declare that its innermost secret is to be found, not in its imagery, but in its syntax and rhythms. Those long, winding sentences, full of subordinate clauses, questions, exclamations, parentheses, and participles, often extending throughout a whole poem, communicate, as Mr Belmore has said,[1] not merely a result but a process: Rilke's attempt to analyse as accurately as possible, and with the maximum fullness compatible with the maximum concentration, precisely what and how a particular 'thing felt' came to be and to mean for him at a particular moment. The 'what', one might perhaps say, making a rather crude distinction, could be communicated by images (although in some of the finest poems a comparatively small part is played by imagery), but the 'how', the inner vibration, could be communicated only by rhythm, a rhythm whose complexity often required a correspondingly elaborate syntax. A good and characteristic example is *The Lace* (p. 99), a poem consisting of two parts, of which the first contains thirteen lines, while the second, which contains fourteen, is technically, like no less than fifty of *New Poems*, a sonnet.[2] In the first poem Rilke considers the possibility that the maker of a piece of lace he is contemplating may have sacrificed her sight to make it, although within this thing made she has incorporated, rescuing it from transience, her happiness and even her soul. In the second poem he considers (to speak somewhat old-fashionedly) the moral of this, its applicability to life in general: when life comes to assume *this sort* of meaninglessness, a thing *like this* can give it *this sort* of meaning; when life feels like *that*, such a thing can make it feel like *this*. The mere *what*, the mere idea, that the maker's life, or some of it, can achieve permanence in a thing made, and that a work of art, a thing made, is more meaningful than life itself as we commonly experience it – this is almost trite;

[1] *Op. cit.*, p. 84.
[2] Several other poems might be regarded as sonnets with codas: *e.g.*, *The Merry-go-round*, p. 125.

36

Rilke's whole emphasis is upon the *how*: *how* the contrast between the general meaninglessness of life and the meaningfulness of a piece of lace presented itself to him at a particular moment, what inner vibrations it set up in him; and these inner vibrations he can communicate only in and through a complex rhythmical pattern and a complex syntax. The poem begins with a sentence occupying eight lines, in which he tries to collect and hold together the essential elements of this contrast as he has felt them at a particular moment.

> And if one day our doing and our ado's
> and all that happens to us should appear
> trivial and strange, and it were far from clear
> why we should struggle out of children's shoes
> merely for that – would not, perhaps, this run
> of yellowed lace, this finely woven length
> of flowery lace, then have sufficient strength
> to keep us here? For look, it all got done.
>
> A life perhaps was slighted, who can know?
> A chance of happiness let slip – yet, spite
> of all, there still emerged, however slow,
> this thing, not easier than life, but quite
> perfect, and, oh, so beautiful – as though
> *now* were no more too soon for smiles and flight.

It is this continual outstretching and in-grasping, reflected in the contest between the metrical pattern and the rhythmical, or sentence, pattern, that gives to so many of Rilke's poems their peculiar tension, a tension that might almost be called dramatic. In this contrast between the metrical pattern and the rhythmical pattern there is a remarkable affinity between Rilke and some of our own seventeenth-century poets, especially Donne, the Donne of the *Songs and Sonets*. In a brilliant, though somewhat unsympathetic, essay on Donne, Professor J. E. V. Crofts says of those highly intricate and exacting metrical patterns which Donne apparently invented for himself:

What makes it more curious is that, having gone to the trouble of inventing these patterns, he persistently effaces and makes us forget them by allowing the natural rhythm of his language to pour over them, like a flood over a harrow, drowning them out of sight. . . He seems to have regarded the pattern of verse (when he thought

about it) not as an aid or an instrument of expression, but as a kind
of obstacle, like the intricate wards of a lock; and the game of
versification consisted in cutting the key of words so cunningly that
it would move through them all without touching, as though they
were not there.[1]

The odd thing is that, in describing what seems to him a mere
exhibition of puzzling perversity, Professor Crofts has most ad-
mirably reminded us of the characteristic virtue of many of
Donne's poems: the fact that the 'naturalness' of their speech-
rhythms is enormously heightened, set off, made twice as natural
by the 'artificiality' of his metrical patterns, by the contrast between the informality of his sentences and the formality of his
metrical forms, and that the fitting of these long, complex, yet
natural-sounding sentences into elaborate verse-patterns trans-
figures prose and common speech and the rhythms of common
speech into the most unquestionable poetry. Prose defiantly and
triumphantly compels us to recognise it as poetry. Rilke, like
Donne, is a tremendous virtuoso, continually wagering, as it
were, that he can transform prose into poetry, and compelling
us to admit that he has succeeded. And the contrast, the tension, between informality and formality is even more surprising
and exciting in Rilke's poetry than in Donne's, since Rilke's
rhymes, partly because of the frequent alternation between masculine and feminine ones, are generally more conspicuous (it
has been recorded that, in reciting his poetry, he put great
emphasis upon them), besides being often astonishingly daring
or ingenious; and by means of these emphatic rhymes the metrical pattern keeps vigorously re-asserting itself against the inun-
dating rhythm. There is a similar virtuosity in Yeats's mature
poetry, a similar surprising contrast between the colloquiality
of his sentences and the formality of his verse-forms, although
Yeats was both a less exact and a less ingenious rhymer than
Rilke, and his rhythms, though essentially speech-rhythms, tend
to be more consistently oratorical, or even solemn, than Rilke's,
whose voice, even within a single short poem, can reveal an
astonishing range and variety of inflection. Some, perhaps,
might be inclined to regard it as a characteristically feminine

[1] 'John Donne', in *Essays and Studies by Members of the English Association*,
1937, pp. 138-9.

rather than a characteristically masculine voice – one is often reminded of the excited and exciting comments and reflections of Virginia Woolf. *Du Uns-Sagender*, 'you us-expresser', he makes the women exclaim at the end of his *Song of Women to the Poet* (p. 71).

Yeats has told us[1] how he only gradually came to recognise that, for his special purpose, he must use nothing but the common syntax; and in some of the best seventeenth-century poems, including those of Donne himself, the effectiveness of that peculiar contrast I have been describing is too often impaired by the use of inversions for the sake of rhyme, or even for the sake of mere metrical convenience. In *New Poems* Rilke only occasionally departs from normal word order, and then nearly always for the sake of some special emphasis. His vocabulary is large, with numerous words borrowed from French, and with several of his own invention, but the relationship between the language of his poetry and what Wordsworth called 'the language really used by men', a relationship which, as Professor Zinn has remarked in his epilogue to the fourth volume of the new edition of Rilke's Collected Works, even Germans have found it so hard to describe, is not one that can be exhibited by means of inventories and lists. Looked at from the reader's point of view, it is a relationship in which we are perpetually, simultaneously, and, I think, exceptionally aware of likeness and unlikeness, of resemblance in difference and difference in resemblance. The words and the rhythms are those of cultivated speech, idealised, transfigured, and, as it were, resurrected by elaborate rhythmical and metrical patterns. There are some most interesting remarks about poetry and the language of poetry in some of the letters which, during the last years of his life, Rilke wrote to Countess Margot Sizzo, who in the summer of 1921 had sent him her manuscript translation of his *Cornet* into French. In a letter of 17 March 1922, speaking of the poet Richard Dehmel, who was always urging writers to get away from their desks and out into what he called 'life', as though mere writing were something that came of itself, and not a craft that had to be learnt like any other, Rilke passionately declared that

---

[1] *Autobiographies*, 1926, p. 190.

No word in a poem (I mean here every 'and' or 'the' or 'that') is *identical* with the like-sounding word in ordinary usage and conversation; the purer legitimacy, the large relationship, the constellation which receives it in verse or in artistic prose alters it to the very kernel of its nature, makes it useless, unfit for mere intercourse, inviolable and lasting.

He then recalled how Dehmel, before the War, had reproached him for spending so much of his life abroad, to which he had contented himself with replying that abroad he enjoyed the great advantage of not hearing German, usually spoken so badly and so carelessly, spoken around him, and of allowing it to achieve a singular concentration and clarity *within* him.[1]

At the risk of appearing egotistical, I will conclude these remarks and this Introduction with a confession and a personal experience. I had been inclined to regard Rilke's remarks to the Countess Sizzo about the difference between words in poetry and words in common speech as a piece of pardonable exaggeration, until, quite recently, I was visiting a woman friend, a great lover of poetry, who, as she was accustomed to do, asked me to read aloud some of my unpublished translations. I read some of my versions of *New Poems*, including *Eve* (p. 207), which especially pleased her and which she asked me to read again and yet again. There is only one simile in this poem, and, except for its opening lines, the effect of it depends hardly at all upon imagery and almost entirely upon rhythm; for, if Rilke has here 'depicted' anything, it is Eve's sigh on leaving Paradise, and how can a sigh be represented except either by musical sounds (the penultimate movement of Beethoven's C sharp minor quar-

---

[1] *Die Briefe an Gräfin Sizzo*, 1950, pp. 20-21. Lou Andreas-Salomé has recorded that she once expressed the fear that his long residence in Paris might prevent him from achieving the finest and last degree of intimacy with the German language, to which Rilke replied: 'Oh no! That intimacy thrives on it! Just think how many, many words I *save* for myself through not using them up on everyday banalities!' (*Rainer Maria Rilke*, 1929, pp. 90-91). On 1 July 1920 he wrote to Kippenberg from Venice, which he had been able to re-visit briefly from Switzerland: 'How I long to be out in the world again, among the similes I used to receive from it, in foreign-speaking regions where no one knows me and where language, my own, will shine out again in perpetual relief as material for my work' (*Briefe an seinen Verleger*, 1934, p. 306; 1949, Bd. II, p. 358).

tet is a superb example) or by rhythmically ordered words, which have received from the poet and which transmit to the reader what I can best describe as a certain inner vibration? In translating this poem I had tried to follow Rilke's rhythms as closely as I could, and, while retaining a natural word-order, to entice from the simplest words the maximum vibration.

> Ah, she could have stayed so gladly, though . . .

This, it seemed to me, sounded 'natural', 'like' a sort of idealised common speech; but how did my friend spontaneously express her admiration for it? 'How different those words are from ours!', she exclaimed. I was momentarily astonished by this remark; then I suddenly recalled what Rilke had written to the Countess Sizzo, with, as it had hitherto seemed to me, some exaggeration. Had he, then, not been exaggerating, and was what I had been trying to sound 'like' not, after all, common speech, or common speech so idealised that it no longer sounded 'like' but 'how different!'? And had I, for once, at any rate, succeeded, by means of rhythm and context, in altering words such as 'so', 'though', 'longer', 'go', and 'with' 'to the very kernel of their nature'? To some extent, perhaps. And yet, how often, when re-reading something with which I had for long been tolerably satisfied, have I not recalled another passage in a letter to the Countess Sizzo (15 December 1921). Just because her translation of his *Cornet* had achieved some measure of success, he must, Rilke declared, judge it all the more severely:

> For when anywhere in the realm of art a certain achievement is reached, there forthwith presents itself the demand for perfection, or at least for what we are more or less ready to call by that name. And the longer one practises this singular métier of artistic activity, the severer one becomes towards all who meddle with it, and has, if one finally grows relentless, only the one excuse: that one is no less so towards oneself.

New Poems
First Part

Karl und Elisabeth von der Heydt
in Freundschaft

FRÜHER APOLLO

WIE manches Mal durch das noch unbelaubte
Gezweig ein Morgen durchsieht, der schon ganz
im Frühling ist: so ist in seinem Haupte
nichts, was verhindern könnte, daß der Glanz

aller Gedichte uns fast tödlich träfe;
denn noch kein Schatten ist in seinem Schaun,
zu kühl für Lorbeer sind noch seine Schläfe,
und später erst wird aus den Augenbraun

hochstämmig sich der Rosengarten heben,
aus welchem Blätter, einzeln, ausgelöst
hintreiben werden auf des Mundes Beben,

der jetzt noch still ist, niegebraucht und blinkend
und nur mit seinem Lächeln etwas trinkend
als würde ihm sein Singen eingeflößt.

MÄDCHEN-KLAGE

DIESE Neigung, in den Jahren,
da wir alle Kinder waren,
viel allein zu sein, war mild;
andern ging die Zeit im Streite,
und man hatte seine Seite,
seine Nähe, seine Weite,
einen Weg, ein Tier, ein Bild.

Und ich dachte noch, das Leben
hörte niemals auf zu geben,
daß man sich in sich besinnt.
Bin ich in mir nicht im Größten?
Will mich Meines nicht mehr trösten
und verstehen wie als Kind?

Plötzlich bin ich wie verstoßen,
und zu einem Übergroßen

EARLY APOLLO

As framing boughs, still leafless, can exhibit
a morning that's already all in Spring,
there's nothing in his head that could prohibit
the splendour of all poems from centering

upon us with an almost fatal shining;
for in his gaze as yet no shadow plays,
his temples are too cool for laurel's twining,
and from his eyebrows not till later days

will that tall-stemmed rose garden be uplifting,
and loosened petals, one by one, be drifting
along the tremors of the mouth below,

as yet still silent, sparkling and unused,
just drinking something with its smile, as though
its singing were being gradually infused.

Paris, 11 July 1906

GIRL'S LAMENT

THIS inclining to be lonely,
in those years when we were only
small, was gentle after all;
others' time was all resistance,
and one had one's own consistence,
one's own nearness, one's own distance,
picture, pathway, animal.

And I still believed that living
always would continue giving
times for self-withdrawingness.
Is some greater still outside me?
Will what's mine no more provide me
calm and comprehendingness?

Suddenly I seem outhounded,
and to something too unbounded

47

wird mir diese Einsamkeit,
wenn, auf meiner Brüste Hügeln
stehend, mein Gefühl nach Flügeln
oder einem Ende schreit.

LIEBES-LIED

Wie soll ich meine Seele halten, daß
sie nicht an deine rührt? Wie soll ich sie
hinheben über dich zu andern Dingen?
Ach gerne möcht ich sie bei irgendwas
Verlorenem im Dunkel unterbringen
an einer fremden stillen Stelle, die
nicht weiterschwingt, wenn deine Tiefen schwingen.
Doch alles, was uns anrührt, dich und mich,
nimmt uns zusammen wie ein Bogenstrich,
der aus zwei Saiten *eine* Stimme zieht.
Auf welches Instrument sind wir gespannt?
Und welcher Geiger hat uns in der Hand?
O süßes Lied.

these my solitudes extend,
when on my breasts' eminences
stands my feeling and commences
crying for wings or for an end.

Paris, c. 1 July 1906

LOVE-SONG

How shall I hold my soul, that it may not
be touching yours? How shall I lift it then
above you to where other things are waiting?
Ah, gladly would I lodge it, all-forgot,
with some lost thing the dark is isolating
on some remote and silent spot that, when
your depths vibrate, is not itself vibrating.
You and me – all that lights upon us, though,
brings us together like a fiddle-bow
drawing *one* voice from two strings it glides along.
Across what instrument have we been spanned?
And what violinist holds us in his hand?
O sweetest song.

Capri, mid-March 1907

ERANNA AN SAPPHO

O DU wilde weite Werferin:
Wie ein Speer bei andern Dingen
lag ich bei den Meinen. Dein Erklingen
warf mich weit. Ich weiß nicht, *wo* ich bin.
Mich kann keiner wiederbringen.

Meine Schwestern denken mich und weben,
und das Haus ist voll vertrauter Schritte.
Ich allein bin fern und fortgegeben,
und ich zittere wie eine Bitte;
denn die schöne Göttin in der Mitte
ihrer Mythen glüht und lebt mein Leben.

SAPPHO AN ERANNA

UNRUH will ich über dich bringen,
schwingen will ich dich, umrankter Stab.
Wie das Sterben will ich dich durchdringen
und dich weitergeben wie das Grab
an das Alles: allen diesen Dingen.

ERANNA TO SAPPHO

O you wild adept at throwing!
Like a spear by other things, I'd lain
there beside my next of kin. Your strain
flung me far. To *where*'s beyond my knowing.
None can bring me back again.

Sisters think upon me as they twine,
and the house is full of warm relation.
I alone am out of the design,
and I tremble like a supplication;
for the lovely goddess all creation
bowers in legend lives this life of mine.

SAPPHO TO ERANNA

With unrest I want to inundate you,
want to brandish you, you vine-wreathed stave.
Want, like death itself, to penetrate you
and to pass you onwards like the grave
to the All: to all these things that wait you.

Meudon, winter 1905-6

SAPPHO AN ALKAÏOS

FRAGMENT

UND was hättest du mir denn zu sagen,
und was gehst du meine Seele an,
wenn sich deine Augen niederschlagen
vor dem nahen Nichtgesagten? Mann,

sieh, uns hat das Sagen dieser Dinge
hingerissen und bis in den Ruhm.
Wenn ich denke: unter euch verginge
dürftig unser süßes Mädchentum,

welches wir, ich Wissende und jene
mit mir Wissenden, vom Gott bewacht,
trugen unberührt, daß Mytilene
wie ein Apfelgarten in der Nacht
duftete vom Wachsen unsrer Brüste –.

Ja, auch dieser Brüste, die du nicht
wähltest wie zu Fruchtgewinden, Freier
mit dem weggesenkten Angesicht.
Geh und laß mich, daß zu meiner Leier
komme, was du abhältst: alles steht.

Dieser Gott ist nicht der Beistand Zweier,
aber wenn er durch den Einen geht

. . . . . .

SAPPHO TO ALCAEUS

FRAGMENT

WHAT, though, would you have to tell me really,
what are you to my soul anyway,
when your eyes sink down before that nearly
uttered something that you never say?

Look, man, these are just the things whose saying,
till we're famed, has so enraptured us.
When I think: with you would be decaying
that sweet maidenhood which now we've thus, –

I the seer and all those who've been illumined by me, to a god's delight, –
borne inviolate, till Mytilene,
like an apple-orchard in the night,
with the ripening of our breasts is fragrant. –

Yes, with these breasts too that you have passed
over for your fruit-wreaths, wooer there,
standing with the countenance downcast.
Leave me, so that what you will not spare,
to my lyre may come: all's unbegun.

This god's no assistance to a pair;
when, though, he shall deign to pass through one

. . . .

Paris, 24 July 1907

A letter to his wife on the day after he had written this poem reveals that it was
inspired by an ancient vase-painting – almost certainly that of the fifth century B.C.
in the Glyptothek at Munich – which represents Sappho and Alcaeus, with lyres in
their hands, confronting each other, Alcaeus with bowed head. This may perhaps
be regarded as an illustration of some verses attributed to Alcaeus and Sappho by
Aristotle and quoted by him in the *Rhetoric* (I, ix, 20) as an example of the kind of
things that make us feel ashamed. Alcaeus says: 'I want to tell you something, but
shame restrains me'; to which Sappho replies (I translate that version of the text
which had reached Rilke): 'If your wish had been for things good or noble and
your tongue had not been concocting for its utterance something base, shame
would not have cast down your eyes, but you would have rightly spoken of it.' For
a full discussion of the fragment see Denys Page, *Sappho and Alcaeus*, 1955, pp. 104ff.

GRABMAL
EINES JUNGEN MÄDCHENS

WIR gedenkens noch. Das ist, als müßte
alles diese einmal wieder sein.
Wie ein Baum an der Limonenküste
trugst du deine kleinen leichten Brüste
in das Rauschen seines Bluts hinein:

– jenes Gottes.
                    Und es war der schlanke
Flüchtling, der Verwöhnende der Fraun.
Süß und glühend, warm wie dein Gedanke,
überschattend deine frühe Flanke
und geneigt wie deine Augenbraun.

OPFER

O WIE blüht mein Leib aus jeder Ader
duftender, seitdem ich dich erkenn;
sieh, ich gehe schlanker und gerader,
und du wartest nur – : wer bist du denn?

Sieh: ich fühle, wie ich mich entferne,
wie ich Altes, Blatt um Blatt, verlier.
Nur dein Lächeln steht wie lauter Sterne
über dir und bald auch über mir.

Alles was durch meine Kinderjahre
namenlos noch und wie Wasser glänzt,
will ich nach dir nennen am Altare,
der entzündet ist von deinem Haare
und mit deinen Brüsten leicht bekränzt.

FUNERAL MONUMENT OF
A YOUNG GIRL

WE recall it still. As though once more
all of it must sometime come to be.
Like a tree along the lemon-shore,
those small lightsome breasts of yours you bore
out towards his blood's insurgency:

– that divinity's.
                    That slim, appealing
fugitive, so spoiling womenkind.
Sweet and glowing, warm as your own feeling,
overshadowing your unconcealing
flanks and, like those brows of yours, inclined.

Meudon, winter 1905-6

SACRIFICE

How my body flowers with ever-greater
fragrance since you came into my ken;
look, my walk is slimmer now and straighter,
and you merely wait: – Who are you, then?

Look: I feel how far I am already,
shedding, leaf on leaf, what used to be.
Your smile only like a star hangs steady
over you and soon will over me.

What through childish years I can but claim to
see like nameless water glittering,
on that altar I will give your name to,
altar which your hair has set a flame to
and your breasts are lightly garlanding.

Meudon, winter 1905-6

ÖSTLICHES TAGLIED

Ist dieses Bette nicht wie eine Küste,
ein Küstenstreifen nur, darauf wir liegen?
Nichts ist gewiß als deine hohen Brüste,
die mein Gefühl in Schwindeln überstiegen.

Denn diese Nacht, in der so vieles schrie,
in der sich Tiere rufen und zerreißen,
ist sie uns nicht entsetzlich fremd? Und wie:
was draußen langsam anhebt, Tag geheißen,
ist das uns denn verständlicher als sie?

Man müßte so sich ineinanderlegen
wie Blütenblätter um die Staubgefäße:
so sehr ist überall das Ungemäße
und häuft sich an und stürzt sich uns entgegen.

Doch während wir uns aneinander drücken,
um nicht zu sehen, wie es ringsum naht,
kann es aus dir, kann es aus mir sich zücken:
denn unsre Seelen leben von Verrat.

EASTERN AUBADE

Does it not, though, like a coast appear,
a strip of coast, this bed on which we're lying?
Those lofty breasts of yours alone are clear
to my grown-dizzy feeling's dim descrying.

For, oh, this night in which so much was screaming,
in which beasts called and rent themselves in prey,
is it not grimly strange to us? And, gleaming
outside so slowly there and called the day,
is that too really more familiar-seeming?

One needs to be as much within another
as anthers are in petals: so unending
around us things immeasurably transcending
accumulate until they almost smother.

While, though, with these embraces we are keeping
unnoticed that in-closing enmity,
from you, from me, it still can be outleaping:
for, oh, our spirits live by treachery.

Paris, May-June 1906

57

ABISAG

I

SIE lag. Und ihre Kinderarme waren
von Dienern um den Welkenden gebunden,
auf dem sie lag die süßen langen Stunden,
ein wenig bang vor seinen vielen Jahren.

Und manchmal wandte sie in seinem Barte
ihr Angesicht, wenn eine Eule schrie;
und alles, was die Nacht war, kam und scharte
mit Bangen und Verlangen sich um sie.

Die Sterne zitterten wie ihresgleichen,
ein Duft ging suchend durch das Schlafgemach,
der Vorhang rührte sich und gab ein Zeichen,
und leise ging ihr Blick dem Zeichen nach –.

Aber sie hielt sich an dem dunkeln Alten
und, von der Nacht der Nächte nicht erreicht,
lag sie auf seinem fürstlichen Erkalten
jungfräulich und wie eine Seele leicht.

II

Der König saß und sann den leeren Tag
getaner Taten, ungefühlter Lüste
und seiner Lieblingshündin, der er pflag –.
Aber am Abend wölbte Abisag
sich über ihm. Sein wirres Leben lag
verlassen wie verrufne Meeresküste
unter dem Sternbild ihrer stillen Brüste.

Und manchmal, als ein Kundiger der Frauen,
erkannte er durch seine Augenbrauen
den unbewegten, küsselosen Mund;
und sah: ihres Gefühles grüne Rute
neigte sich nicht herab zu seinem Grund.
Ihn fröstelte. Er horchte wie ein Hund
und suchte sich in seinem letzten Blute.

ABISAG

I

SHE lay. Those childish arms of hers were tied
by servants round that witherer-away,
on whom throughout the long sweet hours she lay,
by his great age a little terrified.

And now and then her countenance would stir
within his beard there when an owl had hooted;
and all that ever Night was convoluted
in anxiousness and longing over her.

The stars were quivering as with like emotion,
a scent passed through the chamber seekingly,
a sign was given by the curtain's motion,
sign which her glance had followed furtively. –

But still she clung against his sombre oldness,
and, all-unreached by Night's benightingness,
lay there upon his royal growing-coldness
with maidenly and spirit lightsomeness.

II

The King sat thinking through the empty day
of doings done, of unfelt delectation,
and sometimes with his favourite dog would play.
Abisag, though, when light was growing grey,
arched over him. His mazy being lay
like some avoided coast-line's isolation
beneath her quiet breasts' twin-constellation.

And now and then, as one in women wise,
through his thick eyebrows he would recognise
the all-unmoved, unkissing mouth; and found
her feeling's green divining rod was showing
no inclination to his under-ground.
Chill came on him. He hearkened like a hound
and sought himself within his blood's last flowing.

Meudon, winter 1905-6
I Kings, i, 1-4.

DAVID SINGT VOR SAUL

I

KÖNIG, hörst du, wie mein Saitenspiel
Fernen wirft, durch die wir uns bewegen:
Sterne treiben uns verwirrt entgegen,
und wir fallen endlich wie ein Regen,
und es blüht, wo dieser Regen fiel.

Mädchen blühen, die du noch erkannt,
die jetzt Frauen sind und mich verführen;
den Geruch der Jungfraun kannst du spüren,
und die Knaben stehen, angespannt
schlank und atmend, an verschwiegnen Türen.

Daß mein Klang dir alles wiederbrächte.
Aber trunken taumelt mein Getön:
Deine Nächte, König, deine Nächte –,
und wie waren, die dein Schaffen schwächte,
o wie waren alle Leiber schön.

Dein Erinnern glaub ich zu begleiten,
weil ich ahne. Doch auf welchen Saiten
greif ich dir ihr dunkles Lustgestöhn? –

II

König, der du alles dieses hattest
und der du mit lauter Leben mich
überwältigest und überschattest:
komm aus deinem Throne und zerbrich
meine Harfe, die du so ermattest.

Sie ist wie ein abgenommner Baum:
durch die Zweige, die dir Frucht getragen,
schaut jetzt eine Tiefe wie von Tagen,
welche kommen –, und ich kenn sie kaum.

Laß mich nicht mehr bei der Harfe schlafen;
sieh dir diese Knabenhand da an:
glaubst du, König, daß sie die Oktaven
eines Leibes noch nicht greifen kann?

DAVID SINGS BEFORE SAUL

I

CAN you hear, King, how my instrument
flings out distances through which we're wending?
Stars encounter us uncomprehending,
and at last like rain we are descending,
and a flowering follows that descent.

Girls you still were able to possess
flower from women tempting my defences;
scent of virgins re-assails your senses;
slender boys stand, all excitedness,
panting where some hidden stair commences.

Would my strings could bring back everything!
But my music's reeling drunkenly.
Ah, those nights of yours, those nights, my King, –
and, grown heavier from your handselling,
how superb those bodies all could be!

I can match you their remembered splendour,
since I can divine it. How, though, render
for you their dark groans of ecstasy?

II

King, who had such blessings here below,
and who now with life that never ceases
overshadow me and overthrow:
come down from your throne and break in pieces
this my harp you are exhausting so.

Look, it's like an amputated tree:
through its boughs, where fruits for you were growing,
depths now, as of days to come, are showing, –
scarcely recognisable by me.

Let me by its side no more be sleeping;
look, King, at this boyish hand: do you
really think it cannot yet be leaping
through the octaves of a body too?

III

König, birgst du dich in Finsternissen,
und ich hab dich doch in der Gewalt.
Sieh, mein festes Lied ist nicht gerissen,
und der Raum wird um uns beide kalt.
Mein verwaistes Herz und dein verworrnes
hängen in den Wolken deines Zornes,
wütend ineinander eingebissen
und zu einem einzigen verkrallt.

Fühlst du jetzt, wie wir uns umgestalten?
König, König, das Gewicht wird Geist.
Wenn wir uns nur aneinanderhalten,
du am Jungen, König, ich am Alten,
sind wir fast wie ein Gestirn das kreist.

III

Though you're hiding in the dark somewhere,
King, I have you still within my hold.
Look, my firm-spun song's without a tear,
and the space around us both grows cold.
My deserted heart and your untended
in your anger's clouds are both suspended,
madly bit into each other there
and into a single heart uprolled.

How we change each other, can you clearly
feel now? Burden's being inspirited.
If we hold to one another merely,
you to youth, King, I to age, we're nearly
like a star that's circling overhead.

Meudon, winter 1905-6
I Samuel, xvi, 14-23.

JOSUAS LANDTAG

So wie der Strom am Ausgang seine Dämme
durchbricht mit seiner Mündung Übermaß,
so brach nun durch die Ältesten der Stämme
zum letzten Mal die Stimme Josuas.

Wie waren die geschlagen, welche lachten,
wie hielten alle Herz und Hände an,
als hübe sich der Lärm von dreißig Schlachten
in einem Mund; und dieser Mund begann.

Und wieder waren Tausende voll Staunen
wie an dem großen Tag vor Jericho,
nun aber waren in ihm die Posaunen,
und ihres Lebens Mauern schwankten so,

daß sie sich wälzten von Entsetzen trächtig
und wehrlos schon und überwältigt, eh
sie's noch gedachten, wie er eigenmächtig
zu Gibeon die Sonne anschrie: steh!

Und Gott ging hin, erschrocken wie ein Knecht,
und hielt die Sonne, bis ihm seine Hände
wehtaten, ob dem schlachtenden Geschlecht,
nur weil da einer wollte, daß sie stände.

Und das war dieser; dieser Alte wars,
von dem sie meinten, daß er nicht mehr gelte
inmitten seines hundertzehnten Jahrs.
Da stand er auf und brach in ihre Zelte.

Er ging wie Hagel nieder über Halmen:
Was wollt ihr Gott versprechen? Ungezählt
stehn um euch Götter, wartend, daß ihr wählt.
Doch wenn ihr wählt, wird euch der Herr zermalmen.

Und dann, mit einem Hochmut ohnegleichen:
Ich und mein Haus, wir bleiben ihm vermählt.

Da schrien sie alle: Hilf uns, gieb ein Zeichen
und stärke uns zu unserer schweren Wahl.

Aber sie sahn ihn, wie seit Jahren schweigend,
zu seiner festen Stadt am Berge steigend;
und dann nicht mehr. Es war das letzte Mal.

JOSHUA'S COUNCIL

As some outflowing river breaks its tether,
pouring in pomp of waters from afar,
so broke upon the elders met together
for the last time the voice of Joshua.

How those who had been laughing were discounted,
how hearts and hands were checked by every man,
as though the din of thirty battles mounted
within one mouth, and that one mouth began.

And once again the thousands were astounded
as on the great day before Jericho,
though now it was in him the trumpets sounded
and their own lives the walls that tottered so

that not till rolling in the pangs of fear,
defencelessly, they seemed to understand
that this was he who, born to domineer,
had shouted to the sun in Gideon: Stand!

And God had gone off in humiliation,
and held the sun, until his hands were tired,
above that immolating generation,
only because one man had so required.

And this was he – whose blood, though they had ceased
to care about him in their calculations,
his five score years and ten had not decreased.
He rose and broke upon their habitations.

Like hail on standing harvests he descended:
What would ye promise God? On every side
uncounted gods await what ye decide.
Choose, and be crushed by Him ye have offended.

And then, with arrogance till then unspoken:
I and my house have been and are his bride.

Whereat they all cried: Help us, give some token,
that this hard choice may not bring punishment.

But they saw him, silent, without pity,
reascending to his mountain city;
then no more. It was the last descent.

Paris, shortly before 9 July 1906
Joshua, xxiii and xxiv.

DER AUSZUG
DES VERLORENEN SOHNES

Nun fortzugehn von alledem Verworrnen,
das unser ist und uns doch nicht gehört,
das, wie das Wasser in den alten Bornen,
uns zitternd spiegelt und das Bild zerstört;
von allem diesen, das sich wie mit Dornen
noch einmal an uns anhängt – fortzugehn
und Das und Den,
die man schon nicht mehr sah
(so täglich waren sie und so gewöhnlich),
auf einmal anzuschauen: sanft, versöhnlich
und wie an einem Anfang und von nah;
und ahnend einzusehn, wie unpersönlich,
wie über alle hin das Leid geschah,
von dem die Kindheit voll war bis zum Rand –:
Und dann doch fortzugehen, Hand aus Hand,
als ob man ein Geheiltes neu zerrisse,
und fortzugehn: wohin? Ins Ungewisse,
weit in ein unverwandtes warmes Land,
das hinter allem Handeln wie Kulisse
gleichgültig sein wird: Garten oder Wand;
und fortzugehn: warum? Aus Drang, aus Artung,
aus Ungeduld, aus dunkler Erwartung,
aus Unverständlichkeit und Unverstand:

Dies alles auf sich nehmen und vergebens
vielleicht Gehaltnes fallen lassen, um
allein zu sterben, wissend nicht warum –

Ist das der Eingang eines neuen Lebens?

THE DEPARTURE
OF THE PRODIGAL SON

Now to depart from all this incoherence
that's ours, but which we can't appropriate,
and, like old well-springs, mirrors our appearance
in trembling outlines that disintegrate;
from all this, that with bramble-like adherence
is once more clinging to us – to depart,
and then to start
bestowing on this and that you'd ceased to see
(so took for granted was their ministration)
a sudden gaze: all reconciliation,
tender and close and new-beginningly;
and to divine the whelming desolation,
the inexorable impersonality,
of all that childhood needed to withstand: –
And even then depart, hand out of hand,
as though you tore a wound that had been healing,
and to depart: whither? To unrevealing
distance, to some warm, unrelated land,
that, back-clothwise, will stay, without all feeling,
behind all action: garden, sea or sand;
and to depart: why? Impulse, generation,
impatience, obscure hope, and desperation
not to be understood or understand:

To take on all this, and, in vain persistence,
let fall, perhaps what you have held, to die
alone and destitute, not knowing why –

Is this the way into some new existence?

Paris, June 1906
Luke, xv, 11-32.

DER ÖLBAUM-GARTEN

Er ging hinauf unter dem grauen Laub
ganz grau und aufgelöst im Ölgelände
und legte seine Stirne voller Staub
tief in das Staubigsein der heißen Hände.

Nach allem dies. Und dieses war der Schluß.
Jetzt soll ich gehen, während ich erblinde,
und warum willst Du, daß ich sagen muß
Du seist, wenn ich Dich selber nicht mehr finde.

Ich finde Dich nicht mehr. Nicht in mir, nein.
Nicht in den andern. Nicht in diesem Stein.
Ich finde Dich nicht mehr. Ich bin allein.

Ich bin allein mit aller Menschen Gram,
den ich durch Dich zu lindern unternahm,
der Du nicht bist. O namenlose Scham...

Später erzählte man: ein Engel kam –.

Warum ein Engel? Ach es kam die Nacht
und blätterte gleichgültig in den Bäumen.
Die Jünger rührten sich in ihren Träumen.
Warum ein Engel? Ach es kam die Nacht.

Die Nacht, die kam, war keine ungemeine;
so gehen hunderte vorbei.
Da schlafen Hunde und da liegen Steine.
Ach eine traurige, ach irgendeine,
die wartet, bis es wieder Morgen sei.

Denn Engel kommen nicht zu solchen Betern,
und Nächte werden nicht um solche groß.
Die sich-Verlierenden läßt alles los,
und sie sind preisgegeben von den Vätern
und ausgeschlossen aus der Mütter Schooß.

THE OLIVE GARDEN

AND still he climbed, and through the grey leaves thrust,
quite grey and lost in the grey olive lands,
and laid his burning forehead full of dust
deep in the dustiness of burning hands.

After all, this. And, this, then, was the end.
Now I'm to go, while I am going blind;
and, oh, why wilt Thou have me still contend
Thou art, whom I myself no longer find.

No more I find Thee. In myself no tone
of Thee; nor in the rest; nor in this stone.
I can find Thee no more. I am alone.

I am alone with all that human fate
I undertook through Thee to mitigate,
Thou who art not. Oh, shame too consummate . . .

An angel came, those afterwards relate.

Wherefore an angel? Oh, there came the night,
and turned the leaves of trees indifferently,
and the disciples stirred uneasily.
Wherefore an angel? Oh, there came the night.

The night that came requires no specifying;
just so a hundred nights go by,
while dogs are sleeping and while stones are lying –
just any melancholy night that, sighing,
lingers till morning mount the sky.

For angels never come to such men's prayers,
nor nights for them mix glory with their gloom.
Forsakenness is the self-loser's doom,
and such are absent from their father's cares
and disincluded from their mother's womb.

Paris, May-June 1906
Luke, xxii, 39-46.

PIETÀ

So seh ich, Jesus, deine Füße wieder,
die damals eines Jünglings Füße waren,
da ich sie bang entkleidete und wusch;
wie standen sie verwirrt in meinen Haaren
und wie ein weißes Wild im Dornenbusch.

So seh ich deine niegeliebten Glieder
zum erstenmal in dieser Liebesnacht.
Wir legten uns noch nie zusammen nieder,
und nun wird nur bewundert und gewacht.

Doch, siehe, deine Hände sind zerrissen –:
Geliebter, nicht von mir, von meinen Bissen.
Dein Herz steht offen und man kann hinein:
das hätte dürfen nur mein Eingang sein.

Nun bist du müde, und dein müder Mund
hat keine Lust zu meinem wehen Munde –.
O Jesus, Jesus, wann war unsre Stunde?
Wie gehn wir beide wunderlich zugrund.

GESANG DER FRAUEN AN DEN DICHTER

Sieh, wie sich alles auftut: so sind wir;
denn wir sind nichts als solche Seligkeit.
Was Blut und Dunkel war in einem Tier,
das wuchs in uns zur Seele an und schreit

als Seele weiter. Und es schreit nach dir.
Du freilich nimmst es nur in dein Gesicht
als sei es Landschaft: sanft und ohne Gier.
Und darum meinen wir, du bist es nicht,

nach dem es schreit. Und doch, bist du nicht der,
an den wir uns ganz ohne Rest verlören?
Und werden wir in irgend einem *mehr?*

Mit uns geht das Unendliche *vorbei.*
Du aber sei, du Mund, daß wir es hören,
du aber, du Uns-Sagender: du sei.

PIETÀ

So, Jesus, once again I am beholding
those feet that seemed so youthful to me there
when I unshod and washed them, greatly fearing;
oh, how they stood entangled in my hair,
like some white wild thing from a thorn-bush peering.

Those limbs, from every lover so withholding,
for the first time in this love-night I view.
We've never felt each other's arms enfolding,
and now I only weep and watch for you.

But, look, how torn your hands have come to be: –
not from my bites, beloved, not by me.
Your heart stands open now for all to share:
I only should have had the entry there.

Now you are tired, and your tired mouth is urged
by no desire for my sad mouth, alas! –
O Jesus, Jesus, when did our time pass?
How strangely both of us are being submerged.

Paris, May-June 1906

SONG OF WOMEN TO THE POET

Look, how all's now unfolding: we are too,
for we are nothing but such blissfulness.
What in the brutes was blood and darkness grew
in us to soul, and its outcryingness

as soul continues. And it's crying for you.
You, though, ingaze it in a mild repose,
uncravingly, as if it were a view.
And therefore it's not you, we must suppose,

it's crying for. And yet, are you not he
on whom we could be utterly expended?
And more than that in whom else shall we be?

With us the Infinite keeps going again.
You, though, you mouth, that we may apprehend it,
you, though, you us-expresser, must remain.

Capri, mid-March 1907

71

DER TOD DES DICHTERS

Er lag. Sein aufgestelltes Antlitz war
bleich und verweigernd in den steilen Kissen,
seitdem die Welt und dieses von-ihr-Wissen,
von seinen Sinnen abgerissen,
zurückfiel an das teilnahmslose Jahr.

Die, so ihn leben sahen, wußten nicht,
wie sehr er Eines war mit allem diesen;
denn Dieses: diese Tiefen, diese Wiesen
und diese Wasser *waren* sein Gesicht.

O sein Gesicht war diese ganze Weite,
die jetzt noch zu ihm will und um ihn wirbt;
und seine Maske, die nun bang verstirbt,
ist zart und offen wie die Innenseite
von einer Frucht, die an der Luft verdirbt.

BUDDHA

Als ob er horchte. Stille: eine Ferne...
Wir halten ein und hören sie nicht mehr.
Und er ist Stern. Und andre große Sterne,
die wir nicht sehen, stehen um ihn her.

O er ist alles. Wirklich, warten wir,
daß er uns sähe? Sollte er bedürfen?
Und wenn wir hier uns vor ihm niederwürfen,
er bliebe tief und träge wie ein Tier.

Denn das, was uns zu seinen Füßen reißt,
das kreist in ihm seit Millionen Jahren.
Er, der vergißt was wir erfahren
und der erfährt was uns verweist.

THE POET'S DEATH

HE lay. His high-propped face could only peer
in pale refusal at the silent cover,
now that the world and all this knowledge of her,
torn from the senses of her lover,
had fallen back to the unfeeling year.

Those who had seen him living saw no trace
of his deep unity with all that passes;
for these, these valleys here, these meadow-grasses,
these streams of running water, *were* his face.

Oh yes, his face was this remotest distance,
that seeks him still and woos him in despair;
and his mere mask, timidly dying there,
tender and open, has no more consistence
than broken fruit corrupting in the air.

Paris, May-June 1906
Probably suggested by Rodin's sculpture, *La Mort du Poète*.

BUDDHA

As though he listened. Stillness: something far . . .
We hold our breath; our hearing, though, 's too dim.
And he is star. And many a mighty star,
beyond our vision, is attending him.

Oh, he is all. Lingering, have we the least
hope that he'll notice? Could he ever need?
And if we fell before him here to plead,
he'd still sit deep and idle as a beast.

For that in him which drags us to his feet
has circled in him for a million years.
He who forgets our hopes and fears
in thoughts from which our thoughts retreat.

Meudon, end of 1905
On a little mound in Rodin's garden at Meudon stood an image of Buddha, which
Rilke could see from his window and to which he often refers in his letters.

L'ANGE DU MÉRIDIEN

Im Sturm, der um die starke Kathedrale
wie ein Verneiner stürzt der denkt und denkt,
fühlt man sich zärtlicher mit einem Male
von deinem Lächeln zu dir hingelenkt:

lächelnder Engel, fühlende Figur,
mit einem Mund, gemacht aus hundert Munden:
gewahrst du gar nicht, wie dir unsre Stunden
abgleiten von der vollen Sonnenuhr,

auf der des Tages ganze Zahl zugleich,
gleich wirklich, steht in tiefem Gleichgewichte,
als wären alle Stunden reif und reich.

Was weißt du, Steinerner, von unserm Sein?
und hältst du mit noch seligerm Gesichte
vielleicht die Tafel in die Nacht hinein?

L'ANGE DU MÉRIDIEN

CHARTRES

In storm, that round the strong cathedral rages
like a denier thinking through and through,
your tender smiling suddenly engages
our hearts and lifts them up to you:

O smiling angel, sympathetic stone,
with mouth as from a hundred mouths distilled:
do you not mark how, from your ever-filled
sundial, our hours are gliding one by one –

that so impartial sundial, upon which
the day's whole sum is balanced equally,
as though all hours alike were ripe and rich?

What do you know, stone-nurtured, of our plight?
With face that's even blissfuller, maybe,
you hold your tables out into the night.

Paris, May-June 1906

75

DIE KATHEDRALE

In jenen kleinen Städten, wo herum
die alten Häuser wie ein Jahrmarkt hocken,
der *sie* bemerkt hat plötzlich und, erschrocken,
die Buden zumacht und, ganz zu und stumm,

die Schreier still, die Trommeln angehalten,
zu ihr hinaufhorcht aufgeregten Ohrs – :
dieweil sie ruhig immer in dem alten
Faltenmantel ihrer Contreforts
dasteht und von den Häusern gar nicht weiß:

in jenen kleinen Städten kannst du sehn,
wie sehr entwachsen ihrem Umgangskreis
die Kathedralen waren. Ihr Erstehn
ging über alles fort, so wie den Blick
des eignen Lebens viel zu große Nähe
fortwährend übersteigt, und als geschähe
nichts anderes; als wäre Das Geschick,
was sich in ihnen aufhäuft ohne Maßen,
versteinert und zum Dauernden bestimmt,
nicht Das, was unten in den dunkeln Straßen
vom Zufall irgendwelche Namen nimmt
und darin geht, wie Kinder Grün und Rot
und was der Krämer hat als Schürze tragen.
Da war Geburt in diesen Unterlagen,
und Kraft und Andrang war in diesem Ragen
und Liebe überall wie Wein und Brot,
und die Portale voller Liebesklagen.
Das Leben zögerte im Stundenschlagen,
und in den Türmen, welche voll Entsagen
auf einmal nicht mehr stiegen, war der Tod.

THE CATHEDRAL

IN those small towns where, clustered round about,
old houses squat and jostle like a fair,
that's just caught sight of *it*, and then and there
shut up the stalls, and, silenced every shout,

the criers still, the drum-sticks all suspended,
stands gazing up at it with straining ears:
while it, as calm as ever, in the splendid
wrinkled buttress-mantle rears
itself above the homes it never knew:

in those small towns you come to realise
how the cathedrals utterly outgrew
their whole environment. Their birth and rise,
as our own life's too great proximity
will mount beyond our vision and our sense
of other happenings, took precedence
of all things; as though that were history,
piled up in their immeasurable masses
in petrification safe from circumstance,
not that, which down among the dark streets passes
and takes whatever name is given by chance
and goes in that, as children green or red,
or what the dealer has, wear in rotation.
For birth was here, within this deep foundation,
and strength and purpose in this aspiration,
and love, like bread and wine, was all around,
and porches full of lovers' lamentation.
In the tolled hours was heard life's hestitation,
and in those towers that, full of resignation,
ceased all at once from climbing, death was found.

Paris, c. 1 July 1906
Last 2 lines: Rilke had been struck by the contrast between the spireless towers of
so many medieval French cathedrals (Chartres, Notre-Dame, Rheims Amiens,
etc.) and the spired towers of most German and Austrian ones.

77

DAS PORTAL

I

Da blieben sie, als wäre jene Flut
zurückgetreten, deren großes Branden
an diesen Steinen wusch, bis sie entstanden;
sie nahm im Fallen manches Attribut

aus ihren Händen, welche viel zu gut
und gebend sind, um etwas festzuhalten.
Sie blieben, von den Formen in Basalten
durch einen Nimbus, einen Bischofshut,

bisweilen durch ein Lächeln unterschieden,
für das ein Antlitz seiner Stunden Frieden
bewahrt hat als ein stilles Zifferblatt;

jetzt fortgerückt ins Leere ihres Tores,
waren sie einst die Muschel eines Ohres
und fingen jedes Stöhnen dieser Stadt.

II

Sehr viele Weite ist gemeint damit:
so wie mit den Kulissen einer Szene
die Welt gemeint ist; und so wie durch jene
der Held im Mantel seiner Handlung tritt:–

so tritt das Dunkel dieses Tores handelnd
auf seiner Tiefe tragisches Theater,
so grenzenlos und wallend wie Gott-Vater
und so wie Er sich wunderlich verwandelnd

in einen Sohn, der aufgeteilt ist hier
auf viele kleine beinah stumme Rollen,
genommen aus des Elends Zubehör.

Denn nur noch so entsteht (das wissen wir)
aus Blinden, Fortgeworfenen und Tollen
der Heiland wie ein einziger Akteur.

III

So ragen sie, die Herzen angehalten
(sie stehn auf Ewigkeit und gingen nie);
nur selten tritt aus dem Gefäll der Falten
eine Gebärde, aufrecht, steil wie sie,

THE PORCH

I

THEY'VE lingered there, as though it had receded,
that tide which once so thunderously surged
against these massive stones till they emerged;
and with it many an emblem's ebbed unheeded

out of their hands, so much too liberal
and kindly to retain their grasp of things.
They've lingered, from a cliff's ensculpturings
distinguished only by vestigial

nimbus or mitre or, at times, a smile,
for which a face, to serve as silent dial,
has saved up all the peace its hours once brought.

Rapt now into their porch's emptiness,
they used to be an ear's wide-openedness
wherewith this city's every groan was caught.

II

Therewith great distantness is signified:
as with some stage-set we are looking at
the world is signified, and as through that
the hero, mantled in his act, will stride,

the tragic stage of its profundity
by this great door's enacting dark is trod,
as boundless and as fluctuant as God,
and, like him, self-transforming wondrously

into a Son, disseminated there
in multitudes of small parts, almost mute,
taken from misery's repertoire of woes.

For now it's only thus (we're well aware)
that out of those blind, mad, and destitute
the Saviour, like a single actor, grows.

III

And thus they tower with arrested hearts
(they'll stand for ever and for ever stay);
though sometimes from the fall of folds outstarts
a sudden gesture, upright, steep as they,

79

und bleibt nach einem halben Schritte stehn
wo die Jahrhunderte sie überholen.
Sie sind im Gleichgewicht auf den Konsolen,
in denen eine Welt, die sie nicht sehn,

die Welt der Wirrnis, die sie nicht zertraten,
Figur und Tier, wie um sie zu gefährden,
sich krümmt und schüttelt und sie dennoch hält:

weil die Gestalten dort wie Akrobaten
sich nur so zuckend und so wild gebärden,
damit der Stab auf ihrer Stirn nicht fällt.

DIE FENSTERROSE

DA drin: das träge Treten ihrer Tatzen
macht eine Stille, die dich fast verwirrt;
und wie dann plötzlich eine von den Katzen
den Blick an ihr, der hin und wieder irrt,

gewaltsam in ihr großes Auge nimmt, –
den Blick, der, wie von eines Wirbels Kreis
ergriffen, eine kleine Weile schwimmt
und dann versinkt und nichts mehr von sich weiß,

wenn dieses Auge, welches scheinbar ruht,
sich auftut und zusammenschlägt mit Tosen
und ihn hineinreißt bis ins rote Blut –:

So griffen einstmals aus dem Dunkelsein
der Kathedralen große Fensterrosen
ein Herz und rissen es in Gott hinein.

and, after half a step, will stop, until
it's overtaken by the centuries.
They're poised on brackets whose interstices
a world they do not see enlivens still,

that wildering world they have not trodden out,
where shape and beast, as though imperilling,
writhe and upsurge and yet uphold them all:

because, like acrobats, that monstrous rout
only indulge in such wild gesturing
so that the brow-supported staff shan't fall.

Paris, 8-11 July 1906
Chartres.

THE ROSE WINDOW

IN there: the lazy-pacing paws are making
a silence almost dizzying you; and then
how suddenly one cat-like creature's taking
the glance that strays to it and back again

into its great eye irresistibly, –
the glance which, grasped as in a whirlpool's twist,
floats for a little while revolvingly
and then sinks down and ceases to exist,

when that eye, whose reposefulness but seems,
opens and closes with a raging clasp
and hales it in to where the red blood streams: –

Thus from the darkness there in days gone by
would the cathedrals' great rose-windows grasp
a heart and hale it into God on high.

Paris, shortly before 8 July 1906

DAS KAPITÄL

WIE sich aus eines Traumes Ausgeburten
aufsteigend aus verwirrendem Gequäl
der nächste Tag erhebt: so gehn die Gurten
der Wölbung aus dem wirren Kapitäl

und lassen drin, gedrängt und rätselhaft
verschlungen, flügelschlagende Geschöpfe:
ihr Zögern und das Plötzliche der Köpfe
und jene starken Blätter, deren Saft

wie Jähzorn steigt, sich schließlich überschlagend
in einer schnellen Geste, die sich ballt
und sich heraushält –: alles aufwärtsjagend,

was immer wieder mit dem Dunkel kalt
herunterfällt, wie Regen Sorge tragend
für dieses alten Wachstums Unterhalt.

GOTT IM MITTELALTER

UND sie hatten Ihn in sich erspart
und sie wollten, daß er sei und richte,
und sie hängten schließlich wie Gewichte
(zu verhindern seine Himmelfahrt)

an ihn ihrer großen Kathedralen
Last und Masse. Und er sollte nur
über seine grenzenlosen Zahlen
zeigend kreisen und wie eine Uhr

Zeichen geben ihrem Tun und Tagwerk.
Aber plötzlich kam er ganz in Gang,
und die Leute der entsetzten Stadt

ließen ihn, vor seiner Stimme bang,
weitergehn mit ausgehängtem Schlagwerk
und entflohn vor seinem Zifferblatt.

THE CAPITAL

As, mounting from those monsterly assaultings
with which confusing dreams can so appal,
next day arises, so proceed the vaulting's
encinctures from the mazy capital,

and leave therein a pinion-beating press
of shapes mysteriously engarlanded,
their hesitance and suddenness of head,
and those stout leaves, whose sap, like angriness,

has mounted to a final overspill
in the swift gesture of a fist outthrust,
forever chasing upwards all that still,

with the oncoming darkness, will persist
in falling coldly back, because it must,
like rain, take care that this old growth subsist.

Paris, 8-11 July 1906

GOD IN THE MIDDLE AGES

AND they'd got him in themselves upstored,
and they wanted him to reign forever,
and they hung on him (a last endeavour
to withhold his journey heavenward

and to have him near them in their slumbers)
their cathedrals' massive weights. He must
merely wheel across his boundless numbers
pointingly and, like a clock, adjust

what they daily toiled at or transacted.
But he suddenly got into gear,
and the people of the stricken town

left him – for his voice inspired such fear –
running with his striking-works extracted,
and absconded from his dial's frown.

Paris, 19-23 July 1907

MORGUE

DA liegen sie bereit, als ob es gälte,
nachträglich eine Handlung zu erfinden,
die mit einander und mit dieser Kälte
sie zu versöhnen weiß und zu verbinden;

denn das ist alles noch wie ohne Schluß.
Wasfür ein Name hätte in den Taschen
sich finden sollen? An dem Überdruß
um ihren Mund hat man herumgewaschen:

er ging nicht ab; er wurde nur ganz rein.
Die Bärte stehen, noch ein wenig härter,
doch ordentlicher im Geschmack der Wärter,

nur um die Gaffenden nicht anzuwidern.
Die Augen haben hinter ihren Lidern
sich umgewandt und schauen jetzt hinein.

MORGUE

HERE they lie ready, as though what were still
needful were that some action be invented
whereby with one another and this chill
they might become united and contented;

for all is still as though without conclusion.
What names, we'd like to know, may have been found
inside their pockets? All the disillusion
about their mouths has been washed round and round:

it didn't go; it merely came quite clean.
Their beards are left them, just a bit less pendant,
but tidier, as it seems to the attendant,

so that the starers shan't be disconcerted.
The eyes beneath their eyelids have averted
their gaze from outwardness to that within.

Paris, beginning of July 1906

DER GEFANGENE

I

MEINE Hand hat nur noch eine
Gebärde, mit der sie verscheucht;
auf die alten Steine
fällt es aus Felsen feucht.

Ich höre nur dieses Klopfen,
und mein Herz hält Schritt
mit dem Gehen der Tropfen
und vergeht damit.

Tropften sie doch schneller,
käme doch wieder ein Tier.
Irgendwo war es heller –.
Aber was wissen wir.

II

Denk dir, das was jetzt Himmel ist und Wind,
Luft deinem Mund und deinem Auge Helle,
das würde Stein bis um die kleine Stelle
an der dein Herz und deine Hände sind.

Und was jetzt in dir morgen heißt und: dann
und: späterhin und nächstes Jahr und weiter –
das würde wund in dir und voller Eiter
und schwäre nur und bräche nicht mehr an.

Und das was war, das wäre irre und
raste in dir herum, den lieben Mund
der niemals lachte, schäumend von Gelächter.

Und das was Gott war, wäre nur dein Wächter
und stopfte boshaft in das letzte Loch
ein schmutziges Auge. Und du lebtest doch.

THE PRISONER

ONE gesture alone, for scaring
away, my hand now owns;
droppings from rock are wearing
the ancient paving-stones.

That is the only knock here;
my heart in step keeps on
with those drops from the rock here
and goes where they have gone.

If only they'd drop more fast, though,
if an animal came again.
Somewhere it was brighter. – At last, though,
all is beyond our ken.

II

Suppose that what's now sky and wind for you,
air for your mouth and brightness for your vision,
turned into stone all round that small provision
of space your heart and hands were welcome to.

And what's *to-morrow* in you now and *then*
and *later* and *next year* and *something waiting*
became all sore in you and suppurating
and festered on and never dawned again.

And what had been became insane and raged
within you, and your mouth, so disengaged
from laughter, were now laughing long and hard.

And what had once been God were just your guard,
attempting with a dirty eye to fill
the last hole up. And yet you lived on still.

Probably first half of 1906

DER PANTHER

SEIN Blick ist vom Vorübergehn der Stäbe
so müd geworden, daß er nichts mehr hält.
Ihm ist, als ob es tausend Stäbe gäbe
und hinter tausend Stäben keine Welt.

Der weiche Gang geschmeidig starker Schritte,
der sich im allerkleinsten Kreise dreht,
ist wie ein Tanz von Kraft um eine Mitte,
in der betäubt ein großer Wille steht.

Nur manchmal schiebt der Vorhang der Pupille
sich lautlos auf –. Dann geht ein Bild hinein,
geht durch der Glieder angespannte Stille –
und hört im Herzen auf zu sein.

DIE GAZELLE

Gazella Dorcas

VERZAUBERTE: wie kann der Einklang zweier
erwählter Worte je den Reim erreichen,
der in dir kommt und geht, wie auf ein Zeichen.
Aus deiner Stirne steigen Laub und Leier,

und alles Deine geht schon im Vergleich
durch Liebeslieder, deren Worte, weich
wie Rosenblätter, dem, der nicht mehr liest,
sich auf die Augen legen, die er schließt:

um dich zu sehen: hingetragen, als
wäre mit Sprüngen jeder Lauf geladen
und schösse nur nicht ab, solang der Hals

das Haupt ins Horchen hält: wie wenn beim Baden
im Wald die Badende sich unterbricht:
den Waldsee im gewendeten Gesicht.

THE PANTHER

JARDIN DES PLANTES, PARIS

His gaze those bars keep passing is so misted
with tiredness, it can take in nothing more.
He feels as though a thousand bars existed,
and no more world beyond them than before.

Those supply-powerful paddings, turning there
in tiniest of circles, well might be
the dance of forces round a centre where
some mighty will stands paralyticly.

Just now and then the pupil's noiseless shutter
is lifted. – Then an image will indart,
down through the limbs' intensive stillness flutter,
and end its being in the heart.

Paris, 1903 or (possibly) end of 1902
First published September 1903. The earliest of *New Poems*.

THE GAZELLE

Gazella Dorcas

Enchanted thing: however can the chime
of two selected words attain the true
rhyme that, as beckoned, comes and goes in you?
Out of your forehead leaf and lyre climb,

and all you are has been in simile
passing through those love-songs continually
whose words will cover, light as leaves of rose,
the no-more-reader's eyes, which he will close:

only to look upon you: so impelled
as though each limb of yours with leaps were laden,
and held its fire but while the neck upheld

the head in hearkening: as when a maiden
breaks off from bathing in some lonely place,
the forest-lake within her swift-turned face.

Paris, 17 July 1907
A month earlier (13 June) Rilke had written to his wife: 'Yesterday, by the way, I
spent the whole morning in the Jardin des Plantes, in front of the gazelles... I saw
only one of them stand up for a moment, it lay down again immediately; but I
saw, while they were stretching and testing themselves, the magnificent workman-
ship of those limbs: (they are like guns, from which leaps are fired).'

DAS EINHORN

Der Heilige hob das Haupt, und das Gebet
fiel wie ein Helm zurück von seinem Haupte:
denn lautlos nahte sich das niegeglaubte,
das weiße Tier, das wie eine geraubte
hülflose Hindin mit den Augen fleht.

Der Beine elfenbeinernes Gestell
bewegte sich in leichten Gleichgewichten,
ein weißer Glanz glitt selig durch das Fell,
und auf der Tierstirn, auf der stillen, lichten,
stand, wie ein Turm im Mond, das Horn so hell,
und jeder Schritt geschah, es aufzurichten.

Das Maul mit seinem rosagrauen Flaum
war leicht gerafft, so daß ein wenig Weiß
(weißer als alles) von den Zähnen glänz'e;
die Nüstern nahmen auf und lechzten leis.
Doch seine Blicke, die kein Ding begrenzte,
warfen sich Bilder in den Raum
und schlossen einen blauen Sagenkreis.

SANKT SEBASTIAN

Wie ein Liegender so steht er; ganz
hingehalten von dem großen Willen.
Weitentrückt wie Mütter, wenn sie stillen,
und in sich gebunden wie ein Kranz.

Und die Pfeile kommen: jetzt und jetzt
und als sprängen sie aus seinen Lenden,
eisern bebend mit den freien Enden.
Doch er lächelt dunkel, unverletzt.

Einmal nur wird seine Trauer groß,
und die Augen liegen schmerzlich bloß,
bis sie etwas leugnen, wie Geringes,
und als ließen sie verächtlich los
die Vernichter eines schönen Dinges.

THE UNICORN

AND then the saint looked up, and in surprise
the prayer fell like a helmet from his head:
for softly neared that never-credited
white creature, which, like some unparented,
some helpless hind, beseeches with its eyes.

The ivory framework of the limbs so light
moved like a pair of balances deflected,
there glided through the coat a gleam of white,
and on the forehead, where the beams collected,
stood, like a moon-lit tower, the horn so bright,
at every footstep proudly re-erected.

Its mouth was slightly open, and a trace
of white through the soft down of grey and rose
(whitest of whites) came from the gleaming teeth;
its nostrils panted gently for repose.
Its gaze, though, checked by nothing here beneath,
projecting pictures into space,
brought a blue saga-cycle to a close.

Meudon, winter 1905-6

SAINT SEBASTIAN

LIKE one lying down he stands there, all
target-proffered by his mighty will.
Far-removed, like mothers when they still,
self-inwoven like a coronal.

And the arrows come, and, as if straight
out of his own loins originating,
cluster with their feathered ends vibrating.
But he darkly smiles, inviolate.

Only once his eyes show deep distress,
gazing in a painful nakedness;
then, as though ashamed of noticing,
seem to let go with disdainfulness
those destroyers of a lovely thing.

Meudon, winter 1905-6

There are many representations of the martyrdom of St. Sebastian by Renaissance
artists, but Rilke would seem to have had more particularly in mind that by
Botticelli in the Kaiser Friedrich Museum at Berlin.

DER STIFTER

DAS war der Auftrag an die Malergilde.
Vielleicht daß ihm der Heiland nie erschien;
vielleicht trat auch kein heiliger Bischof milde
an seine Seite wie in diesem Bilde
und legte leise seine Hand auf ihn.

Vielleicht war dieses alles: *so* zu knien
(so wie es alles ist, was wir erfuhren):
zu knien: daß man die eigenen Konturen,
die auswärtswollenden, ganz angespannt
im Herzen hält, wie Pferde in der Hand.

Daß wenn ein Ungeheueres geschähe,
das nicht versprochen ist und nieverbrieft,
wir hoffen könnten, daß es uns nicht sähe
und näher käme, ganz in unsre Nähe,
mit sich beschäftigt und in sich vertieft.

DER ENGEL

MIT einem Neigen seiner Stirne weist
er weit von sich was einschränkt und verpflichtet;
denn durch sein Herz geht riesig aufgerichtet
das ewig Kommende das kreist.

Die tiefen Himmel stehn ihm voll Gestalten,
und jede kann ihm rufen: komm, erkenn –.
Gieb seinen leichten Händen nichts zu halten
aus deinem Lastenden. Sie kämen denn

bei Nacht zu dir, dich ringender zu prüfen,
und gingen wie Erzürnte durch das Haus
und griffen dich als ob sie dich erschüfen
und brächen dich aus deiner Form heraus.

THE DONOR

THE painters' guild was given this commission.
His Lord, perhaps, he did not really see;
perhaps, as he was kneeling in submission,
no saintly bishop stood in this position
and laid his hand upon him silently.

To kneel like this was everything, maybe
(just as it's all that we ourselves have known):
to kneel: and hold with choking breath one's own
contracted contours, trying to expand,
tight in one's heart like horses in one's hand.

So that, if something awesome should appear,
something unpromised and unprophesied,
we might dare hope it would not see nor hear,
and might approach, until it came quite near,
deep in itself and self-preoccupied.

Paris, mid-July 1906

THE ANGEL

BOWING his head a little, he absolves
himself from things that limit and direct,
for through his heart moves, mightily erect,
the eternal future, that revolves.

Before him full of shapes deep heaven stands,
and each can call to him with pleading claim.
Put nothing into his unburdened hands
from your encumbrancy. Unless they came

by night for wrestlinger investigating,
and crossed like raging furies your threshold
and seized on you as though they were creating
and breaking you from your retaining mould.

Paris, early summer 1906

RÖMISCHE SARKOPHAGE

Was aber hindert uns zu glauben, daß
(so wie wir hingestellt sind und verteilt)
nicht eine kleine Zeit nur Drang und Haß
und dies Verwirrende in uns verweilt,

wie einst in dem verzierten Sarkophag
bei Ringen, Götterbildern, Gläsern, Bändern,
in langsam sich verzehrenden Gewändern
ein langsam Aufgelöstes lag –

bis es die unbekannten Munde schluckten,
die niemals reden. (Wo besteht und denkt
ein Hirn, um ihrer einst sich zu bedienen?)

Da wurde von den alten Aquädukten
ewiges Wasser in sie eingelenkt – :
das spiegelt jetzt und geht und glänzt in ihnen.

DER SCHWAN

Diese Mühsal, durch noch Ungetanes
schwer und wie gebunden hinzugehn,
gleicht dem ungeschaffnen Gang des Schwanes.

Und das Sterben, dieses Nichtmehrfassen
jenes Grunds, auf dem wir täglich stehn,
seinem ängstlichen Sich-Niederlassen – :

in die Wasser, die ihn sanft empfangen
und die sich, wie glücklich und vergangen,
unter ihm zurückziehn, Flut um Flut;
während er unendlich still und sicher
immer mündiger und königlicher
und gelassener zu ziehn geruht.

ROMAN SARCOPHAGI

WHY should we too, though, not anticipate
(set down here and assigned our places thus)
that only for a short time rage and hate
and this bewildering will remain in us,

as in the ornate sarcophagus, enclosed
with images of gods, rings, glasses, trappings,
there lay in slowly self-consuming wrappings
something being slowly decomposed –

till swallowed by those unknown mouths at last,
that never speak. (Where bides a brain that may
yet trust the utterance of its thinking to them?)

Then from the ancient aqueducts there passed
eternal water into them one day: –
that mirrors now and moves and sparkles through them.

Paris, May-June 1906
In many parts of Italy stone sarcophagi are used as troughs or basins from which
running water may be drawn. See *Sonnets to Orpheus*, I, x, of which this poem is a
kind of pre-echo.

THE SWAN

THIS laborious going on and on,
bound and heavy, through the still-to-do is
like the unshaped walking of the swan.

Dying too, that no more hold-providing
by the ground we daily trusted to, is
like his so unconfident subsiding

into waters that receive him gently
and, as though departed and contently,
wave on wave retire from under him;
while he, infinitely still and surely,
ever kinglier and more maturely,
more composedly, condescends to swim.

Meudon, winter 1905-6

KINDHEIT

Es wäre gut viel nachzudenken, um
von so Verlornem etwas auszusagen,
von jenen langen Kindheit-Nachmittagen,
die so nie wiederkamen – und warum?

Noch mahnt es uns –: vielleicht in einem Regnen,
aber wir wissen nicht mehr was das soll;
nie wieder war das Leben von Begegnen,
von Wiedersehn und Weitergehn so voll

wie damals, da uns nichts geschah als nur
was einem Ding geschieht und einem Tiere:
da lebten wir, wie Menschliches, das Ihre
und wurden bis zum Rande voll Figur.

Und wurden so vereinsamt wie ein Hirt
und so mit großen Fernen überladen
und wie von weit berufen und berührt
und langsam wie ein langer neuer Faden
in jene Bilder-Folgen eingeführt,
in welchen nun zu dauern uns verwirrt.

DER DICHTER

Du entfernst dich von mir, du Stunde.
Wunden schlägt mir dein Flügelschlag.
Allein: was soll ich mit meinem Munde?
mit meiner Nacht? mit meinem Tag?

Ich habe keine Geliebte, kein Haus,
keine Stelle, auf der ich lebe.
Alle Dinge, an die ich mich gebe,
werden reich und geben mich aus.

CHILDHOOD

By much reflection it were good to try
and find some words for what's so gone for ever
with those long childhood-afternoons, that never
came back again in just that way – and why?

It still reminds us: – maybe when rain's falling,
though we no longer know what it can mean;
never again has life been so enthralling
with meeting, re-encounter, change of scene

as then, when nothing more of happening
befell us than what thing or creature shares:
we lived, as it were human, what was theirs,
and got all brim-full of imagining.

And got as lonesome as a shepherd may
whom great horizons have so overfreighted,
and touched and summoned as from far away
and like a long new thread insinuated
into those picture-series where to-day
it so bewilders us to have to stay.

Paris, c. 1 July 1906

THE POET

You're leaving me, hour, without hesitation.
I'm bruised by the beat of your winged away.
What shall I now in my isolation
do with my mouth? my night? my day?

I've no beloved, no own roof-tree,
no spot whereon to be living.
All those things to which I keep giving
myself grow wealthy and squander me.

Meudon, winter 1905-6

DIE SPITZE

I

MENSCHLICHKEIT: Namen schwankender Besitze,
noch unbestätigter Bestand von Glück:
ist das unmenschlich, daß zu dieser Spitze,
zu diesem kleinen dichten Spitzenstück
zwei Augen wurden? – Willst du sie zurück?

Du Langvergangene und schließlich Blinde,
ist deine Seligkeit in diesem Ding,
zu welcher hin, wie zwischen Stamm und Rinde,
dein großes Fühlen, kleinverwandelt, ging?

Durch einen Riß im Schicksal, eine Lücke
entzogst du deine Seele deiner Zeit;
und sie ist so in diesem lichten Stücke,
daß es mich lächeln macht vor Nützlichkeit.

II

Und wenn uns eines Tages dieses Tun
und was an uns geschieht gering erschiene
und uns so fremd, als ob es nicht verdiene,
daß wir so mühsam aus den Kinderschuhn
um seinetwillen wachsen –: Ob die Bahn
vergilbter Spitze, diese dichtgefügte
blumige Spitzenbahn, dann nicht genügte,
uns hier zu halten? Sieh: sie ward *getan*.

Ein Leben ward vielleicht verschmäht, wer weiß?
Ein Glück war da und wurde hingegeben,
und endlich wurde doch, um jeden Preis,
dies Ding daraus, nicht leichter als das Leben
und doch vollendet und so schön als sei's
nicht mehr zu früh, zu lächeln und zu schweben.

THE LACE

I

HUMANNESS: name for wavering possession,
still undetermined term of happiness:
is it inhuman that there went to fashion
this piece of lace-work's fine enwovenness
two eyes? – Do you regret their absentness?

You long-departed and at last benighted,
is all your heaven in this thing, where went,
as between trunk and bark, your lofty-flighted
feeling in magical diminishment?

Through some small chink in destiny, some gaping,
you drew your soul from temporality;
and it's so present in this airy shaping,
I have to smile at the expediency.

Paris, early summer 1906

II

And if one day our doing and our ado's
and all that happens to us should appear
trivial and strange, and it were far from clear
why we should struggle out of children's shoes
merely for that – would not, perhaps, this run
of yellowed lace, this finely woven length
of flowery lace, then have sufficient strength
to keep us here? For look, it all got done.

A life perhaps was slighted, who can know?
A chance of happiness let slip – yet, spite
of all, there still emerged, however slow,
this thing, not easier than life, but quite
perfect, and, oh, so beautiful – as though
now were no more too soon for smiles and flight.

Capri, c. 10 February 1907

99

EIN FRAUEN-SCHICKSAL

So wie der König auf der Jagd ein Glas
ergreift, daraus zu trinken, irgendeines, –
und wie hernach der welcher es besaß
es fortstellt und verwahrt, als wär es keines:

so hob vielleicht das Schicksal, durstig auch,
bisweilen Eine an den Mund und trank,
die dann ein kleines Leben, viel zu bang
sie zu zerbrechen, abseits vom Gebrauch

hinstellte in die ängstliche Vitrine,
in welcher seine Kostbarkeiten sind
(oder die Dinge, die für kostbar gelten).

Da stand sie fremd wie eine Fortgeliehne
und wurde einfach alt und wurde blind
und war nicht kostbar und war niemals selten.

DIE GENESENDE

Wie ein Singen kommt und geht in Gassen
und sich nähert und sich wieder scheut,
flügelschlagend, manchmal fast zu fassen
und dann wieder weit hinausgestreut:

spielt mit der Genesenden das Leben;
während sie, geschwächt und ausgeruht,
unbeholfen, um sich hinzugeben,
eine ungewohnte Geste tut.

Und sie fühlt es beinah wie Verführung,
wenn die hartgewordne Hand, darin
Fieber waren voller Widersinn,
fernher, wie mit blühender Berührung,
zu liebkosen kommt ihr hartes Kinn.

A FEMININE DESTINY

As when, out shooting with his friends, the king
picks up a glass to drink from, any sort, –
and afterwards the owner of the thing
preserves it like the rarest ever wrought:

Fate, also thirsty, now and then maybe
has raised a woman to its lips and drunk,
whom then some little life has too much shrunk
from fear of breaking and has carefully

placed in that tremulous vitrine, wherein
its various preciousnesses are consigned
(or objects such as pass for precious there).

As strange as if on loan she's stood therein
and simply gone on growing old and blind
and wasn't precious and was never rare.

Paris, c. 1 July 1906

THE CONVALESCENT

As a street-song comes and goes in snatches,
now approaching, now again in doubt,
fluttering, till at times one almost catches,
and then once again all scattered out:

life is playing with the convalescent,
while she, weakened and recovering,
clumsily, to be more acquiescent,
makes some unaccustomed gesturing.

And she feels it almost like temptation
when that hard-grown hand of hers, wherein
such irrational fevers used to spin,
comes, all blossoming with new sensation,
from afar to stroke her hardened chin.

Early 1906

DIE ERWACHSENE

Das alles stand auf ihr und war die Welt
und stand auf ihr mit allem, Angst und Gnade,
wie Bäume stehen, wachsend und gerade,
ganz Bild und bildlos wie die Bundeslade
und feierlich, wie auf ein Volk gestellt.

Und sie ertrug es; trug bis obenhin
das Fliegende, Entfliehende, Entfernte,
das Ungeheuere, noch Unerlernte
gelassen wie die Wasserträgerin
den vollen Krug. Bis mitten unterm Spiel,
verwandelnd und auf andres vorbereitend,
der erste weiße Schleier, leise gleitend,
über das aufgetane Antlitz fiel

fast undurchsichtig und sich nie mehr hebend
und irgendwie auf alle Fragen ihr
nur eine Antwort vage wiedergebend:
In dir, du Kindgewesene, in dir.

TANAGRA

Ein wenig gebrannter Erde,
wie von großer Sonne gebrannt.
Als wäre die Gebärde
einer Mädchenhand
auf einmal nicht mehr vergangen;
ohne nach etwas zu langen,
zu keinem Dinge hin
aus ihrem Gefühle führend,
nur an sich selber rührend
wie eine Hand ans Kinn.

Wir heben und wir drehen
eine und eine Figur;
wir können fast verstehen
weshalb sie nicht vergehen, –
aber wir sollen nur
tiefer und wunderbarer
hängen an dem was war
und lächeln: ein wenig klarer
vielleicht als vor einem Jahr.

THE GROWN-UP

ALL that was standing on her and composed
the world, and all its dread and graciousness,
standing like trees in straight upshootingness,
all image, like God's ark, yet imageless,
and solemn, as upon a race imposed.

And she could bear it; bore high over her
the flying, fleeing, far away extended,
the unimagined, still unapprehended
as calmly as a water-carrier
her jar. Till midst of that activity,
transforming and for something else disposing,
the first white veil, scarce-feelably enclosing,
over that opened face fell suddenly,

almost opaque and lifting nevermore,
and somehow to all questioning anew
giving the same vague answer as before:
In you yourself, you once a child, in you.

Paris, 19 July 1907

TANAGRA

A LITTLE burnt earth, as fired
by an almighty sun.
As though the once here-inspired
gesture her hand begun
had suddenly grown eternal;
reaching for nothing external,
leading but from within
her feeling into her feeling,
over her own self stealing
like a hand around a chin.

We lift and keep revolving
figure on figure thus;
we're almost near resolving
why they are undissolving, –
yet it's but given us
deeplier and still more dearly
to cling to what once was here,
and smile: just a bit more clearly,
maybe, than we did last year.

Paris, beginning of July 1906

DIE ERBLINDENDE

Sie saß so wie die anderen beim Tee.
Mir war zuerst, als ob sie ihre Tasse
ein wenig anders als die andern fasse.
Sie lächelte einmal. Es tat fast weh.

Und als man schließlich sich erhob und sprach
und langsam und wie es der Zufall brachte
durch viele Zimmer ging (man sprach und lachte),
da sah ich sie. Sie ging den andern nach,

verhalten, so wie eine, welche gleich
wird singen müssen und vor vielen Leuten;
auf ihren hellen Augen die sich freuten
war Licht von außen wie auf einem Teich.

Sie folgte langsam und sie brauchte lang
als wäre etwas noch nicht überstiegen;
und doch: als ob, nach einem Übergang,
sie nicht mehr gehen würde, sondern fliegen.

IN EINEM FREMDEN PARK

BORGEBY-GÅRD

Zwei Wege sinds. Sie führen keinen hin.
Doch manchmal, in Gedanken, läßt der eine
dich weitergehn. Es ist, als gingst du fehl;
aber auf einmal bist du im Rondel
alleingelassen wieder mit dem Steine
und wieder auf ihm lesend: Freiherrn
Brite Sophie – und wieder mit dem Finger
abfühlend die zerfallne Jahreszahl –.
Warum wird dieses Finden nicht geringer?

Was zögerst du ganz wie zum ersten Mal
erwartungsvoll auf diesem Ulmenplatz,
der feucht und dunkel ist und niebetreten?

GOING BLIND

SHE'D sat just like the others there at tea.
And then I'd seemed to notice that her cup
was being a little differently picked up.
She'd smiled once. It had almost hurt to see.

And when eventually they rose and talked
and slowly, and as chance led, were dispersing
through several rooms there, laughing and conversing,
I noticed her. Behind the rest she walked

subduedly, like someone who presently
will have to sing, and with so many listening;
on those bright eyes of hers, with pleasure glistening,
played, as on pools, an outer radiancy.

She followed slowly and she needed time,
as though some long ascent were not yet by;
and yet: as though, when she had ceased to climb,
she would no longer merely walk, but fly.

Paris, end of June 1906

IN A FOREIGN PARK

BORGEBY-GÅRD

TWO paths. They're speeding no one's business.
One, though, at times, when pensively alone,
lets you go on. You feel you've lost your bearing;
till suddenly you find you're once more sharing
the solitary round-plot with the stone
and once more reading on it: Baroness
Brita Sophie – and once more with your finger
outfeeling the dilapidated year. –
Why does the newness of this find still linger?

Why do you linger like your first time here
under these elm trees so expectantly,
on this damp, sombre turf none ever treads?

Und was verlockt dich für ein Gegensatz,
etwas zu suchen in den sonnigen Beeten,
als wärs der Name eines Rosenstocks?

Was stehst du oft? Was hören deine Ohren?
Und warum siehst du schließlich, wie verloren,
die Falter flimmern um den hohen Phlox.

ABSCHIED

Wɪᴇ hab ich das gefühlt, was Abschied heißt.
Wie weiß ichs noch: ein dunkles unverwundnes
grausames Etwas, das ein Schönverbundnes
noch einmal zeigt und hinhält und zerreißt.

Wie war ich ohne Wehr, dem zuzuschauen,
das, da es mich, mich rufend, gehen ließ,
zurückblieb, so als wärens alle Frauen
und dennoch klein und weiß und nichts als dies:

Ein Winken, schon nicht mehr auf mich bezogen,
ein leise Weiterwinkendes –, schon kaum
erklärbar mehr: vielleicht ein Pflaumenbaum,
von dem ein Kuckuck hastig abgeflogen.

TODES-ERFAHRUNG

Wɪʀ wissen nichts von diesem Hingehn, das
nicht mit uns teilt. Wir haben keinen Grund,
Bewunderung und Liebe oder Haß
dem Tod zu zeigen, den ein Maskenmund

tragischer Klage wunderlich entstellt.
Noch ist die Welt voll Rollen, die wir spielen.
Solang wir sorgen, ob wir auch gefielen,
spielt auch der Tod, obwohl er nicht gefällt.

And what's enticing you, contrastingly,
to seek for something in the sunny beds,
as though some rose-tree's name were fascinating?

Why do you stop so? What sound's reaching you?
And why so lostly does your gaze pursue
the butterflies round the tall phlox rotating?

Paris, mid-July 1906

Borgeby-Gård was a country house in Sweden where Rilke had stayed for more
than two months in the summer of 1904. In his letters he had often mentioned its
park, and in one of 9 July to his wife he had described the stone in memory of
Brita Sophie.

PARTING

How I have felt that thing that's called 'to part',
and feel it still: a dark, invincible,
cruel something by which what was joined so well
is once more shown, held out, and torn apart.

In what defenceless gaze at that I've stood,
which, as it, calling to me, let me go,
stayed there, as though it were all womanhood,
yet small and white and nothing more than, oh,

a waving, now already unrelated
to me, a slight, continuing wave, – scarce now
explainable: perhaps a plum-tree bough
some perching cuckoo's hastily vacated.

Early 1906

DEATH EXPERIENCED

We know just nothing of this going hence
that so excludes us. We've no grounds at all
to greet with plaudits or malevolence
the Death whom that mask-mouth of tragical

lament disfigures so incredibly.
The world's still full of parts being acted by us.
Till pleasing in them cease to occupy us,
Death will act too, although unpleasingly.

Doch als du gingst, da brach in diese Bühne
ein Streifen Wirklichkeit durch jenen Spalt
durch den du hingingst: Grün wirklicher Grüne,
wirklicher Sonnenschein, wirklicher Wald.

Wir spielen weiter. Bang und schwer Erlerntes
hersagend und Gebärden dann und wann
aufhebend; aber dein von uns entferntes,
aus unserm Stück entrücktes Dasein kann

uns manchmal überkommen, wie ein Wissen
von jener Wirklichkeit sich niedersenkend,
so daß wir eine Weile hingerissen
das Leben spielen, nicht an Beifall denkend.

BLAUE HORTENSIE

So wie das letzte Grün in Farbentiegeln
sind diese Blätter, trocken, stumpf und rauh,
hinter den Blütendolden, die ein Blau
nicht auf sich tragen, nur von ferne spiegeln.

Sie spiegeln es verweint und ungenau,
als wollten sie es wiederum verlieren,
und wie in alten blauen Briefpapieren
ist Gelb in ihnen, Violett und Grau;

Verwaschnes wie an einer Kinderschürze,
Nichtmehrgetragnes, dem nichts mehr geschieht:
wie fühlt man eines kleinen Lebens Kürze.

Doch plötzlich scheint das Blau sich zu verneuen
in einer von den Dolden, und man sieht
ein rührend Blaues sich vor Grünem freuen.

When, though, you went, there broke upon this scene
a shining segment of realities
in at the crack you disappeared through: green
of real green, real sunshine, real trees.

We go on acting. Uttering what exacted
such painful learning, gesturing now and then;
but your existence and the part you acted,
withdrawn now from our play and from our ken,

sometimes recur to us like intimations
of that reality and of its laws,
and we transcend awhile our limitations
and act our lives unthinking of applause.

Capri, 24 January 1907
In memory of Countess Luise Schwerin, who had died 24 January 1906.

BLUE HYDRANGEA

THESE leaves are like the green paint's last persistence
in colour-pans, harsh, lustreless and dried,
behind the umbelled blooms, whose blue's not dyed
into themselves but mirrored from a distance.

Mirrored in some tear-dimmed, uncertain way,
as though they wanted it to leave their faces,
and, as in old blue note-paper, ther're traces
of yellow in them, violet, and grey;

the washed-out look of many a childish dress,
the no-more-worn no more can happen to:
how much you feel a small life's fleetingness!

But suddenly the blue appears more keen
within one umbel, and there's shown to you
a moving blue's delight in front of green.

Paris, mid-July 1906

VOR DEM SOMMERREGEN

Auf einmal ist aus allem Grün im Park
man weiß nicht was, ein Etwas, fortgenommen;
man fühlt ihn näher an die Fenster kommen
und schweigsam sein. Inständig nur und stark

ertönt aus dem Gehölz der Regenpfeifer,
man denkt an einen Hieronymus:
so sehr steigt irgend Einsamkeit und Eifer
aus dieser einen Stimme, die der Guß

erhören wird. Des Saales Wände sind
mit ihren Bildern von uns fortgetreten,
als dürften sie nicht hören was wir sagen.

Es spiegeln die verblichenen Tapeten
das ungewisse Licht von Nachmittagen,
in denen man sich fürchtete als Kind.

IM SAAL

Wie sind sie alle um uns, diese Herrn
in Kammerherrentrachten und Jabots,
wie eine Nacht um ihren Ordensstern
sich immer mehr verdunkelnd, rücksichtslos,
und diese Damen, zart, fragile, doch groß
von ihren Kleidern, eine Hand im Schooß,
klein wie ein Halsband für den Bologneser;
wie sind sie da um jeden: um den Leser,
um den Betrachter dieser Bibelots,
darunter manches ihnen noch gehört.

Sie lassen, voller Takt, uns ungestört
das Leben leben wie wir es begreifen
und wie sie's nicht verstehn. Sie wollten blühn,
und blühn ist schön sein; doch wir wollen reifen,
und das heißt dunkel sein und sich bemühn.

BEFORE SUMMER RAIN

Quite suddenly, from all the green around,
something – you hardly know just what – has gone;
you feel the park itself drawing in upon
the windows and growing silent. The last sound

is the rain-piping dotterel in the wood,
reminding you of somebody's *Jerome* –
there rises so much zeal and solitude
from that one voice the downpour soon will come

responding to. The lofty walls, arrayed
with ancient portraits, as though recollecting
they should not listen to our talk, withdraw.

The faded tapestries are now reflecting
the uncertain light we in our childhood saw
those afternoons when we were so afraid.

Paris, beginning of July 1906
Written after a visit to the château at Chantilly.

IN THE DRAWING-ROOM

How presently around us they all are,
these noblemen in ruffs and courtier's dress,
each like an evening round his order-star
darkening with ever more remorselessness;
these ladies, slender, fragile, whom their clothes
so much enlarge, with one hand in repose,
small as the collar for a tiny hound:
how they stand round us: round the reader, round
the contemplator of these bibelots,
among which there are some they still possess.

They let us go on, in their tactfulness,
living the kind of life we find alluring
and they can't grasp. They chose florescency,
and flowers are beautiful; we choose maturing,
and that means effort and obscurity.

Paris, beginning of July 1906
Probably, like the preceding poem, inspired by a visit to Chantilly.

LETZTER ABEND

AUS DEM BESITZE FRAU NONNAS

Und Nacht und fernes Fahren; denn der Train
des ganzen Heeres zog am Park vorüber.
Er aber hob den Blick vom Clavecin
und spielte noch und sah zu ihr hinüber

beinah wie man in einen Spiegel schaut:
so sehr erfüllt von seinen jungen Zügen
und wissend, wie sie seine Trauer trügen,
schön und verführender bei jedem Laut.

Doch plötzlich wars, als ob sich das verwische:
sie stand wie mühsam in der Fensternische
und hielt des Herzens drängendes Geklopf.

Sein Spiel gab nach. Von draußen wehte Frische.
Und seltsam fremd stand auf dem Spiegeltische
der schwarze Tschako mit dem Totenkopf.

JUGEND-BILDNIS MEINES VATERS

Im Auge Traum. Die Stirn wie in Berührung
mit etwas Fernem. Um den Mund enorm
viel Jugend, ungelächelte Verführung,
und vor der vollen schmückenden Verschnürung
der schlanken adeligen Uniform
der Säbelkorb und beide Hände –, die
abwarten, ruhig, zu nichts hingedrängt.
Und nun fast nicht mehr sichtbar: als ob sie
zuerst, die Fernes greifenden, verschwänden.
Und alles andre mit sich selbst verhängt
und ausgelöscht als ob wirs nicht verständen
und tief aus seiner eignen Tiefe trüb –.

Du schnell vergehendes Daguerreotyp
in meinen langsamer vergehenden Händen.

LAST EVENING

BY PERMISSION OF FRAU NONNA

AND night and distant travel; for the train
of the whole army swept along the park.
He looked up from the harpsichord again
and played and glanced at her without remark,

almost like looking in a mirror's round:
so filled with his young features was that face,
features that bore his sadness with a grace
suing more seductively at every sound.

Then all at once that seemed to disappear:
she stood, as though with a great effort, near
the window-seat, and clasped her beating breast.

His playing stopped. Outside a fresh wind blew.
And on the mirror-table, strange and new,
stood the black shako with the death's head crest.

Paris, June 1906
'Frau Nonna' was Rilke's friend Julie Frelfrau von Nordeck zur Rabenau, whose
first husband had fallen in the battle of Königgrätz, 3 July 1866.

PORTRAIT OF MY FATHER AS
A YOUNG MAN

DREAM in the eyes. The brow as in relation
with something distant. Mouth with more than norm
of youth, unsmilingly diffused temptation,
and, placed before the corded decoration
of the slim, gentlemanly uniform,
the sabre-hilt and those two hands, that stay
quiescent, – with no passionate intent.
And hardly to be seen now: as if they
were first to vanish, grasping the unscanned.
And all the rest in self-envelopment
and quenched as if we didn't understand
and deeply, from its very depth, opaque.

You swiftly fading daguerrotype I take
in my more gradually fading hand.

Paris, 27 June 1906

SELBSTBILDNIS AUS DEM JAHRE 1906

Des alten lange adligen Geschlechtes
Feststehendes im Augenbogenbau.
Im Blicke noch der Kindheit Angst und Blau
und Demut da und dort, nicht eines Knechtes,
doch eines Dienenden und einer Frau.
Der Mund als Mund gemacht, groß und genau,
nicht überredend, aber ein Gerechtes
Aussagendes. Die Stirne ohne Schlechtes
und gern im Schatten stiller Niederschau.

Das, als Zusammenhang, erst nur geahnt;
noch nie im Leiden oder im Gelingen
zusammgefaßt zu dauerndem Durchdringen,
doch so, als wäre mit zerstreuten Dingen
von fern ein Ernstes, Wirkliches geplant.

DER KÖNIG

Der König ist sechzehn Jahre alt.
Sechzehn Jahre und schon der Staat.
Er schaut, wie aus einem Hinterhalt,
vorbei an den Greisen vom Rat

in den Saal hinein und irgendwohin
und fühlt vielleicht nur dies:
an dem schmalen langen harten Kinn
die kalte Kette vom Vlies.

Das Todesurteil vor ihm bleibt
lang ohne Namenszug.
Und sie denken: wie er sich quält.

Sie wüßten, kennten sie ihn genug,
daß er nur langsam bis siebzig zählt
eh er es unterschreibt.

SELF-PORTRAIT FROM THE YEAR 1906

THE old, long-noble race's unregressing
distinction in the eye-brows' archingness.
The gaze with childhood's blue and anxiousness
still in it, far from servile, but confessing
a server's and a woman's humbleness.
The mouth made like a mouth, large, strict, and less
apt for persuading than for just expressing
what's right. The forehead, not unprepossessing,
at home in quiet down-looking shadowedness.

This, as coherence, only just divined;
never, as yet, in suffering or elation
collected for some lasting culmination;
as if from far, though, with stray things, creation
of something real and serious were designed.

Paris, spring 1906 (probably)

THE KING

THE age of the King is sixteen years.
Sixteen, and already the state.
As though from an ambuscade he peers
past where his grey councillors wait

into the hall and some point therein,
and only feels, maybe,
against his narrow, long, hard chin
the Fleece press chillingly.

Before him the death-warrant they submit
for long remains unsigned.
And they're thinking: It plagues him sore.

They'd know, if they knew enough of his mind,
he's but slowly counting to seventy before
setting his hand to it.

Paris, c. 1 July 1906
Suggested by a picture of Edward VI, *The Death Warrant*, by John Pettie (1839-93),
which Rilke had seen in the Hamburg Kunsthalle.

AUFERSTEHUNG

Der Graf vernimmt die Töne,
er sieht einen lichten Riß;
er weckt seine dreizehn Söhne
im Erb-Begräbnis.

Er grüßt seine beiden Frauen
ehrerbietig von weit –;
und alle, voll Vertrauen,
stehn auf zur Ewigkeit

und warten nur noch auf Erich
und Ulriken Dorotheen,
die, sieben- und dreizehnjährig,
    (sechzehnhundertzehn)
verstorben sind in Flandern,
um heute vor den andern
unbeirrt herzugehn.

DER FAHNENTRÄGER

Die Andern fühlen alles an sich rauh
und ohne Anteil: Eisen, Zeug und Leder.
Zwar manchmal schmeichelt eine weiche Feder,
doch sehr allein und lieb-los ist ein jeder;
er aber trägt – als trüg er eine Frau –
die Fahne in dem feierlichen Kleide.
Dicht hinter ihm geht ihre schwere Seide,
die manchmal über seine Hände fließt.

Er kann allein, wenn er die Augen schließt,
ein Lächeln sehn: er darf sie nicht verlassen. –

Und wenn es kommt in blitzenden Kürassen
und nach ihr greift und ringt und will sie fassen –:

dann darf er sie abreißen von dem Stocke
als riß er sie aus ihrem Mädchentum,
um sie zu halten unterm Waffenrocke.

Und für die Andern ist das Mut und Ruhm.

RESURRECTION

THE Count hears sounds outbreaking
and sees a glimmering rent;
his thirteen sons he's waking
in the family monument.

He greets from afar his pair
of spouses respectfully; –
and all with a confident air
get up for Eternity;

and wait but till Eric appears
and Ulrica Dorothy,
he who at seventeen years
died, and at thirteen she
(sixteen-ten, in Flanders),
who'll lead these older upstanders
to-day unfalteringly.

Paris, c. 1 July 1906

There is an interesting 'explanation' of the last stanza in a letter of Rilke's to
Hedwig von Boddien, 10 August 1913.

THE ENSIGN

THE others feel in all they are arrayed
no touch of sympathy: iron, cloth and leather.
There is at times the flattery of a feather,
but each is lone and loveless altogether;
he carries though – as if it were a maid –
the precious ensign in her gala dress.
Sometimes he feels her heavy silk's caress
flowing along his fingers fold on fold.

Shutting his eyes, he only can behold
a smile, a smile; never must he forsake her. –

And if a flashing of cuirasses shake her
and grasp at her and strive and try to take her: –

then he may tear her boldly from the lance,
as though he tore her from her virgin name,
to hold beneath his tunic in a trance.

The others call that bravery and fame.

Paris, 11-19 July 1906

DER LETZTE GRAF VON BREDERODE
ENTZIEHT SICH TÜRKISCHER
GEFANGENSCHAFT

SIE folgten furchtbar; ihren bunten Tod
von ferne nach ihm werfend, während er
verloren floh, nichts weiter als: bedroht.
Die Ferne seiner Väter schien nicht mehr

für ihn zu gelten; denn um so zu fliehn,
genügt ein Tier vor Jägern. Bis der Fluß
aufrauschte nah und blitzend. Ein Entschluß
hob ihn samt seiner Not und machte ihn

wieder zum Knaben fürstlichen Geblütes.
Ein Lächeln adeliger Frauen goß
noch einmal Süßigkeit in sein verfrühtes

vollendetes Gesicht. Er zwang sein Roß,
groß wie sein Herz zu gehn, sein blutdurchglühtes:
es trug ihn in den Strom wie in sein Schloß.

DIE KURTISANE

VENEDIGS Sonne wird in meinem Haar
ein Gold bereiten: aller Alchemie
erlauchten Ausgang. Meine Brauen, die
den Brücken gleichen, siehst du sie

hinführen ob der lautlosen Gefahr
der Augen, die ein heimlicher Verkehr
an die Kanäle schließt, so daß das Meer
in ihnen steigt und fällt und wechselt. Wer

mich einmal sah, beneidet meinen Hund,
weil sich auf ihm oft in zerstreuter Pause
die Hand, die nie an keiner Glut verkohlt,

die unverwundbare, geschmückt, erholt –.
Und Knaben, Hoffnungen aus altem Hause,
gehn wie an Gift an meinem Mund zugrund.

THE LAST COUNT OF BREDERODE
ESCAPES FROM TURKISH CAPTIVITY

THEY followed fearsomely; from distantness
hurling their motley death at him, while he
fled lost, with nothing but his threatenedness.
It seemed the farness of his ancestry

for him had ceased to count; for so to flee
needs but a hunted animal. Until
the stream roared near and bright. An act of will
raised him and his distress and suddenly

made him again a boy of princely race.
A smile of noble women gone before him
once more poured sweetness into that young face

too soon complete. He forced his horse to pace
as grandly as his blood-glowing heart: it bore him
into the stream as into his own place.

Capri, mid-March 1907

THE COURTESAN

THE sun of Venice in my hair's preparing
a gold where lustrously shall culminate
all alchemy. My brows, which emulate
her bridges, you can contemplate

over the silent perilousness repairing
of eyes which some communion secretly
unites with her canals, so that the sea
rises and ebbs and changes in them. He

who once has seen me falls to envying
my dog, because, in moments of distraction,
this hand no fieriness incinerates,

scathless, bejewelled, there recuperates. –
And many a hopeful youth of high extraction
will not survive my mouth's envenoming.

Capri, mid-March 1907

DIE TREPPE DER ORANGERIE

VERSAILLES

WIE Könige, die schließlich nur noch schreiten
fast ohne Ziel, nur um von Zeit zu Zeit
sich den Verneigenden auf beiden Seiten
zu zeigen in des Mantels Einsamkeit –:

so steigt, allein zwischen den Balustraden,
die sich verneigen schon seit Anbeginn,
die Treppe: langsam und von Gottes Gnaden
und auf den Himmel zu und nirgends hin;

als ob sie allen Folgenden befahl
zurückzubleiben, – so daß sie nicht wagen
von ferne nachzugehen; nicht einmal
die schwere Schleppe durfte einer tragen.

DER MARMOR-KARREN

PARIS

AUF Pferde, sieben ziehende, verteilt,
verwandelt Niebewegtes sich in Schritte;
denn was hochmütig in des Marmors Mitte
an Alter, Widerstand und All verweilt,

das zeigt sich unter Menschen. Siehe, nicht
unkenntlich, unter irgend einem Namen,
nein: wie der Held das Drängen in den Dramen
erst sichtbar macht und plötzlich unterbricht:

so kommt es durch den stauenden Verlauf
des Tages, kommt in seinem ganzen Staate,
als ob ein großer Triumphator nahte

langsam zuletzt; und langsam vor ihm her
Gefangene, von seiner Schwere schwer.
Und naht noch immer und hält alles auf.

THE STEPS OF THE ORANGERY

VERSAILLES

LIKE kings who simply pace at certain hours
with no more purpose than the habitude
of showing the double-rank of courtly bowers
their presence in their mantle's solitude: –

even so this flight of steps ascends in lonely
pomp between pillars bowing eternally:
slowly and By the Grace of God and only
to Heaven and nowhere intermediately;

as having ordered all its retinue
to stay behind, – and they're not even daring
to follow at a distance; none may do
so much as hold the heavy train it's wearing.

Paris, mid-July 1906

THE MARBLE-WAGON

PARIS

DISTRIBUTED to seven steeds to haul,
the never-moved is changing into paces;
for what the marble hiddenly embraces
of haughty age, resistancy, and All,

shows among men. Yes, recognisably,
allowing at least some sort of name's emergence:
yes, as the hero makes the drama's urgence
seen when he interrupts it suddenly,

it's coming through the locked upgathering
of the day's course, with all its pomp appearing,
as though some mighty triumpher were nearing

slowly at last; and slowly before him
captives who feel his weight in every limb.
And keeps on nearing and halts everything.

Paris, 28 June 1907

Judith Cladel, *Auguste Rodin. L'œuvre et l'homme*, Brussels 1908, p. 50, describes how every spring an enormous wagon, drawn by ten or twelve horses, used to collect from the studios in the rue de l' Université, leased by the Dépôt des Marbres, sculptures and paintings destined for various exhibitions.

BUDDHA

Schon von ferne fühlt der fremde scheue
Pilger, wie es golden von ihm träuft;
so als hätten Reiche voller Reue
ihre Heimlichkeiten aufgehäuft.

Aber näher kommend wird er irre
vor der Hoheit dieser Augenbraun:
denn das sind nicht ihre Trinkgeschirre
und die Ohrgehänge ihrer Fraun.

Wüßte einer denn zu sagen, welche
Dinge eingeschmolzen wurden, um
dieses Bild auf diesem Blumenkelche

aufzurichten: stummer, ruhiggelber
als ein goldenes und rundherum
auch den Raum berührend wie sich selber.

RÖMISCHE FONTÄNE

BORGHESE

Zwei Becken, eins das andre übersteigend
aus einem alten runden Marmorrand,
und aus dem oberen Wasser leis sich neigend
zum Wasser, welches unten wartend stand,

dem leise redenden entgegenschweigend
und heimlich, gleichsam in der hohlen Hand,
ihm Himmel hinter Grün und Dunkel zeigend
wie einen unbekannten Gegenstand;

sich selber ruhig in der schönen Schale
verbreitend ohne Heimweh, Kreis aus Kreis,
nur manchmal träumerisch und tropfenweis

sich niederlassend an den Moosbehängen
zum letzten Spiegel, der sein Becken leis
von unten lächeln macht mit Übergängen.

BUDDHA

FROM afar the awe-struck pilgrim senses
how it trickles from him goldenly;
as if realms of ripened penitences
had upheaped there all their secrecy.

When he's nearer, though, the elevation
of those brows casts doubt into his mind:
this is not their cups' co-operation
with the ear-rings of their womenkind.

Is there one, then, who could reckon up
what things have been melted down to found
just this image on this flower-cup:

muter, of a yellow more reposing
than a golden one's, and all around
touching, like itself, the space enclosing?

Paris. 19 July 1906

ROMAN FOUNTAIN

BORGHESE

TWO basins, this one over that, ascending
from an old marbled pool's embosoming,
and, from the upper, water gently bending
to water which below stood proffering

that gentle murmurer silence for reply there,
and, as in hollowed hand, clandestinely
showing it a green- and darkness-curtained sky there
like some unrecognised reality;

itself serenely in its lovely chalice
unhomesickly outspreading, ring on ring,
just sometimes dreamily downladdering,

drop after drop, along the mossy tresses
to the last mirror, that would gently bring
its bowl's convex to smile with changefulnesses.

Paris, 8 July 1906

DAS KARUSSELL

JARDIN DU LUXEMBOURG

MIT einem Dach und seinem Schatten dreht
sich eine kleine Weile der Bestand
von bunten Pferden, alle aus dem Land,
das lange zögert, eh es untergeht.
Zwar manche sind an Wagen angespannt,
doch alle haben Mut in ihren Mienen;
ein böser roter Löwe geht mit ihnen
und dann und wann ein weißer Elefant.

Sogar ein Hirsch ist da, ganz wie im Wald,
nur daß er einen Sattel trägt und drüber
ein kleines blaues Mädchen aufgeschnallt.

Und auf dem Löwen reitet weiß ein Junge
und hält sich mit der kleinen heißen Hand,
dieweil der Löwe Zähne zeigt und Zunge.

Und dann und wann ein weißer Elefant.

Und auf den Pferden kommen sie vorüber,
auch Mädchen, helle, diesem Pferdesprunge
fast schon entwachsen; mitten in dem Schwunge
schauen sie auf, irgendwohin, herüber –

Und dann und wann ein weißer Elefant.

Und das geht hin und eilt sich, daß es endet,
und kreist und dreht sich nur und hat kein Ziel.
Ein Rot, ein Grün, ein Grau vorbeigesendet,
ein kleines kaum begonnenes Profil –.
Und manchesmal ein Lächeln, hergewendet,
ein seliges, das blendet und verschwendet
an dieses atemlose blinde Spiel . . .

THE MERRY-GO-ROUND

JARDIN DU LUXEMBOURG

WITH roof and shadow for a while careers
the stud of horses, variously bright,
all from that land that long remains in sight
before it ultimately disappears.
Several indeed pull carriages, with tight-
held rein, but all have boldness in their bearing;
with them a wicked scarlet lion's faring
and now and then an elephant all white.

Just as in woods, a stag comes into view,
save that it has a saddle and tied fast
thereon a little maiden all in blue.

And on the lion a little boy is going,
whose small hot hands hold on with all his might,
while raging lion's tongue and teeth are showing.

And now and then an elephant all white.

And on the horses they come riding past,
girls too, bright-skirted, whom the horse-jumps here
scarce now preoccupy: in full career
elsewhither, hitherwards, a glance they cast –

And now and then an elephant all white.

And on it goes and hastens to be ended,
and aimlessly rotates until it's done.
A red, a green, a grey is apprehended,
a little profile, scarcely yet begun. –
And now and then a smile, for us intended,
blissfully happy, dazzlingly expended
upon this breathless, blindly followed fun . . .

Paris, June 1906

l. 3, 'that land' is Childhood, and the image is that of a coastline gradually sinking
beneath the horizon from the gaze of a departing voyager.

SPANISCHE TÄNZERIN

Wɪᴇ in der Hand ein Schwefelzündholz, weiß,
eh es zur Flamme kommt, nach allen Seiten
zuckende Zungen streckt –: beginnt im Kreis
naher Beschauer hastig, hell und heiß
ihr runder Tanz sich zuckend auszubreiten.

Und plötzlich ist er Flamme, ganz und gar.

Mit einem Blick entzündet sie ihr Haar
und dreht auf einmal mit gewagter Kunst
ihr ganzes Kleid in diese Feuersbrunst,
aus welcher sich, wie Schlangen die erschrecken,
die nackten Arme wach und klappernd strecken.

Und dann: als würde ihr das Feuer knapp,
nimmt sie es ganz zusamm und wirft es ab
sehr herrisch, mit hochmütiger Gebärde
und schaut: da liegt es rasend auf der Erde
und flammt noch immer und ergiebt sich nicht –.
Doch sieghaft, sicher und mit einem süßen
grüßenden Lächeln hebt sie ihr Gesicht
und stampft es aus mit kleinen festen Füßen.

DER TURM

TOUR ST.-NICOLAS, FURNES

Eʀᴅ-Iɴɴᴇʀᴇs. Als wäre dort, wohin
du blindlings steigst, erst Erdenoberfläche,
zu der du steigst im schrägen Bett der Bäche,
die langsam aus dem suchenden Gerinn

der Dunkelheit entsprungen sind, durch die
sich dein Gesicht, wie auferstehend, drängt
und die du plötzlich *siehst*, als fiele sie
aus diesem Abgrund, der dich überhängt

und den du, wie er riesig über dir
sich umstürzt in dem dämmernden Gestühle,
erkennst, erschreckt und fürchtend, im Gefühle:
o wenn er steigt, behangen wie ein Stier –:

SPANISH DANCER

As in the hand a sulphur match, sheer white
before it flames, will stretch out scintillating
tongues on all sides, her round dance, in the tight
ring of spectators, hasty, hot, alight,
has started scintillatingly dilating.

And suddenly it's only flame that's there.

With one glance she has set alight her hair,
and all at once with daring artfulness
spins her whole dress into this fieriness,
from which, like serpents terribly abashing,
her naked arms stretch out aroused and gnashing.

And then, as though her fire would not suffice,
she gathers it all up, and in a trice
flings it away with proud gesticulation
and gazes: still in raging conflagration
it's writhing on the ground unyieldingly. –
She, though, inflexible and with a sweet
saluting smile, looks up victoriously
and stamps it out with little steadfast feet.

Paris, June 1906

THE TOWER

TOUR ST.-NICOLAS, FURNES

EARTH-INNESS. As if not till where you still
so blindly climb to were the Earth's outside:
climb in this criss-cross watercourse supplied
by slow upwellings from the groping rill

of darkness which your face is pressing through
like face of one arising from the dead,
and which can suddenly be *seen* by you,
as though it fell from that high-overhead

hanging abyss, which, in the glimmering
belfry gigantically overheeling,
you recognise with start of terror, feeling:
'If, belled there like a bull, it's clambering!' –

Da aber nimmt dich aus der engen Endung
windiges Licht. Fast fliegend siehst du hier
die Himmel wieder, Blendung über Blendung,
und dort die Tiefen, wach und voll Verwendung,

und kleine Tage wie bei Patenier,
gleichzeitige, mit Stunde neben Stunde,
durch die die Brücken springen wie die Hunde,
dem hellen Wege immer auf der Spur,

den unbeholfne Häuser manchmal nur
verbergen, bis er ganz im Hintergrunde
beruhigt geht durch Buschwerk und Natur.

DER PLATZ

FURNES

WILLKÜRLICH von Gewesnem ausgeweitet:
von Wut und Aufruhr, von dem Kunterbunt
das die Verurteilten zu Tod begleitet,
von Buden, von der Jahrmarktsrufer Mund,
und von dem Herzog der vorüberreitet
und von dem Hochmut von Burgund,

(auf allen Seiten Hintergrund):

ladet der Platz zum Einzug seiner Weite
die fernen Fenster unaufhörlich ein,
während sich das Gefolge und Geleite
der Leere langsam an den Handelsreihn

verteilt und ordnet. In die Giebel steigend,
wollen die kleinen Häuser alles sehn,
die Türme vor einander scheu verschweigend,
die immer maßlos hinter ihnen stehn.

You're drawn, though, from the narrow termination
by gusty light. Near-flying, can see here
the sky's scarce-bearable illumination,
and there the depths, all wakeful application,

and little days, like those of Patenir,
with hours all simultaneously appearing,
through which, like hounds, the bridges are careering
incessantly along the bright road's trail,

which clumsy houses sometimes just avail
to hide till in the far background it's steering
calmly through copses and the open dale.

Paris, 18 July 1907

l. 12, *belled there like a bull*. The only situation it would seem, in which a bull can
be naturally imagined as both *belled* and *climbing* is that of an Alpine bull leading
its herd up to the summer pastures. The paradox is that of an inverted ('overheeling'), a rising instead of a falling, abyss.

l. 17, *Patenir*: a Flemish Painter (c. 1475 - 1525), perhaps the first in whose paintings landscape assumed a more than incidental and decorative importance.

THE SQUARE

FURNES

WIDENED capriciously by what would ply there:
by rage and tumult, by the pageantry
accompanying those condemned to die there,
by booths, by all the mouths of marketry,
and by the ducal ruler riding-by there
and by the pride of Burgundy

(background on all sides equally):

the square keeps on perpetually inviting
the distant windows to its spaciousness,
while vacancy's whole retinue's uniting
slowly with that round-dance of business.

Climbing to gable-height in their endeavour
to see, the little houses aren't inclined
to speak before each other of those ever-
immeasurable towers that stand behind.

Paris, 21 July 1907

QUAI DU ROSAIRE

BRÜGGE

Die Gassen haben einen sachten Gang
(wie manchmal Menschen gehen im Genesen
nachdenkend: was ist früher hier gewesen?)
und die an Plätze kommen, warten lang

auf eine andre, die mit einem Schritt
über das abendklare Wasser tritt,
darin, je mehr sich rings die Dinge mildern,
die eingehängte Welt von Spiegelbildern
so wirklich wird wie diese Dinge nie.

Verging nicht diese Stadt? Nun siehst du, wie
(nach einem unbegreiflichen Gesetz)
sie wach und deutlich wird im Umgestellten,
als wäre dort das Leben nicht so selten;
dort hängen jetzt die Gärten groß und gelten,
dort dreht sich plötzlich hinter schnell erhellten
Fenstern der Tanz in den Estaminets.

Und oben blieb? – Die Stille nur, ich glaube,
und kostet langsam und von nichts gedrängt
Beere um Beere aus der süßen Traube
des Glockenspiels, das in den Himmeln hängt.

BÉGUINAGE

BÉGUINAGE SAINTE-ELISABETH, BRÜGGE

I

Das hohe Tor scheint keine einzuhalten,
die Brücke geht gleich gerne hin und her,
und doch sind sicher alle in dem alten
offenen Ulmenhof und gehn nicht mehr
aus ihren Häusern, als auf jenem Streifen
zur Kirche hin, um besser zu begreifen
warum in ihnen so viel Liebe war.

Dort knieen sie, verdeckt mit reinem Leinen,
so gleich, als wäre nur das Bild der einen
tausendmal im Choral, der tief und klar
zu Spiegeln wird an den verteilten Pfeilern;

QUAI DU ROSAIRE

BRUGES

THE streets are moving with a gentle gait
(like invalids the first time out of door
trying to remember: What was here before?)
and those that come to squares will long await

another street, that, with a single stride,
crosses the water evening's clarified,
wherein, the more things round about are waning,
the mirrored world inhung will be attaining
reality those things have never known.

Did not this city vanish? Now you're shown
it growing (in some unfathomable way)
alert and lucid in transposal there,
as though that life were no such strange affair;
there hang the gardens now with grander air,
there behind windows suddenly aflare
revolves the dance in the estaminets.

Above remained? – Just silence, I opine,
now slowly tasting, with no tasks to ply,
berry on berry from the sweet grape-vine-
cluster of chime that's hanging in the sky.

Paris, 18 or 19 July 1907

BÉGUINAGE

BÉGUINAGE SAINTE-ELISABETH, BRUGES

I

THE lofty gateway seems not to immure,
the bridge is going like-gladly to and fro;
in that old, open elm-court, though, secure
are one and all, and now no longer go
out of their little houses, save when wending
along that strip to church, for comprehending
better why so much love in them arose.

They kneel there in their linen's pure protection,
as like as if a single one's reflection
were myriadly in that chorale that grows
a clear deep mirror columns are suspending;

131

und ihre Stimmen gehn den immer steilern
Gesang hinan und werfen sich von dort,
wo es nicht weitergeht, vom letzten Wort,
den Engeln zu, die sie nicht wiedergeben.

Drum sind die unten, wenn sie sich erheben
und wenden, still. Drum reichen sie sich schweigend
mit einem Neigen, Zeigende zu zeigend
Empfangenden, geweihtes Wasser, das
die Stirnen kühl macht und die Munde blaß.

Und gehen dann, verhangen und verhalten,
auf jenem Streifen wieder überquer –
die Jungen ruhig, ungewiß die Alten
und eine Greisin, weilend, hinterher –
zu ihren Häusern, die sie schnell verschweigen
und die sich durch die Ulmen hin von Zeit
zu Zeit ein wenig reine Einsamkeit,
in einer kleinen Scheibe schimmernd, zeigen.

II

Was aber spiegelt mit den tausend Scheiben
das Kirchenfenster in den Hof hinein,
darin sich Schweigen, Schein und Widerschein
vermischen, trinken, trüben, übertreiben,
phantastisch alternd wie ein alter Wein.

Dort legt sich, keiner weiß von welcher Seite,
Außen auf Inneres und Ewigkeit
auf Immer-Hingehn, Weite über Weite,
erblindend, finster, unbenutzt, verbleit.

Dort bleibt, unter dem schwankenden Dekor
des Sommertags, das Graue alter Winter:
als stünde regungslos ein sanftgesinnter
langmütig lange Wartender dahinter
und eine weinend Wartende davor.

and their unwearied voices keep ascending
the ever-steeper hymn, and plunge from where
it goes no further, from the last word there,
into the angels' un-let-going embraces.

Hence these below, when they uplift their faces
and turn, are still. With silent bows they're giving
(pointers at sisters pointingly receiving)
each other of the holy water now,
that makes the mouth more pale and cools the brow.

And then once more, enveloped and demurely,
across that strip of turf they take their way –
the younger tranquilly, the old unsurely,
and, lingeringly behind them, one going grey –
into the houses that so quickly hide them
and show each other through the elminess
at times a bit of purest loneliness
glimmering through some small window from inside them.

II

What, though, with thousand panes, is it reflecting
into the court, that window in the shrine,
wherein such silence, shine and counter-shine
are mingling, drowning, dimming, resurrecting,
fantastically ageing like old wine?

There's laid there, from which side there's no insistence,
outer on inner, everlastingness
on ever-passing, distance upon distance,
bedazzling, sombre, unused, lustreless.

There among all the summer's swaying decor
gone winters' grey is still procrastinating:
as though behind it, all-unindicating,
stood one long-sufferingly long-awaiting,
and, weeping, an awaiteress before.

Paris, 19-20 July 1907

133

DIE MARIEN-PROZESSION

GENT

Aus allen Türmen stürzt sich, Fluß um Fluß,
hinwallendes Metall in solchen Massen
als sollte drunten in der Form der Gassen
ein blanker Tag erstehn aus Bronzeguß,

an dessen Rand, gehämmert und erhaben,
zu sehen ist der buntgebundne Zug
der leichten Mädchen und der neuen Knaben,
und wie er Wellen schlug und trieb und trug,
hinabgehalten von dem ungewissen
Gewicht der Fahnen und von Hindernissen
gehemmt, unsichtbar wie die Hand des Herrn;

und drüben plötzlich beinah mitgerissen
vom Aufstieg aufgescheuchter Räucherbecken,
die fliegend, alle sieben, wie im Schrecken
an ihren Silberketten zerrn.

Die Böschung Schauender umschließt die Schiene,
in der das alles stockt und rauscht und rollt:
das Kommende, das Chryselephantine,
aus dem sich zu Balkonen Baldachine
aufbäumen, schwankend im Behang von Gold.

Und sie erkennen über all dem Weißen,
getragen und im spanischen Gewand,
das alte Standbild mit dem kleinen heißen
Gesichte und dem Kinde auf der Hand
und knieen hin, je mehr es naht und naht,
in seiner Krone ahnungslos veraltend
und immer noch das Segnen hölzern haltend
aus dem sich groß gebärdenden Brokat.

Da aber, wie es an den Hingeknieten
vorüberkommt, die scheu von unten schaun,
da scheint es seinen Trägern zu gebieten
mit einem Hochziehn seiner Augenbraun,

PROCESSION OF THE VIRGIN

FROM all the city's towers, surge on surge,
such masses of onseething metal thunder
as if within the street-formed mould thereunder
a day of glittering bronze were to emerge,

along whose border, splendidly indented,
the parti-colourfully posied train
of new-sprung girls and boys should be presented,
how it would toss and billow and sustain,
now underheld by the uncalculated
weight of the banners and coagulated
by hindrance hidden as God's hands remain,

now suddenly almost precipitated
aloft by the upstartled censers' flight,
all seven on the wing and, as in fright,
each tugging at its silver chain.

The backward-sloped embankment of the peering
contains the channel rustlingly downrolled
by that chryselephantine pomp that's nearing,
whence up to height of balconies are rearing
the swaying canopies festooned with gold.

And, topping all the whiteness, they're discerning,
high-carried and in Spanish garb arrayed,
the ancient image with the little burning
face and the infant on its hand displayed,
and throngedlier kneel the nearer it's conveyed,
unconscious, in its crown, of obsolescing,
and woodenly distributing its blessing
out of the grandly-posturing brocade.

And then, while passing by the kneeling prayers,
who timidly glance upwards from below,
it seems to be commanding its conveyers
with an uplifting of its eyebrows, so

hochmütig, ungehalten und bestimmt:
so daß sie staunen, stehn und überlegen
und schließlich zögernd gehn. Sie aber nimmt

in sich die Schritte dieses ganzen Stromes
und geht, allein, wie auf erkannten Wegen
dem Glockendonnern des großoffnen Domes
auf hundert Schultern frauenhaft entgegen.

st. 4, l. 3, *Chryselephantine*. In a letter of 25 July 1907 Rilke informed his wife that
this word meant 'made of gold and ivory', that it had been applied by ancient
writers to the statues of Phidias, and that 'hier soll der Ausdruck helfen, das Weiße
und Goldene der Prozession rasch, mit einem Schlage, heraufzurufen'.

DIE INSEL

NORDSEE

I

DIE nächste Flut verwischt den Weg im Watt,
und alles wird auf allen Seiten gleich;
die kleine Insel draußen aber hat
die Augen zu; verwirrend kreist der Deich

um ihre Wohner, die in einen Schlaf
geboren werden, drin sie viele Welten
verwechseln, schweigend; denn sie reden selten,
und jeder Satz ist wie ein Epitaph

für etwas Angeschwemmtes, Unbekanntes,
das unerklärt zu ihnen kommt und bleibt.
Und so ist alles, was ihr Blick beschreibt

von Kindheit an: nicht auf sie Angewandtes,
zu Großes, Rücksichtsloses, Hergesandtes,
das ihre Einsamkeit noch übertreibt.

II

Als läge er in einem Krater-Kreise
auf einem Mond: ist jeder Hof umdämmt,
und drin die Gärten sind auf gleiche Weise
gekleidet und wie Waisen gleich gekämmt

von jenem Sturm, der sie so rauh erzieht
und tagelang sie bange macht mit Toden.
Dann sitzt man in den Häusern drin und sieht
in schiefen Spiegeln was auf den Kommoden

imperious and irate and unmistaking,
they have to stare and stand and think for long,
then hesitantly move. She, though, is making

into her own the steps of all this throng
and going alone, as on familiar-feeling
ways, to the open minster's thundrous pealing
on hundred shoulders womanly along.

Paris, 20 July 1907

THE ISLAND

NORTH SEA

I

ACROSS the mud-flat track the next tide sweeps,
and everything on all sides grows alike;
the little island over there, though, keeps
its eyes shut; dizzy-makingly its dyke

circles the dwellers there, born into dreams
where quietly universe with universe
will get confused; for seldom they converse,
and like an epitaph each sentence seems

for something unfamiliar, inundated,
that comes to them mysteriously and stays.
And such is everything that meets their gaze

from childhood on: something all-unrelated
to them, too big, regardless, transmigrated,
making still lonelier their lonely days.

Paris, 23 July 1906

II

As though it lay within some lunar crater's
outthrust, each farm's surrounded by a dyke,
and garths are costumed by their cultivators
the same way and, like orphans, combed alike

by that storm-wind, so roughly educating
and cowing for days on end with perishings.
One sits inside the house then, contemplating
in mirrors hung aslant what far-fetched things

137

Seltsames steht. Und einer von den Söhnen
tritt abends vor die Tür und zieht ein Tönen
aus der Harmonika wie Weinen weich;

so hörte ers in einem fremden Hafen –.
Und draußen formt sich eines von den Schafen
ganz groß, fast drohend, auf dem Außendeich.

III

Nah ist nur Innres; alles andre fern.
Und dieses Innere gedrängt und täglich
mit allem überfüllt und ganz unsäglich.
Die Insel ist wie ein zu kleiner Stern

welchen der Raum nicht merkt und stumm zerstört
in seinem unbewußten Furchtbarsein,
so daß er, unerhellt und überhört,
allein

damit dies alles doch ein Ende nehme,
dunkel auf einer selbsterfundnen Bahn
versucht zu gehen, blindlings, nicht im Plan
der Wandelsterne, Sonnen und Systeme.

HETÄREN-GRÄBER

In ihren langen Haaren liegen sie
mit braunen, tief in sich gegangenen Gesichtern.
Die Augen zu wie vor zu vieler Ferne.
Skelette, Munde, Blumen. In den Munden
die glatten Zähne wie ein Reise-Schachspiel
aus Elfenbein in Reihen aufgestellt.
Und Blumen, gelbe Perlen, schlanke Knochen,
Hände und Hemden, welkende Gewebe
über dem eingestürzten Herzen. Aber
dort unter jenen Ringen, Talismanen
und augenblauen Steinen (Lieblings-Angedenken)
steht noch die stille Krypta des Geschlechtes,
bis an die Wölbung voll mit Blumenblättern.
Und wieder gelbe Perlen, weitverrollte, –
Schalen gebrannten Tones, deren Bug

stand on the dresser. And when day is done
one son will draw from his accordion
before the door a sound that seems to weep –

such, in some foreign port, it reached his ears. –
And huge and almost threateningly appears
on that surrounding dyke one of the sheep.

Paris, 24 July 1906

III

Only within is near; all else is far.
And this within crowded, and day by day
too filled with all, and what no words can say.
The island's like a too exiguous star

which unperceiving space, without a word,
has shattered in unconscious frightfulness
so that it, unillumined and unheard,
with no ambitiousness

save that all this may somewhere find an end,
goes struggling on some self-discovered line
in darkness, blindly, out of the design
wherein the planets, suns, and systems wend.

Paris, 23-4 July 1906 (ll. 1-5) and 20 August 1907 (the rest)

TOMBS OF THE HETÆRÆ

THEY lie in their long hair, and their brown faces
have now withdrawn deep, deep into themselves.
Eyes closed, as though confronting too much distance.
Skeletons, mouths, and flowers. Within the mouths
the smooth teeth like a set of pocket-chessmen
marshalled together in two ivory rows.
And flowers, yellow pearls, and slender bones,
and hands, and tunics – withering warp and woof
above the inward-fallen heart. But there,
beneath those rings, beneath the talismans
and eye-blue stones (those cherished souvenirs),
there still remains the silent crypt of sex,
filled to its vaulted roof with flower petals.
And once more yellow pearls, rolled far asunder, –
dishes of hard-burnt clay, whose rondure once

139

ihr eignes Bild geziert hat, grüne Scherben
von Salben-Vasen, die wie Blumen duften,
und Formen kleiner Götter: Hausaltäre,
Hetärenhimmel mit entzückten Göttern.
Gesprengte Gürtel, flache Skarabäen,
kleine Figuren riesigen Geschlechtes,
ein Mund der lacht und Tanzende und Läufer,
goldene Fibeln, kleinen Bogen ähnlich
zur Jagd auf Tier- und Vogelamulette,
und lange Nadeln, zieres Hausgeräte
und eine runde Scherbe roten Grundes,
darauf, wie eines Eingangs schwarze Aufschrift,
die straffen Beine eines Viergespannes.
Und wieder Blumen, Perlen, die verrollt sind,
die hellen Lenden einer kleinen Leier,
und zwischen Schleiern, die gleich Nebeln fallen,
wie ausgekrochen aus des Schuhes Puppe:
des Fußgelenkes leichter Schmetterling.

So liegen sie mit Dingen angefüllt,
kostbaren Dingen, Steinen, Spielzeug, Hausrat,
zerschlagnem Tand (was alles in sie abfiel),
und dunkeln wie der Grund von einem Fluß.

Flußbetten waren sie,
darüber hin in kurzen schnellen Wellen
(die weiter wollten zu dem nächsten Leben)
die Leiber vieler Jünglinge sich stürzten
und in denen der Männer Ströme rauschten.
Und manchmal brachen Knaben aus den Bergen
der Kindheit, kamen zagen Falles nieder
und spielten mit den Dingen auf dem Grunde,
bis das Gefälle ihr Gefühl ergriff:

Dann füllten sie mit flachem klaren Wasser
die ganze Breite dieses breiten Weges
und trieben Wirbel an den tiefen Stellen;
und spiegelten zum erstenmal die Ufer
und ferne Vogelrufe –, während hoch
die Sternennächte eines süßen Landes
in Himmel wuchsen, die sich nirgends schlossen.

her image decorated, – green remains
of unguent vases that once smelt like flowers, –
figures of little gods, too: household altars,
Hetæræ-heavens with ecstatic gods!
The unsprung girdle, the flat scarabæus,
and little figures of gigantic sex;
a mouth that laughs, and dancing girls, and runners,
and golden clasps that might be little bows
for hunting beast- and bird-shaped amulets;
and long pins, quaintly fashioned crockery,
and a round potsherd with a reddish ground
whereon, like dark inscriptions over entries,
appear the taut legs of a team of horses.
And flowers again, pearls that have rolled apart,
the shining loins of a tiny lyre,
and then, between the veils that fall like vapours,
crept, as it were, from chrysalidal shoe,
the ankle, like an airy butterfly.

And thus they lie, filled to the brim with things,
with precious things, with jewels, toys, bric-à-brac,
with broken trash (all that fell into them),
and sombre as the bottom of a river.

Yes, they were river beds:
over and over them in short, swift waves
(all pressing onwards to some life that waited)
bodies of many youths would hurtle headlong,
and manly rivers, too, would roar within them.
And sometimes boys, emerging from the mountains
of Childhood, would descend in timid torrents,
and play with what they found upon the bottom,
till all at once the falling gradient gripped them:

And then they'd fill with shallow crystal water
the whole expanse of these broad watercourses,
and set up eddies in the deeper places;
and mirror, for the first time, the wide-spreading
banks and far cries of birds, while, high above them,
the starry nights of a sweet country blossomed
into a heaven that could nowhere close.

Rome, beginning of 1904

ORPHEUS. EURYDIKE. HERMES

Das war der Seelen wunderliches Bergwerk.
Wie stille Silbererze gingen sie
als Adern durch sein Dunkel. Zwischen Wurzeln
entsprang das Blut, das fortgeht zu den Menschen,
und schwer wie Porphyr sah es aus im Dunkel.
Sonst war nichts Rotes.

Felsen waren da
und wesenlose Wälder. Brücken über Leeres
und jener große graue blinde Teich,
der über seinem fernen Grunde hing
wie Regenhimmel über einer Landschaft.
Und zwischen Wiesen, sanft und voller Langmut,
erschien des einen Weges blasser Streifen,
wie eine lange Bleiche hingelegt.

Und dieses einen Weges kamen sie.

Voran der schlanke Mann im blauen Mantel,
der stumm und ungeduldig vor sich aussah.
Ohne zu kauen fraß sein Schritt den Weg
in großen Bissen; seine Hände hingen
schwer und verschlossen aus dem Fall der Falten
und wußten nicht mehr von der leichten Leier,
die in die Linke eingewachsen war
wie Rosenranken in den Ast des Ölbaums.
Und seine Sinne waren wie entzweit:
indes der Blick ihm wie ein Hund vorauslief,
umkehrte, kam und immer wieder weit
und wartend an der nächsten Wendung stand, –
blieb sein Gehör wie ein Geruch zurück.
Manchmal erschien es ihm als reichte es
bis an das Gehen jener beiden andern,
die folgen sollten diesen ganzen Aufstieg.
Dann wieder wars nur seines Steigens Nachklang
und seines Mantels Wind was hinter ihm war.
Er aber sagte sich, sie kämen doch;
sagte es laut und hörte sich verhallen.
Sie kämen doch, nur wärens zwei
die furchtbar leise gingen. Dürfte er
sich einmal wenden (wäre das Zurückschaun
nicht die Zersetzung dieses ganzen Werkes,
das erst vollbracht wird), müßte er sie sehen,
die beiden Leisen, die ihm schweigend nachgehn:

ORPHEUS. EURYDICE. HERMES

THAT was the so unfathomed mine of souls.
And they, like silent veins of silver ore,
were winding through its darkness. Between roots
welled up the blood that flows on to mankind,
like blocks of heavy porphyry in the darkness.
Else there was nothing red.

But there were rocks
and ghostly forests. Bridges over voidness
and that immense, grey, unreflecting pool
that hung above its so far distant bed
like a grey rainy sky above a landscape.
And between meadows, soft and full of patience,
appeared the pale strip of the single pathway,
like a long line of linen laid to bleach.

And on this single pathway they approached.

In front the slender man in the blue mantle,
gazing in dumb impatience straight before him.
His steps devoured the way in mighty chunks
they did not pause to chew; his hands were hanging,
heavy and clenched, out of the falling folds,
no longer conscious of the lightsome lyre,
the lyre which had grown into his left
like twines of rose into a branch of olive.
It seemed as though his senses were divided:
for, while his sight ran like a dog before him,
turned round, came back, and stood, time and again,
distant and waiting, at the path's next turn,
his hearing lagged behind him like a smell.
It seemed to him at times as though it stretched
back to the progress of those other two
who should be following up this whole ascent.
Then once more there was nothing else behind him
but his climb's echo and his mantle's wind.
He, though, assured himself they still were coming;
said it aloud and heard it die away.
They still were coming, only they were two
that trod with fearful lightness. If he durst
but once look back (if only looking back
were not undoing of this whole enterprise
still to be done), he could not fail to see them,
the two light-footers, following him in silence:

Den Gott des Ganges und der weiten Botschaft,
die Reisehaube über hellen Augen,
den schlanken Stab hertragend vor dem Leibe
und flügelschlagend an den Fußgelenken;
und seiner linken Hand gegeben: *sie.*

Die So-geliebte, daß aus einer Leier
mehr Klage kam als je aus Klagefrauen;
daß eine Welt aus Klage ward, in der
alles noch einmal da war: Wald und Tal
und Weg und Ortschaft, Feld und Fluß und Tier;
und daß um diese Klage-Welt, ganz so
wie um die andre Erde, eine Sonne
und ein gestirnter stiller Himmel ging,
ein Klage-Himmel mit entstellten Sternen –:
Diese So-geliebte.

Sie aber ging an jenes Gottes Hand,
den Schritt beschränkt von langen Leichenbändern,
unsicher, sanft und ohne Ungeduld.
Sie war in sich, wie Eine hoher Hoffnung,
und dachte nicht des Mannes, der voranging,
und nicht des Weges, der ins Leben aufstieg.
Sie war in sich. Und ihr Gestorbensein
erfüllte sie wie Fülle.
Wie eine Frucht von Süßigkeit und Dunkel,
so war sie voll von ihrem großen Tode,
der also neu war, daß sie nichts begriff.

Sie war in einem neuen Mädchentum
und unberührbar; ihr Geschlecht war zu
wie eine junge Blume gegen Abend,
und ihre Hände waren der Vermählung
so sehr entwöhnt, daß selbst des leichten Gottes
unendlich leise, leitende Berührung
sie kränkte wie zu sehr Vertraulichkeit.

Sie war schon nicht mehr diese blonde Frau,
die in des Dichters Liedern manchmal anklang,
nicht mehr des breiten Bettes Duft und Eiland
und jenes Mannes Eigentum nicht mehr.

Sie war schon aufgelöst wie langes Haar
und hingegeben wie gefallner Regen
und ausgeteilt wie hundertfacher Vorrat.

Sie war schon Wurzel.

144

The god of faring and of distant message,
the travelling-hood over his shining eyes,
the slender wand held out before his body,
the wings around his ankles lightly beating,
and in his left hand, as entrusted, *her*.

She, so belov'd, that from a single lyre
more mourning rose than from all women-mourners, –
that a whole world of mourning rose, wherein
all things were once more present: wood and vale
and road and hamlet, field and stream and beast, –
and that around this world of mourning turned,
even as around the other earth, a sun
and a whole silent heaven full of stars,
a heaven of mourning with disfigured stars: –
she, so beloved.

But hand in hand now with that god she walked,
her paces circumscribed by lengthy shroudings,
uncertain, gentle, and without impatience.
Wrapt in herself, like one whose time is near,
she thought not of the man who went before them,
nor of the road ascending into life.
Wrapt in herself she wandered. And her deadness
was filling her like fullness.
Full as a fruit with sweetness and with darkness
was she with her great death, which was so new
that for the time she could take nothing in.

She had attained a new virginity
and was intangible; her sex had closed
like a young flower at the approach of evening,
and her pale hands had grown so disaccustomed
to being a wife, that even the slim god's
endlessly gentle contact as he led her
disturbed her like a too great intimacy.

Even now she was no longer that blonde woman
who'd sometimes echoed in the poet's poems,
no longer the broad couch's scent and island,
nor yonder man's possession any longer.

She was already loosened like long hair,
and given far and wide like fallen rain,
and dealt out like a manifold supply.

She was already root.

Und als plötzlich jäh
der Gott sie anhielt und mit Schmerz im Ausruf
die Worte sprach: Er hat sich umgewendet –,
begriff sie nichts und sagte leise: *Wer?*

Fern aber, dunkel vor dem klaren Ausgang,
stand irgend jemand, dessen Angesicht
nicht zu erkennen war. Er stand und sah,
wie auf dem Streifen eines Wiesenpfades
mit trauervollem Blick der Gott der Botschaft
sich schweigend wandte, der Gestalt zu folgen,
die schon zurückging dieses selben Weges,
den Schritt beschränkt von langen Leichenbändern,
unsicher, sanft und ohne Ungeduld.

ALKESTIS

DA plötzlich war der Bote unter ihnen,
hineingeworfen in das Überkochen
des Hochzeitsmahles wie ein neuer Zusatz.
Sie fühlten nicht, die Trinkenden, des Gottes
heimlichen Eintritt, welcher seine Gottheit
so an sich hielt wie einen nassen Mantel
und ihrer einer schien, der oder jener,
wie er so durchging. Aber plötzlich sah
mitten im Sprechen einer von den Gästen
den jungen Hausherrn oben an dem Tische
wie in die Höh gerissen, nicht mehr liegend,
und überall und mit dem ganzen Wesen
ein Fremdes spiegelnd, das ihn furchtbar ansprach.
Und gleich darauf, als klärte sich die Mischung,
war Stille; nur mit einem Satz am Boden
von trübem Lärm und einem Niederschlag
fallenden Lallens, schon verdorben riechend
nach dumpfem umgestandenen Gelächter.
Und da erkannten sie den schlanken Gott,
und wie er dastand, innerlich voll Sendung
und unerbittlich, – wußten sie es beinah.
Und doch, als es gesagt war, war es mehr
als alles Wissen, gar nicht zu begreifen.
Admet muß sterben. Wann? In dieser Stunde.

And when, abruptly,
the god had halted her and, with an anguished
outcry, outspoke the words: He has turned round! –
she took in nothing, and said softly: Who?

But in the distance, dark in the bright exit,
someone or other stood, whose countenance
was indistinguishable. Stood and saw
how, on a strip of pathway between meadows,
with sorrow in his look, the god of message
turned silently to go behind the figure
already going back by that same pathway,
its paces circumscribed by lengthy shroudings,
uncertain, gentle, and without impatience.

Rome, beginning of 1904; revised Sweden, autumn 1904

ALCESTIS

THEN all at once the Messenger was there,
flung in among them like a new ingredient
just as the wedding feast was boiling over.
The revellers, they did not feel the god's
secret incoming, for he clasped his godhead
as closely to himself as a wet mantle,
and seemed like one of them, one or another,
as he passed through the hall. But suddenly
one of the guests, talking away there, saw
the hall's young master at the upper table
snatched, as it were, aloft, no more reclining,
and everywhere and with his whole existence
mirroring some strange and terrible demand.
And thereupon, as though the mixture cleared,
was silence: with some dregs, right at the bottom,
of cloudy hubbub, and a sediment
of falling babble, giving off already
the smell of hollow laughter that's gone flat.
And then they recognised the slender god,
and, as he stood there, full of inward mission
and unentreatable, they almost knew.
And yet, when it was uttered, it was far
beyond all knowledge, past all comprehension.
Admetus dies. When? In this very hour.

Der aber brach die Schale seines Schreckens
in Stücken ab und streckte seine Hände
heraus aus ihr, um mit dem Gott zu handeln.
Um Jahre, um ein einzig Jahr noch Jugend,
um Monate, um Wochen, um paar Tage,
ach, Tage nicht, um Nächte, nur um Eine,
um Eine Nacht, um diese nur: um die.
Der Gott verneinte, und da schrie er auf
und schrie's hinaus und hielt es nicht und schrie
wie seine Mutter aufschrie beim Gebären.

Und die trat zu ihm, eine alte Frau,
und auch der Vater kam, der alte Vater,
und beide standen, alt, veraltet, ratlos,
beim Schreienden, der plötzlich, wie noch nie
so nah, sie ansah, abbrach, schluckte, sagte:
Vater,
liegt dir denn viel daran an diesem Rest,
an diesem Satz, der dich beim Schlingen hindert?
Geh, gieß ihn weg. Und du, du alte Frau,
Matrone,
was tust du denn noch hier: du hast geboren.
Und beide hielt er sie wie Opfertiere
in Einem Griff. Auf einmal ließ er los
und stieß die Alten fort, voll Einfall, strahlend
und atemholend, rufend: Kreon, Kreon!
Und nichts als das; und nichts als diesen Namen.
Aber in seinem Antlitz stand das Andere,
das er nicht sagte, namenlos erwartend,
wie ers dem jungen Freunde, dem Geliebten,
erglühend hinhielt übern wirren Tisch.
Die Alten (stand da), siehst du, sind kein Loskauf,
sie sind verbraucht und schlecht und beinah wertlos,
du aber, du, in deiner ganzen Schönheit –

Da aber sah er seinen Freund nicht mehr.
Er blieb zurück, und das was kam war *sie*,
ein wenig kleiner fast als er sie kannte
und leicht und traurig in dem bleichen Brautkleid.
Die andern alle sind nur ihre Gasse,
durch die sie kommt und kommt –: (gleich wird sie da sein
in seinen Armen, die sich schmerzhaft auftun).

He, though, had started breaking, piece by piece,
his shell of fright, and was already stretching
his hands therefrom to bargain with the god.
For years, for yet one single year of youth,
for months, for weeks, for a few days – alas!
not days, – for nights, just for a single one,
for one night, just for this one: just for this.
The god refused, and then he screamed aloud
and screamed it out, withheld it not, and screamed
as his own mother screamed when he was born.

And she came up to him, an aged woman,
and then his father came, his aged father,
and both stood, aged, antiquated, helpless,
beside the screamer, who suddenly, never yet
so closely, looked at them, stopped, gulped, and said:
Father,
does it mean much to you, this residue,
this sediment, that hinders you in swallowing?
Go, pour it out. And you, old woman, you,
Mother,
why are you here still? You have given birth.
And held them both, like sacrificial beasts,
in one hard grip. Then suddenly let go,
pushed the old folk away, radiant, inspired,
and breathing hard, and shouting: Creon, Creon!
and nothing else, and nothing but that name.
But in his face appeared that something else
he did not utter, longing for the moment
when, glowingly, across the tangled table,
he'd proffer it the young friend, the beloved.
Look, the old folk (appeared there) are no ransom,
they are worn out and poor and almost worthless,
but you – it's different, you in all your beauty –

Now, though, he could no longer see his friend.
He stayed behind, and it was she that came,
almost a little smaller than he'd known her,
and light and sad in her pale bridal dress.
The others are all nothing but her street,
down which she comes and comes (she'll soon be there
within his arms, so painfully extended).

Doch wie er wartet, spricht sie; nicht zu ihm.
Sie spricht zum Gotte, und der Gott vernimmt sie,
und alle hörens gleichsam erst im Gotte:

Ersatz kann keiner für ihn sein. Ich *bins*.
Ich bin Ersatz. Denn keiner ist zu Ende
wie ich es bin. Was bleibt mir denn von dem
was ich hier war? Das *ists* ja, daß ich sterbe.
Hat sie dirs nicht gesagt, da sie dirs auftrug,
daß jenes Lager, das da drinnen wartet,
zur Unterwelt gehört? Ich nahm ja Abschied.
Abschied über Abschied.
Kein Sterbender nimmt mehr davon. Ich ging ja,
damit das Alles, unter Dem begraben
der jetzt mein Gatte ist, zergeht, sich auflöst –.
So führ mich hin: ich sterbe ja für ihn.

Und wie der Wind auf hoher See, der umspringt,
so trat der Gott fast wie zu einer Toten
und war auf einmal weit von ihrem Gatten,
dem er, versteckt in einem kleinen Zeichen,
die hundert Leben dieser Erde zuwarf.
Der stürzte taumelnd zu den beiden hin
und griff nach ihnen wie im Traum. Sie gingen
schon auf den Eingang zu, in dem die Frauen
verweint sich drängten. Aber einmal sah
er noch des Mädchens Antlitz, das sich wandte
mit einem Lächeln, hell wie eine Hoffnung,
die beinah ein Versprechen war: erwachsen
zurückzukommen aus dem tiefen Tode
zu ihm, dem Lebenden –

Da schlug er jäh
die Hände vors Gesicht, wie er so kniete,
um nichts zu sehen mehr nach diesem Lächeln.

But while he waits, she speaks, though not to him.
Speaks to the god, and the god listens to her,
and all hear, as it were, within the god:

None can be substitute for him. I'm that.
I'm substitute. For no one's reached the end
of everything as I have. What remains
of all I used to be? What's this but dying?
Did she not tell you, she who sent you hither,
that yonder couch waiting in there for me
belongs to the underworld? I said farewell.
Farewell upon farewell.
None dying could say more. And why I went,
was that all this, buried beneath the man
who's now my husband, might dissolve and fade. –
Lead me away: I'm dying for him already.

And, like a veering wind on the high seas,
the god approached her almost as one dead,
and all at once was far off from her husband,
to whom, concealed within a little token,
he tossed the hundred lives of mortal men.
He stumbled dizzily towards the pair
and grasped at them as in a dream. Already
they'd nearly reached the entrance, where the women
were crowding tearfully. But yet once more
he saw the maiden's face, that turned to him,
smiling a smile as radiant as a hope,
that was almost a promise: to return,
grown up, out of the depths of death again,
to him, the liver –

         Thereupon he flung
his hands, as he knelt there, before his face,
so as to see no more after that smile.

Capri, 7-10 February 1907

151

GEBURT DER VENUS

An diesem Morgen nach der Nacht, die bang
vergangen war mit Rufen, Unruh, Aufruhr, –
brach alles Meer noch einmal auf und schrie.
Und als der Schrei sich langsam wieder schloß
und von der Himmel blassem Tag und Anfang
herabfiel in der stummen Fische Abgrund –:
gebar das Meer.

Von erster Sonne schimmerte der Haarschaum
der weiten Wogenscham, an deren Rand
das Mädchen aufstand, weiß, verwirrt und feucht.
So wie ein junges grünes Blatt sich rührt,
sich reckt und Eingerolltes langsam aufschlägt,
entfaltete ihr Leib sich in die Kühle
hinein und in den unberührten Frühwind.

Wie Monde stiegen klar die Kniee auf
und tauchten in der Schenkel Wolkenränder;
der Waden schmaler Schatten wich zurück,
die Füße spannten sich und wurden licht,
und die Gelenke lebten wie die Kehlen
von Trinkenden.

Und in dem Kelch des Beckens lag der Leib
wie eine junge Frucht in eines Kindes Hand.
In seines Nabels engem Becher war
das ganze Dunkel dieses hellen Lebens.
Darunter hob sich licht die kleine Welle
und floß beständig über nach den Lenden,
wo dann und wann ein stilles Rieseln war.
Durchschienen aber und noch ohne Schatten,
wie ein Bestand von Birken im April,
warm, leer und unverborgen, lag die Scham.

Jetzt stand der Schultern rege Waage schon
im Gleichgewichte auf dem graden Körper,
der aus dem Becken wie ein Springbrunn aufstieg
und zögernd in den langen Armen abfiel
und rascher in dem vollen Fall des Haars.

Dann ging sehr langsam das Gesicht vorbei:
aus dem verkürzten Dunkel seiner Neigung
in klares, waagrechtes Erhobensein.
Und hinter ihm verschloß sich steil das Kinn.

BIRTH OF VENUS

THE morning following that fearful night
that passed with shouting, restlessness, and uproar,
the sea burst open yet again and screamed.
And, as the scream ebbed slowly to its close,
and, from the sky's pale daybreak and beginning,
was falling back to the dumb fishes' darkness –
the sea gave birth.

The first rays shimmered on the foaming hair
of the wide wave-vagina, on whose rim
the maiden rose, white and confused and wet.
And, as a young green leaf bestirs itself,
stretches and slowly opens out encurlment,
her body was unfolded into coolness
and into the unfingered wind of dawn.

Like moons the knees went climbing clearly upwards
to dive into the cloud-brims of the thighs;
the narrow shadow of the calves retreated,
the feet extended and grew luminous,
and all the joints became as much alive
as drinkers' throats.

And in the pelvis-chalice lay the belly,
like a young fruit within a childish hand.
And there, within its navel's narrow goblet,
was all this limpid life contained of darkness.
Thereunder lightly rose the little swell
and lapped continually towards the loins
where now and then a silent trickle glistened.
Translucent, though, and still without a shadow,
lay, like a group of silver birch in April,
warm, empty, all-unhidden, the vagina.

And now the shoulders' mobile balance hung
in equipoise upon the wand-straight body,
which mounted from the pelvis like a fountain,
and in the long arms lingeringly descended,
and swiftlier in the hair's abundant fall.

Then, very slowly came the face's progress,
from the fore-shortened dimness of its drooping
into clear horizontal exaltation,
brought to abrupt conclusion by the chin.

Jetzt, da der Hals gestreckt war wie ein Strahl
und wie ein Blumenstiel, darin der Saft steigt,
streckten sich auch die Arme aus wie Hälse
von Schwänen, wenn sie nach dem Ufer suchen.

Dann kam in dieses Leibes dunkle Frühe
wie Morgenwind der erste Atemzug.
Im zartesten Geäst der Aderbäume
entstand ein Flüstern, und das Blut begann
zu rauschen über seinen tiefen Stellen.
Und dieser Wind wuchs an: nun warf er sich
mit allem Atem in die neuen Brüste
und füllte sie und drückte sich in sie, –
daß sie wie Segel, von der Ferne voll,
das leichte Mädchen nach dem Strande drängten.

So landete die Göttin.

Hinter ihr,
die rasch dahinschritt durch die jungen Ufer,
erhoben sich den ganzen Vormittag
die Blumen und die Halme, warm, verwirrt,
wie aus Umarmung. Und sie ging und lief.

Am Mittag aber, in der schwersten Stunde,
hob sich das Meer noch einmal auf und warf
einen Delphin an jene selbe Stelle.
Tot, rot und offen.

Now, when the neck was stretched out like a jet
and like a flower-stalk where sap is mounting,
the arms began to stretch out too, like necks
of swans, when they are making for the shore.

Then entered the dim dawning of this body,
like matutinal wind, the first deep breath.
Within the tenderest branches of the vein-trees
a whispering arose, and then the blood
began to rustle over deeper places.
And this wind grew and grew, until it hurtled
with all its power of breath at the new breasts
and filled them up and forced itself within them,
and they, like filled sails full of the horizon,
impelled the lightsome maiden to the shore.

And thus the goddess landed.

And behind her,
who swiftly left behind the youthful shores,
kept springing up throughout the whole forenoon
the flowers and the grasses, warm, confused,
as from embracing. And she walked and ran.

At noontide, though, in that most heavy hour,
the sea rose up yet once again and flung
a dolphin out upon that self-same spot.
Dead, red, and open.

Rome, beginning of 1904 (first draft); Sweden, autumn 1904 (final version)

DIE ROSENSCHALE

ZORNIGE sahst du flackern, sahst zwei Knaben
zu einem Etwas sich zusammenballen,
das Haß war und sich auf der Erde wälzte
wie ein von Bienen überfallnes Tier;
Schauspieler, aufgetürmte Übertreiber,
rasende Pferde, die zusammenbrachen,
den Blick wegwerfend, bläkend das Gebiß
als schälte sich der Schädel aus dem Maule.

Nun aber weißt du, wie sich das vergißt:
denn vor dir steht die volle Rosenschale,
die unvergeßlich ist und angefüllt
mit jenem Äußersten von Sein und Neigen,
Hinhalten, Niemals-Gebenkönnen, Dastehn,
das unser sein mag: Äußerstes auch uns.

Lautloses Leben, Aufgehn ohne Ende,
Raum-brauchen ohne Raum von jenem Raum
zu nehmen, den die Dinge rings verringern,
fast nicht Umrissen-sein wie Ausgespartes
und lauter Inneres, viel seltsam Zartes
und Sich-Bescheinendes – bis an den Rand:
ist irgend etwas uns bekannt wie dies?

Und dann wie dies: daß ein Gefühl entsteht,
weil Blütenblätter Blütenblätter rühren?
Und dies: daß eins sich aufschlägt wie ein Lid,
und drunter liegen lauter Augenlider,
geschlossene, als ob sie, zehnfach schlafend,
zu dämpfen hätten eines Innern Sehkraft.
Und dies vor allem: daß durch diese Blätter
das Licht hindurch muß. Aus den tausend Himmeln
filtern sie langsam jenen Tropfen Dunkel,
in dessen Feuerschein das wirre Bündel
der Staubgefäße sich erregt und aufbäumt.

Und die Bewegung in den Rosen, sieh:
Gebärden von so kleinem Ausschlagswinkel,
daß sie unsichtbar blieben, liefen ihre
Strahlen nicht auseinander in das Weltall.

Sieh jene weiße, die sich selig aufschlug
und dasteht in den großen offnen Blättern
wie eine Venus aufrecht in der Muschel;

THE BOWL OF ROSES

You've seen the flare of anger, seen two boys
bunch themselves up into a ball of something
that was mere hate and roll upon the ground
like a dumb animal attacked by bees;
actors, sky-towering exaggerators,
the crashing downfall of careering horses,
casting away their sight, flashing their teeth
as though the skull were peeling from the mouth.

But now you know how such things are forgotten;
for now before you stands the bowl of roses,
the unforgettable, entirely filled
with that extremity of being and bending,
proffer beyond all power of giving, presence,
that might be ours: that might be our extreme.

Living in silence, endless opening out,
space being used, but without space being taken
from that space which the things around diminish;
absence of outline, like untinted groundwork
and mere Within; so much so strangely tender
and self-illumined – to the very verge: –
where do we know of anything like this?

And this: a feeling able to arise
through petals being touched by other petals?
And this: that one should open like an eyelid,
and lying there beneath it simply eyelids,
all of them closed, as though they had to slumber
ten-fold to quench some inward power of vision.
And this, above all: that through all these petals
light has to penetrate. From thousand heavens
they slowly filter out that drop of darkness
within whose fiery glow the mazy bundle
of stamens stirs itself and reaches upwards.

And then the movement in the roses, look:
gestures deflected through such tiny angles,
they'd all remain invisible unless
their rays ran streaming out into the cosmos.

Look at that white one, blissfully unfolded
and standing in the great big open petals
like Venus upright in her mussel shell;

157

und die errötende, die wie verwirrt
nach einer kühlen sich hinüberwendet,
und wie die kühle fühllos sich zurückzieht,
und wie die kalte steht, in sich gehüllt,
unter den offenen, die alles abtun.
Und *was* sie abtun, wie das leicht und schwer,
wie es ein Mantel, eine Last, ein Flügel
und eine Maske sein kann, je nach dem,
und *wie* sie's abtun: wie vor dem Geliebten.

Was können sie nicht sein: war jene gelbe,
die hohl und offen daliegt, nicht die Schale
von einer Frucht; darin dasselbe Gelb,
gesammelter, orangeröter, Saft war?
Und wars für diese schon zu viel, das Aufgehn,
weil an der Luft ihr namenloses Rosa
den bittern Nachgeschmack des Lila annahm?
Und die batistene, ist sie kein Kleid,
in dem noch zart und atemwarm das Hemd steckt,
mit dem zugleich es abgeworfen wurde
im Morgenschatten an dem alten Waldbad?
Und diese hier, opalnes Porzellan,
zerbrechlich, eine flache Chinatasse
und angefüllt mit kleinen hellen Faltern, –
und jene da, die nichts enthält als sich.

Und sind nicht alle so, nur sich enthaltend,
wenn Sich-enthalten heißt: die Welt da draußen
und Wind und Regen und Geduld des Frühlings
und Schuld und Unruh und vermummtes Schicksal
und Dunkelheit der abendlichen Erde
bis auf der Wolken Wandel, Flucht und Anflug,
bis auf den vagen Einfluß ferner Sterne
in eine Hand voll Innres zu verwandeln.

Nun liegt es sorglos in den offnen Rosen.

look how that blusher there, as in confusion,
has turned towards a cooler bloom, and how
the cool one is unfeelingly withdrawing;
and how the cold one stands, wrapped in herself,
among those open roses doffing all.
And *what* they doff – the way it can appear
now light, now heavy – like a cloak, a burden,
a wing, a domino – it all depends –
and *how* they doff it: as before the loved one.

What can they *not* be: was that yellow one
that lies there hollow, open, not the rind
upon a fruit, in which that self-same yellow
was the intenser, orange-ruddier juice?
And did her blowing prove too much for this one,
since, touched by air, her nameless rosiness
assumed the bitter after-taste of lilac?
And is not yonder cambric one a dress,
wherein, still soft and breath-warm, clings the vest
flung off along with it among the shadows
of early morning by the woodland pool?
And what's this opalescent porcelain,
so fragile, but a shallow china cup,
and full of little shining butterflies?
And that, containing nothing but herself?

And are not all just that, just self-containing,
if self-containing means: to take the world
and wind and rain and patience of the spring-time
and guilt and restlessness and muffled fate
and sombreness of evening earth and even
the melting, fleeing, forming of the clouds
and the vague influence of distant stars,
and change it to a handful of Within?

It now lies heedless in those open roses.

Capri, c. New Year 1907

New Poems
Second Part

A mon grand Ami Auguste Rodin

ARCHAÏSCHER TORSO APOLLOS

WIR kannten nicht sein unerhörtes Haupt,
darin die Augenäpfel reiften. Aber
sein Torso glüht noch wie ein Kandelaber,
in dem sein Schauen, nur zurückgeschraubt,

sich hält und glänzt. Sonst könnte nicht der Bug
der Brust dich blenden, und im leisen Drehen
der Lenden könnte nicht ein Lächeln gehen
zu jener Mitte, die die Zeugung trug.

Sonst stünde dieser Stein entstellt und kurz
unter der Schultern durchsichtigem Sturz
und flimmerte nicht so wie Raubtierfelle;

und bräche nicht aus allen seinen Rändern
aus wie ein Stern: denn da ist keine Stelle,
die dich nicht sieht. Du mußt dein Leben ändern.

KRETISCHE ARTEMIS

WIND der Vorgebirge: war nicht ihre
Stirne wie ein lichter Gegenstand?
Glatter Gegenwind der leichten Tiere,
formtest du sie: ihr Gewand

bildend an die unbewußten Brüste
wie ein wechselvolles Vorgefühl?
Während sie, als ob sie alles wüßte,
auf das Fernste zu, geschürzt und kühl,

stürmte mit den Nymphen und den Hunden,
ihren Bogen probend, eingebunden
in den harten hohen Gurt;

ARCHAIC TORSO OF APOLLO

THOUGH we've not known his unimagined head
and what divinity his eyes were showing,
his torso like a branching street-lamp's glowing,
wherein his gaze, only turned down, can shed

light still. Or else the breast's insurgency
could not be dazzling you, or you discerning
in that slight twist of loins a smile returning
to where was centred his virility.

Or else this stone would not stand so intact
beneath the shoulders' through-seen cataract
and would not glisten like a wild beast's skin;

and would not keep from all its contours giving
light like a star: for there's no place therein
that does not see you. You must change your living.

Paris, early summer 1908

l. 3, *wie ein Kandelaber*. In Germany and Austria *Kandelaber* was the usual word for a street-lamp: not for the comparatively short post with a single square lantern, but for the much taller and more elegant sort with two globes, each suspended from either end of a wide semi-circular cross-piece. Gas lamps, in which the main supply was turned on by means of a long pole and ignited from a small, perpetually burning by-pass, had not yet been replaced by electric. Rilke had already used the word in the poem *Night Drive* (p. 233).

CRETAN ARTEMIS

PROMONTORY wind: was not her meeting
brow like some bright obstacle for you?
Counter-wind through which lithe beasts were fleeting,
did you form her, moulding to

those unconscious breasts of hers that flowing
garment like a wild presentiment?
While herself, as though she were all-knowing,
cool and kirtled, all-intent

on the farthest, stormed with nymph and hound,
testing what her bow could do, inbound
into that hard, high upgirth:

manchmal nur aus fremden Siedelungen
angerufen und erzürnt bezwungen
von dem Schreien um Geburt.

LEDA

Als ihn der Gott in seiner Not betrat,
erschrak er fast, den Schwan so schön zu finden;
er ließ sich ganz verwirrt in ihm verschwinden.
Schon aber trug ihn sein Betrug zur Tat,

bevor er noch des unerprobten Seins
Gefühle prüfte. Und die Aufgetane
erkannte schon den Kommenden im Schwane
und wußte schon: er bat um Eins,

das sie, verwirrt in ihrem Widerstand,
nicht mehr verbergen konnte. Er kam nieder,
und halsend durch die immer schwächre Hand

ließ sich der Gott in die Geliebte los.
Dann erst empfand er glücklich sein Gefieder
und wurde wirklich Schwan in ihrem Schooß.

DELPHINE

Jene Wirklichen, die ihrem Gleichen
überall zu wachsen und zu wohnen
gaben, fühlten an verwandten Zeichen
Gleiche in den aufgelösten Reichen,
die der Gott, mit triefenden Tritonen,
überströmt bisweilen übersteigt;
denn da hatte sich das Tier gezeigt:
anders als die stumme, stumpfgemute
Zucht der Fische, Blut von ihrem Blute
und von fern dem Menschlichen geneigt.

Eine Schar kam, die sich überschlug,
froh, als fühlte sie die Fluten glänzend:
Warme, Zugetane, deren Zug

sometimes only hailed from isolated
huts and, to her fury, dominated
by some woman's cry for birth.

Paris, early summer 1908

LEDA

WHEN first the god set foot there in his need,
the swan's great beauty almost frightened him;
he vanished into it with wits a-swim.
But his deceit onswept him to his deed

before the feelings of that life untried
could be experienced. And, all-robeless, she
knew who that comer in the swan must be,
and knew already that he eyed

what her confused endeavour to withstand
no longer could conceal. The god alighted,
and, necking through the ever-weaker hand,

loosed himself into her he doted on.
Then really felt his plumage and, delighted,
became within her lap entirely swan.

Paris, autumn 1907 or Capri, spring 1908

DOLPHINS

THOSE so real, who in such diverse places
credited their like with growth and dwelling,
came to feel through some akinning traces
likenesses within the liquid spaces
which the god, with Triton train upwelling,
would bestride all-overstreamingly;
for the creature showed there suddenly:
different from the dumbly-vegetating
fishy kind – with their own blood pulsating,
and with yearnings for humanity.

Somersaulting came a school one day,
glad as though they felt the waves' resplendence:
warm and closely-clinging, whose array,

wie mit Zuversicht die Fahrt bekränzend,
leichtgebunden um den runden Bug
wie um einer Vase Rumpf und Rundung,
selig, sorglos, sicher vor Verwundung,
aufgerichtet, hingerissen, rauschend
und im Tauchen mit den Wellen tauschend
die Trireme heiter weitertrug.

Und der Schiffer nahm den neugewährten
Freund in seine einsame Gefahr
und ersann für ihn, für den Gefährten,
dankbar eine Welt und hielt für wahr,
daß er Töne liebte, Götter, Gärten
und das tiefe, stille Sternenjahr.

DIE INSEL DER SIRENEN

WENN er denen, die ihm gastlich waren,
spät, nach ihrem Tage noch, da sie
fragten nach den Fahrten und Gefahren,
still berichtete: er wußte nie,

wie sie schrecken und mit welchem jähen
Wort sie wenden, daß sie so wie er
in dem blau gestillten Inselmeer
die Vergoldung jener Inseln sähen,

deren Anblick macht, daß die Gefahr
umschlägt; denn nun ist sie nicht im Tosen
und im Wüten, wo sie immer war.
Lautlos kommt sie über die Matrosen,

welche wissen, daß es dort auf jenen
goldnen Inseln manchmal singt –,
und sich blindlings in die Ruder lehnen,
wie umringt

von der Stille, die die ganze Weite
in sich hat und an die Ohren weht,
so als wäre ihre andre Seite
der Gesang, dem keiner widersteht.

garlanding the voyage with self-dependence,
round the curving prow in loose relay
like some swelling vase's foliation,
happy, care-free, safe from laceration,
leaping up erect, enraptured, surging,
changing with the billows in submerging,
bore the trireme cheerly on its way.

And the sailor took the new-presented
friend on his lone perilous career,
and for his companion there invented
gratefully a world, which his own dear
sounds and gods and gardens elemented
and the deeply-silent stellar year.

Paris, 1 August 1907
'Those so real' (l. 1) are presumably the ancient Greeks.

THE ISLAND OF THE SIRENS

THOUGH he told it those whose feast he shared in
(late, by their own scale of time, since they
pried so into perils he had fared in)
more than once, he never found a way

so to startle and with such surprising
words bewitch them, they should come to see
in the blue reposing island-sea,
as he could, those golden isles arising,

sight of which turns peril inside out;
for it's now no longer in the breaking
water's rage, where it was known about.
All without a sound it's overtaking

sailors knowing that on those golden shores there
singing can at times begin, –
and they blindly bend against their oars there,
as hemmed in

by that silence, wherein's all the misted
distance, and wherewith their ears are fanned
even as though its other side consisted
of the song no mortal can withstand.

Paris, between 22 August and 5 September 1907

169

KLAGE UM ANTINOUS

KEINER begriff mir von euch den bithynischen Knaben
(daß ihr den Strom anfaßtet und von ihm hübt...).
Ich verwöhnte ihn zwar. Und dennoch: wir haben
ihn nur mit Schwere erfüllt und für immer getrübt.

Wer vermag denn zu lieben? Wer kann es? – Noch keiner.
Und so hab ich unendliches Weh getan –.
Nun ist er am Nil der stillenden Götter einer,
und ich weiß kaum welcher und kann ihm nicht nahn.

Und ihr warfet ihn noch, Wahnsinnige, bis in die Sterne,
damit ich euch rufe und dränge: meint ihr den?
Was ist er nicht einfach ein Toter. Er wäre es gerne.
Und vielleicht wäre ihm nichts geschehn.

l. 1: *mir* is an example of the ethic dative, still common in colloquial German, as
it was in Elizabethan English: in Thomas Nashe we find: 'What does me he,
but...' (*Works*, ed. McKerrow, I, 365, l. 27), 'Giue me one of my yoong Maisters
a booke' (I, 242, l. 9), 'Vp starts me he' (III, 70, l. 23), 'Out steps me an infant
squib of the Innes of Court' (III, 213, l. 12), etc. It was also common in Greek and
Latin, and is usually described by grammarians as indicating the speaker's emo-
tional participation in the action.

DER TOD DER GELIEBTEN

ER wußte nur vom Tod, was alle wissen:
daß er uns nimmt und in das Stumme stößt.
Als aber sie, nicht von ihm fortgerissen,
nein, leis aus seinen Augen ausgelöst,

hinüberglitt zu unbekannten Schatten,
und als er fühlte, daß sie drüben nun
wie einen Mond ihr Mädchenlächeln hatten
und ihre Weise wohlzutun:

da wurden ihm die Toten so bekannt,
als wäre er durch sie mit einem jeden
ganz nah verwandt; er ließ die andern reden

und glaubte nicht und nannte jenes Land
das gutgelegene, das immersüße –.
Und tastete es ab für ihre Füße.

LAMENT FOR ANTINOÜS

NONE of you there could grasp the Bithynian youngster's
being. (Could you grasp the stream and upheave it from him?...)
True, I spoilt him. And yet: we've but managed amongst us
to fill him with heaviness and for ever bedim.

Who's able to love? Who can do it? – Not one all the while here.
And so I've inflicted infinite pain. –
Now he's one of the hearkening gods on the Nile here,
and I scarce know which and can't reach him again.

And up to the stars you still must hurtle him madly,
that I might call you and urge: Is it him you mean?
Why isn't he just one dead? He would have been gladly.
And harmless perhaps his lot would have been.

Paris, autumn 1907 or Capri, spring 1908
The beautiful Bithynian youth Antinoüs, favourite of the Emperor Hadrian,
drowned himself in the Nile, and the Emperor (contrary to this characteristically
personal and unhistorical interpretation) honoured his memory with statues and
temples and proclaimed his deification as a constellation.

THE DEATH OF THE BELOVED

HE only knew of death what all men may:
that those it takes it thrusts into dumb night.
When she herself, though, – no, not snatched away,
but tenderly unloosened from his sight,

had glided over to the unknown shades,
and when he felt that he had now resigned
the moonlight of her laughter to their glades,
and all her ways of being kind:

then all at once he came to understand
the dead through her, and joined them in their walk,
kin to them all; he let the others talk,

and paid no heed to them, and called that land
the fortunately-placed, the ever-sweet. –
And groped out all its pathways for her feet.

Paris, 22 August - 5 September 1907

KLAGE UM JONATHAN

ACH sind auch Könige nicht von Bestand
und dürfen hingehn wie gemeine Dinge,
obwohl ihr Druck wie der der Siegelringe
sich widerbildet in das weiche Land.

Wie aber konntest du, so angefangen
mit deines Herzens Initial,
aufhören plötzlich: Wärme meiner Wangen.
O daß dich einer noch einmal
erzeugte, wenn sein Samen in ihm glänzt.

Irgend ein Fremder sollte dich zerstören,
und der dir innig war, ist nichts dabei
und muß sich halten und die Botschaft hören;
wie wunde Tiere auf den Lagern löhren,
möcht ich mich legen mit Geschrei:

denn da und da, an meinen scheusten Orten,
bist du mir ausgerissen wie das Haar,
das in den Achselhöhlen wächst und dorten,
wo ich ein Spiel für Frauen war,

bevor du meine dort verfitzten Sinne
aufsträhntest wie man einen Knaul entflicht;
da sah ich auf und wurde deiner inne: –
Jetzt aber gehst du mir aus dem Gesicht.

st. 3, l. 4, *löhren.* The word occurs in Luther's translation of *Hosea*, vii, 14: 'So
rufen sie mich auch nicht an von Herzen, sondern lören auf ihren Lagern.' In a
letter to Kippenberg, 8 November 1908, Rilke remarked that the word had been
wrongly printed as 'röhren': 'Es mag übertrieben sein, wenn ich diese Abänderung
als wesentlich störend empfinde, aber es ist so: „löhren" enthält so viel von
Tierklage, auch wilder Tiere, hat einen etwas anderen ö-Laut, und das *l* ist an
dieser Stelle ebenso korrespondierend mit „Lagern" und dem „legen" der kommenden Zeile, wie das *r* schwierig und widerstrebend und nach „Lagern" geradezu
unmöglich ist; überdies: röhren ist ein Fachausdruck, nur für bestimmte Wildarten
gültig.'

LAMENT FOR JONATHAN

ARE even kings unable to withstand?
Can they too pass away like common things,
although their pressure, like a signet ring's,
imprints itself into the yielding land?

How could you all at once, though, so begun here
with your heart's initial letter,
stop, you warmer of these cheeks of mine?
Would it were possible some one here
could become your re-begetter
when his seed within him came to shine!

Some unknown hand's accomplished our dividing,
and your own second self is nothing there,
and must contain himself and hear the tiding;
as wounded animals outroar in hiding,
I'd like to lie and scream somewhere:

for here and here, at all my shyest places,
you've been torn from me like the hair that grows
within my arm-pits and like that which laces
the spot whence sport for women rose,

before you skeined up all my therein centred
senses as one unpicks a tangled clew;
my eyes looked up then and your image entered: –
Now, though, they nevermore shall gaze on you.

Paris, early summer 1908
II Samuel, i.

TRÖSTUNG DES ELIA

Er hatte das getan und dies, den Bund
wie jenen Altar wieder aufzubauen,
zu dem sein weitgeschleudertes Vertrauen
zurück als Feuer fiel von ferne, und
hatte er dann nicht Hunderte zerhauen,
weil sie ihm stanken mit dem Baal im Mund,
am Bache schlachtend bis ans Abendgrauen,

das mit dem Regengrau sich groß verband.
Doch als ihn von der Königin der Bote
nach solchem Werktag antrat und bedrohte,
da lief er wie ein Irrer in das Land,

so lange bis er unterm Ginsterstrauche
wie weggeworfen aufbrach in Geschrei
das in der Wüste brüllte: Gott, gebrauche
mich länger nicht. Ich bin entzwei.

Doch grade da kam ihn der Engel ätzen
mit einer Speise, die er tief empfing,
so daß er lange dann an Weideplätzen
und Wassern immer zum Gebirge ging,

zu dem der Herr um seinetwillen kam:
Im Sturme nicht und nicht im Sich-Zerspalten
der Erde, der entlang in schweren Falten
ein leeres Feuer ging, fast wie aus Scham
über des Ungeheuren ausgeruhtes
Hinstürzen zu dem angekommnen Alten,
der ihn im sanften Sausen seines Blutes
erschreckt und zugedeckt vernahm.

CONSOLING OF ELIJAH

He had been very jealous to repair
the covenant, like that altar in decay
to which his far-flung trust from far away
fell back again as fire; and then and there
had he not handed hundreds down to slay,
because their Baal-filled mouths so fouled the air,
beside the rivulet till evening's grey

blended so grandly with the grey of rain?
Yet when, with such day's labour now behind him,
Jezebel's herald told what she designed him,
he fled like one possessed across the plain,

until, as utterly abandoned, under
the juniper, he burst into a cry
that echoed through the wilderness: Most High,
use me no longer. I am torn asunder.

But at that moment came the angel, bearing
a food for him, of which he ate his fill,
so that for days he could continue faring
by streams and pastures to that holy hill

to which the Lord for his sake only came:
Not in the whirlwind nor the open-breaking
of earth, along which empty fire was shaking
its heavy folds, almost as though for shame
at the rejuvenate precipitation
with which the Never-namable was making
for him who in his blood's soft circulation,
covered and terrified, could hear his name.

Paris, early summer 1908
I Kings, xix.

SAUL UNTER DEN PROPHETEN

Meinst du denn, daß man sich sinken sieht?
Nein, der König schien sich noch erhaben,
da er seinen starken Harfenknaben
töten wollte bis ins zehnte Glied.

Erst da ihn der Geist auf solchen Wegen
überfiel und auseinanderriß,
sah er sich im Innern ohne Segen,
und sein Blut ging in der Finsternis
abergläubig dem Gericht entgegen.

Wenn sein Mund jetzt troff und prophezeite,
war es nur, damit der Flüchtling weit
flüchten könne. So war dieses zweite
Mal. Doch einst: er hatte prophezeit

fast als Kind, als ob ihm jede Ader
mündete in einen Mund aus Erz;
Alle schritten, doch er schritt gerader.
Alle schrieen, doch ihm schrie das Herz.

Und nun war er nichts als dieser Haufen
umgestürzter Würden, Last auf Last;
und sein Mund war wie der Mund der Traufen,
der die Güsse, die zusammenlaufen,
fallen läßt, eh er sie faßt.

SAMUELS ERSCHEINUNG VOR SAUL

Da schrie die Frau zu Endor auf: Ich sehe –
Der König packte sie am Arme: Wen?
Und da die Starrende beschrieb, noch ehe,
da war ihm schon, er hätte selbst gesehn:

Den, dessen Stimme ihn noch einmal traf:
Was störst du mich? Ich habe Schlaf.
Willst du, weil dir die Himmel fluchen
und weil der Herr sich vor dir schloß und schwieg,
in meinem Mund nach einem Siege suchen?
Soll ich dir meine Zähne einzeln sagen?

SAUL AMONG THE PROPHETS

Can one, then, perceive his own decline?
No, the King still thought himself unshaken
when his javelin had so nearly taken
that young harper's life and all his line.

Only when, as he was onward pressing,
came the spirit's ravaging descent,
did he see his inward lack of blessing,
and his blood in deepest darkness went
to the judgment guiltily confessing.

If his mouth now dripped with prophesying,
that was just to let his fleer glide
well away. The second testifying
happened thus. Once, though, he'd prophesied

like a child, as if each vein directly
on into a mouth of bronze outstreamed;
all were striding, he, though, more erectly,
all were screaming, but his heart outscreamed.

And he now was only what these clutters
of downfallen dignities inhem;
and his mouth was like the mouth of gutters,
letting all the congregating sputters
fall before it's captured them.

Paris, summer 1908
I Samuel, xix, 8-24, x, 1-16.

SAMUEL'S APPEARANCE TO SAUL

And then the Witch of Endor cried: I see –
The monarch seized her by the shoulder: Who?
And even before she was describing, he
already felt that he'd been seeing too:

Him, by whose voice he was once more addressed:
Why do you rouse me? I'm at rest.
Will you, now Heaven's curses press you,
now that to all your prayers the Lord is dumb,
seek in my mouth how victory may bless you?
Shall I tell every tooth that I can trace there?

Ich habe nichts als sie ... Es schwand. Da schrie
das Weib, die Hände vors Gesicht geschlagen,
als ob sie's sehen müßte: Unterlieg –

Und er, der in der Zeit, die ihm gelang,
das Volk wie ein Feldzeichen überragte,
fiel hin, bevor er noch zu klagen wagte:
so sicher war sein Untergang.

Die aber, die ihn wider Willen schlug,
hoffte, daß er sich faßte und vergäße;
und als sie hörte, daß er nie mehr äße,
ging sie hinaus und schlachtete und buk

und brachte ihn dazu, daß er sich setzte;
er saß wie einer, der zu viel vergißt:
alles was war, bis auf das Eine, Letzte.
Dann aß er, wie ein Knecht zu Abend ißt.

EIN PROPHET

AUSGEDEHNT von riesigen Gesichten,
hell vom Feuerschein aus dem Verlauf
der Gerichte, die ihn nie vernichten, –
sind die Augen, schauend unter dichten
Brauen. Und in seinem Innern richten
sich schon wieder Worte auf,

nicht die seinen (denn was wären seine
und wie schonend wären sie vertan),
andre, harte: Eisenstücke, Steine,
die er schmelzen muß wie ein Vulkan,

um sie in dem Ausbruch seines Mundes
auszuwerfen, welcher flucht und flucht;
während seine Stirne, wie des Hundes
Stirne, *das* zu tragen sucht,

was der Herr von seiner Stirne nimmt:
Dieser, Dieser, den sie alle fänden,
folgten sie den großen Zeigehänden,
die Ihn weisen wie Er ist: ergrimmt.

They're all that's left to me ... It vanished. She
then screamed and flung her hands before her face there,
as though she'd been compelled to see: Succumb –

And he, who in the days he prospered so
had towered above his people like a crest,
collapsed before he'd ventured to protest:
so certain was his overthrow.

She, though, who'd struck him down unwillingly,
hoped he'd forgot and was himself again;
and when she heard he'd ceased to eat, she then
went out and killed and plied her cookery

and came to him herself and got him seated;
he sat like one with too much to forget:
all that had been and what had now completed.
Then, as a serf at evening eats, he ate.

Paris, 22 August - 5 September 1907
I Samuel, xxviii.

A PROPHET

SUCH as giant visions have dilated,
scintillating from the fiery train
of the judgments they have contemplated,
gaze his thickly superciliated
eyes, and words are being accumulated
deep within him once again:

not his own (for what could his words settle?
And how temperedly would they be dealt!),
other, harder: chunks of stone and metal,
which, like a volcano, he must melt

till eruptingly he sends them flying
from his mouth whose curses fill the air;
while his forehead like a dog's is trying
conscientiously to bear

what from his the Lord has disengaged:
Him, Him, all would find beyond denial,
if they'd only follow those great dial-
hands that show Him as He is: enraged.

Paris, shortly before 17 August 1907

179

JEREMIA

EINMAL war ich weich wie früher Weizen,
doch, du Rasender, du hast vermocht,
mir das hingehaltne Herz zu reizen,
daß es jetzt wie eines Löwen kocht.

Welchen Mund hast du mir zugemutet,
damals, da ich fast ein Knabe war:
eine Wunde wurde er: nun blutet
aus ihm Unglücksjahr um Unglücksjahr.

Täglich tönte ich von neuen Nöten,
die du, Unersättlicher, ersannst,
und sie konnten mir den Mund nicht töten;
sieh du zu, wie du ihn stillen kannst,

wenn, die wir zerstoßen und zerstören,
erst verloren sind und fernverlaufen
und vergangen sind in der Gefahr:
denn dann will ich in den Trümmerhaufen
endlich meine Stimme wiederhören,
die von Anfang an ein Heulen war.

EINE SIBYLLE

EINST, vor Zeiten, nannte man sie alt.
Doch sie blieb und kam dieselbe Straße
täglich. Und man änderte die Maße,
und man zählte sie wie einen Wald

nach Jahrhunderten. Sie aber stand
jeden Abend auf derselben Stelle,
schwarz wie eine alte Citadelle
hoch und hohl und ausgebrannt;

von den Worten, die sich unbewacht
wider ihren Willen in ihr mehrten,
immerfort umschrieen und umflogen,

während die schon wieder heimgekehrten
dunkel unter ihren Augenbogen
saßen, fertig für die Nacht.

JEREMIAH

TENDER as the wheat upspringing greenly
I began, but, rager, you knew how
to provoke my proffered heart so keenly
that it's boiling like a lion's now.

What a mouth it was that you were needing,
almost since my boyish days, from me:
it became a wound, and now there's bleeding
from it year on year of misery.

Daily I re-echoed new distresses
you would so insatiably devise,
and this mouth of mine survived their stresses;
see if you can still it anywise,

when those we've been cursing and confounding
all shall be dispersed and disappear
in catastrophe that shall not fail:
for it's then I hope again to hear
in the ruins my own voice resounding,
that from the beginning was a wail.

Paris, mid-August 1907

A SIBYL

ONCE, long, long ago, they'd called her old.
She, though, went on living there and ranging
daily through the self-same street. Till, changing
measure, like a forest's now they told

her age by centuries. But she returned
every evening to her wonted station,
black as some primeval castellation,
high and hollow and outburned;

ever circled by the screaming flight
of words that, all unwatched for and unwilled,
lodged within her breast and propagated,

while the home-returningly fulfilled
sombrely beneath her eyebrows waited,
ready for the coming night.

Paris, 22 August - 5 September 1907

ABSALOMS ABFALL

Sie hoben sie mit Geblitz:
der Sturm aus den Hörnern schwellte
seidene, breitgewellte
Fahnen. Der herrlich Erhellte
nahm im hochoffenen Zelte,
das jauchzendes Volk umstellte,
zehn Frauen in Besitz,

die (gewohnt an des alternden Fürsten
sparsame Nacht und Tat)
unter seinem Dürsten
wogten wie Sommersaat.

Dann trat er heraus zum Rate,
wie vermindert um nichts,
und jeder, der ihm nahte,
erblindete seines Lichts.

So zog er auch den Heeren
voran wie ein Stern dem Jahr;
über allen Speeren
wehte sein warmes Haar,
das der Helm nicht faßte,
und das er manchmal haßte,
weil es schwerer war
als seine reichsten Kleider.

Der König hatte geboten,
daß man den Schönen schone.
Doch man sah ihn ohne
Helm an den bedrohten
Orten die ärgsten Knoten
zu roten Stücken von Toten
auseinanderhaun.
Dann wußte lange keiner
von ihm, bis plötzlich einer
schrie: Er hängt dort hinten
an den Terebinthen
mit hochgezogenen Braun.

ABSALOM'S REBELLION

THEY lifted them flashingly:
the blast from the horns was swelling
silken, widely-outwelling
banners. The bright-excelling,
on the roof of the royal dwelling,
round which the glad folk were yelling,
took ten women openly,

who (used to the King's, the ageing's,
minimal night and deed),
under his self-assuagings
billowed like summer seed.

Then forth to the council hied him
with undiminished might,
and everyone that nighed him
was dazzled by his light.

At the head of his troops he advances
like a star bringing in the year,
high above all the lances
his warm hair waving clear,
hair beyond's helmet's hold,
that filled him at times with loathing,
because its weight outtold
that of his richest clothing.

The King had giv'n intimations
to spare his fair son for him.
But helmetless they saw him
ripping at threatened stations
tightest of intrications
up into fragmentations
of redly-quivering dead.
Then where he was they doubted,
till suddenly someone shouted:
He's hanging – can't you see? – there
in that great oak tree there
with eyes half-out of his head.

Das war genug des Winks.
Joab, wie ein Jäger,
erspähte das Haar –: ein schräger
gedrehter Ast: da hings.
Er durchrannte den schlanken Kläger,
und seine Waffenträger
durchbohrten ihn rechts und links.

That was sufficient quite.
Joab, that keen awarer,
espied the hair: – its snarer
the bough where it hung so bright.
He ran through the slim despairer,
and each young weapon-bearer
pierced him from left and right.

Paris, summer 1908
II Samuel, xiv-xviii, especially xiv, 25-26, xvi, 21-22, xviii, 9-15.

ESTHER

Die Dienerinnen kämmten sieben Tage
die Asche ihres Grams und ihrer Plage
Neige und Niederschlag aus ihrem Haar,
und trugen es und sonnten es im Freien
und speisten es mit reinen Spezereien
noch diesen Tag und den: dann aber war

die Zeit gekommen, da sie, ungeboten,
zu keiner Frist, wie eine von den Toten
den drohend offenen Palast betrat,
um gleich, gelegt auf ihre Kammerfrauen,
am Ende ihres Weges *Den* zu schauen,
an dem man stirbt, wenn man ihm naht.

Er glänzte so, daß sie die Kronrubine
aufflammen fühlte, die sie an sich trug;
sie füllte sich ganz rasch mit seiner Miene
wie ein Gefäß und war schon voll genug

und floß schon über von des Königs Macht,
bevor sie noch den dritten Saal durchschritt,
der sie mit seiner Wände Malachit
grün überlief. Sie hatte nicht gedacht,

so langen Gang zu tun mit allen Steinen,
die schwerer wurden von des Königs Scheinen
und kalt von ihrer Angst. Sie ging und ging –

Und als sie endlich, fast von nahe, ihn,
aufruhend auf dem Thron von Turmalin,
sich türmen sah, so wirklich wie ein Ding:

empfing die rechte von den Dienerinnen
die Schwindende und hielt sie zu dem Sitze.
Er rührte sie mit seines Szepters Spitze:
... und sie begriff es ohne Sinne, innen.

ESTHER

THE chamber women combed for seven days
the ashes of her grief and her dismay's
lees and precipitation from her hair,
and carried it and sunned it like a fleece
and fed it with the purest spiceries
for two days longer: then the hour was there

when she must cross, unbidden, unobeying,
unlooked for, like a ghost from graveyard straying,
the doorless threshold of that house of fear,
and, leaning on her women, through the dim
yet shining distance of its halls, see him
by whom men die when they draw near.

He shone so, she could feel the incandescence
of those imperial rubies that she wore;
she took a swift upfilling of his presence
and, like a vessel that could hold no more,

was overflowing already with his might
before she'd passed the third of those great halls
that poured the greenness of its green-stone walls
all over her. She had not guessed aright

that length of way, and all those stones and rings
grown heavier from this shining of the king's,
cold from her fear. She went on traversing. –

And when she felt the shining shafts combine
and centre on the throne of tourmaline,
and saw him towering, real as a thing:

the right-hand maid, whose arms she fainted in,
upheld her to that throne that shone so brightly.
He touched her with his golden sceptre, lightly:
. . . and, senseless there, she understood, within.

Paris, early summer 1908

Esther, iv and v and, especially, in the Apocryphal continuation of that Book (from
the Septuagint), xiv and xv. After Haman had persuaded Ahasuerus to destroy
all the captive Jews in his dominions, his queen Esther came to intercede for her
people at a time when the king had commanded that no one should approach him
unsummoned on pain of death, 'except such to whom the King shall hold out the
golden sceptre, that he may live'.

DER AUSSÄTZIGE KÖNIG

Da trat auf seiner Stirn der Aussatz aus
und stand auf einmal unter seiner Krone
als wär er König über allen Graus,
der in die andern fuhr, die fassungsohne

hinstarrten nach dem furchtbaren Vollzug
an jenem, welcher, schmal wie ein Verschnürter,
erwartete, daß einer nach ihm schlug;
doch noch war keiner Manns genug:
als machte ihn nur immer unberührter
die neue Würde, die sich übertrug.

LEGENDE VON DEN DREI LEBENDIGEN
UND DEN DREI TOTEN

Drei Herren hatten mit Falken gebeizt
und freuten sich auf das Gelag.
Da nahm sie der Greis in Beschlag
und führte. Die Reiter hielten gespreizt
vor dem dreifachen Sarkophag,

der ihnen dreimal entgegenstank,
in den Mund, in die Nase, ins Sehn;
und sie wußten es gleich: da lagen lang
drei Tote mitten im Untergang
und ließen sich gräßlich gehn.

Und sie hatten nur noch ihr Jägergehör
reinlich hinter dem Sturmbandlör;
doch da zischte der Alte sein:
– Sie gingen nicht durch das Nadelöhr
und gehen niemals – hinein.

Nun blieb ihnen noch ihr klares Getast,
das stark war vom Jagen und heiß;
doch das hatte ein Frost von hinten gefaßt
und trieb ihm Eis in den Schweiß.

188

THE LEPER KING

THEN on his brow the leprosy emerged
and stood there all at once beneath his crown
as it were king of all the chill that surged
into the rest, who, courtliness cast down,

stared at the terrible consummacy
on him who, narrow as a pinioned traitor,
waited for one to strike remorselessly;
none, though, as yet could dare sufficiently:
as if he'd only grown inviolater
through conference of this new dignity.

Paris, early summer 1908
Charles VI of France, who is also evoked in *Malte Laurids Brigge*.

LEGEND OF THE THREE LIVING
AND THE THREE DEAD

THREE lords had hawked by a forest side,
and now it was feast they would.
But the hermit seized them and turned them aside,
and the riders halted, each astride,
where the three-fold sarcophagus stood,

and stank at them in a three-fold way,
in the mouth, in the nose, in the eyes;
and they knew at once: for many a day
three dead therein had been wasting away
their substance in hideous wise.

And they'd only their hunters' ears so keen
behind their hat-straps still left clean;
but their guide hissed thereinto:
The needle's eye they have never been,
and never will be, through.

They still retained their sense of touch,
strong and hot from their exercise;
but a frost from behind had that in its clutch
and was turning its sweat to ice.

Paris, early summer 1908
Partly inspired, it would seem, by recollections of one of the frescoes in the Campo
Santo at Pisa.

DER KÖNIG VON MÜNSTER

DER König war geschoren;
nun ging ihm die Krone zu weit
und bog ein wenig die Ohren,
in die von Zeit zu Zeit

gehässiges Gelärme
aus Hungermäulern fand.
Er saß, von wegen der Wärme,
auf seiner rechten Hand,

mürrisch und schwergesäßig.
Er fühlte sich nicht mehr echt:
der Herr in ihm war mäßig,
und der Beischlaf war schlecht.

TOTEN-TANZ

SIE brauchen kein Tanz-Orchester;
sie hören in sich ein Geheule
als wären sie Eulennester.
Ihr Ängsten näßt wie eine Beule,
und der Vorgeruch ihrer Fäule
ist noch ihr bester Geruch.

Sie fassen den Tänzer fester,
den rippenbetreßten Tänzer,
den Galan, den echten Ergänzer
zu einem ganzen Paar.
Und er lockert der Ordensschwester
über dem Haar das Tuch;
sie tanzen ja unter Gleichen.
Und er zieht der wachslichtbleichen
leise die Lesezeichen
aus ihrem Stunden-Buch.

THE KING OF MÜNSTER

THE king had felt the shears;
his crown was now too loose
and somewhat bent his ears,
which now and then abuse

and hostile clamour greeted
from many a starveling band.
For warmth's sake he was seated
upon his own right hand,

peevish and all a-fidget.
He felt no longer right:
the master in him was midget,
and bed-performance slight.

Paris, early summer 1908
John of Leyden, leader and self-elected king of the Anabaptists, who in 1535
seized the city of Münster and held out for some time against the forces of the
Bishop.

DANCE OF DEATH

THEY need no band's fervescence;
they hear in themselves such howls
as though they were nests of owls.
Their dread runs like an excrescence,
and the fore-scent of their putrescence
is still the best scent they share.

They're clasping the dancer faster,
the rib-bebroidered dancer,
the gallant, the true enhancer
into a perfect pair.
And he loosens the nun at last her
linen above the hair:
why, only her like observe her!
And he draws for the wax-pale server
gently each place-preserver
out of her book of prayer.

Bald wird ihnen allen zu heiß,
sie sind zu reich gekleidet;
beißender Schweiß verleidet
ihnen Stirne und Steiß
und Schauben und Hauben und Steine;
sie wünschen, sie wären nackt
wie ein Kind, ein Verrückter und Eine:
die tanzen noch immer im Takt.

DAS JÜNGSTE GERICHT

So erschrocken, wie sie nie erschraken,
ohne Ordnung, oft durchlocht und locker,
hocken sie in dem geborstnen Ocker
ihres Ackers, nicht von ihren Laken

abzubringen, die sie liebgewannen.
Aber Engel kommen an, um Öle
einzuträufeln in die trocknen Pfannen
und um jedem in die Achselhöhle

das zu legen, was er in dem Lärme
damals seines Lebens nicht entweihte;
denn dort hat es noch ein wenig Wärme,

daß es nicht des Herren Hand erkälte
oben, wenn er es aus jeder Seite
leise greift, zu fühlen, ob es gälte.

DIE VERSUCHUNG

Nein, es half nicht, daß er sich die scharfen
Stacheln einhieb in das geile Fleisch;
alle seine trächtigen Sinne warfen
unter kreißendem Gekreisch

Frühgeburten: schiefe, hingeschielte
kriechende und fliegende Gesichte,
Nichte, deren nur auf ihn erpichte
Bosheit sich verband und mit ihm spielte.

They're all too heated now,
too rich is their attiring;
biting sweat's inspiring
disgust with rump and brow,
gowns, coifs, and strings of pearl;
they wish they were all as bare
as a child, as a madman and girl:
as they keep on dancing there.

Paris, August 20 1907

THE LAST JUDGMENT

FRIGHTENED as they've never yet been frighted,
all-disordered, often loose and holed,
there they crouch in the exploded mould
of their acre, far too long united

with their shrouds to suffer separation.
Angels are approaching, though, to drip
oil into each dry articulation
and beneath each pair of arms to slip

what the riser, in his past life's din,
somehow came to leave undesecrated;
for there's still a little warmth therein,

so that it won't chill the Lord's hand through
when by him it's gently extricated
up above, to feel if it will do.

Paris, 20 August 1907

THE TEMPTATION

No, it didn't help him, his inducing
sharp-toothed thorns into his lustful flesh;
all his teeming senses were producing,
with loud screams of labour, fresh

miscreations: leeringly-distorted
faces, partly crawling, partly flying,
nothings, whose maliciousness was eyeing
him alone, with whom it jointly sported.

Und schon hatten seine Sinne Enkel;
denn das Pack war fruchtbar in der Nacht
und in immer bunterem Gesprenkel
hingehudelt und verhundertfacht.
Aus dem Ganzen ward ein Trank gemacht:
seine Hände griffen lauter Henkel,
und der Schatten schob sich auf wie Schenkel
warm und zu Umarmungen erwacht –.

Und da schrie er nach dem Engel, schrie:
Und der Engel kam in seinem Schein
und war da: und jagte sie
wieder in den Heiligen hinein,

daß er mit Geteufel und Getier
in sich weiterringe wie seit Jahren
und sich Gott, den lange noch nicht klaren,
innen aus dem Jäsen destillier.

DER ALCHIMIST

Seltsam verlächelnd schob der Laborant
den Kolben fort, der halbberuhigt rauchte.
Er wußte jetzt, was er noch brauchte,
damit der sehr erlauchte Gegenstand

da drin entstände. Zeiten brauchte er,
Jahrtausende für sich und diese Birne
in der es brodelte; im Hirn Gestirne
und im Bewußtsein mindestens das Meer.

Das Ungeheuere, das er gewollt,
er ließ es los in dieser Nacht. Es kehrte
zurück zu Gott und in sein altes Maß;

er aber, lallend wie ein Trunkenbold,
lag über dem Geheimfach und begehrte
den Brocken Gold, den er besaß.

Now his senses had proliferated;
for the pack was fruitful in the night,
and with stipple was centuplicated
still more parti-colourfully bright.
And a drink was brewed from their grimacing,
and his hands were grasping cup on cup,
and like thighs the shadow opened up,
warm and as awakened for embracing. –

And he screamed then for the angel, screamed:
And the angel, in his shiningness,
came and hounded all that had outstreamed
back into the saint's own inwardness,

that he might contend there, year by year,
as before, with monstrous generation,
and distil from inner fermentation
God, the still as yet so far from clear.

Paris, 21 August 1907

THE ALCHEMIST

WITH a wry smile the artist pushed aside
the alembic that fumed there half-placated.
He knew now what he still desiderated
in order that the thing so glorified

might burgeon in it. Ages there must be,
millennia for himself and this globed vase,
bubbling away there; in his brain the stars
and in his consciousness at least the sea.

The immeasurability of his assay,
he let it go that same night. It returned
to God again and its old measuredness;

he, though, now stammering like a drunkard, lay
above the secret drawer and beyearned
the crumb of gold he did possess.

Paris, 22 August 1907

DER RELIQUIENSCHREIN

DRAUSSEN wartete auf alle Ringe
und auf jedes Kettenglied
Schicksal, das nicht ohne sie geschieht.
Drinnen waren sie nur Dinge, Dinge
die er schmiedete; denn vor dem Schmied
war sogar die Krone, die er bog,
nur ein Ding, ein zitterndes und eines
das er finster wie im Zorn erzog
zu dem Tragen eines reinen Steines.

Seine Augen wurden immer kälter
von dem kalten täglichen Getränk;
aber als der herrliche Behälter
(goldgetrieben, köstlich, vielkarätig)
fertig vor ihm stand, das Weihgeschenk,
daß darin ein kleines Handgelenk
fürder wohne, weiß und wundertätig:

blieb er ohne Ende auf den Knien,
hingeworfen, weinend, nicht mehr wagend,
seine Seele niederschlagend
vor dem ruhigen Rubin,
der ihn zu gewahren schien
und ihn, plötzlich um sein Dasein fragend,
ansah wie aus Dynastien.

DAS GOLD

DENK es wäre nicht: es hätte müssen
endlich in den Bergen sich gebären
und sich niederschlagen in den Flüssen
aus dem Wollen, aus dem Gären

ihres Willens; aus der Zwang-Idee,
daß ein Erz ist über allen Erzen.
Weithin warfen sie aus ihren Herzen
immer wieder Meroë

THE RELIQUARY

OUTSIDE there awaited all the rings,
every chain-link, destiny
which without them could not come to be.
Inside they were only things, just things
which he worked; for, plying his artistry,
even the crown he twisted would appear
just a thing, a trembling thing alone,
which, as grimly as in rage, he'd rear
for the wearing of a purest stone.

And his eyes were growing ever-colder
from the cold diurnal compotation;
when, though, all complete, the glorious holder
(heavily engilded, sumptuous)
stood before him, ripe for consecration,
destined for the future habitation
of a small hand, white, miraculous:

long then he remained upon his knees,
prostrate, weeping, daring now no more,
lowering his soul before
the quiet ruby, by which he's
being noticed, as he thinks he sees,
and, with sudden asking what he's for,
gazed at as from dynasties.

Drafts and provisional version Paris, 5 August 1907; final version probably August 1908

GOLD

THINK it hadn't been: it none the less
must in mountains have been generated
and within the streams precipitated
through the willing, the fermentingness,

of their will, their rooted certainty
of one ore surpassing every ore.
From their hearts they would for evermore
keep projecting Meroë

an den Rand der Lande, in den Äther,
über das Erfahrene hinaus;
und die Söhne brachten manchmal später
das Verheißene der Väter,
abgehärtet und verhehrt, nachhaus;

wo es anwuchs eine Zeit, um dann
fortzugehn von den an ihm Geschwächten,
die es niemals liebgewann.
Nur (so sagt man) in den letzten Nächten
steht es auf und sieht sie an.

DER STYLIT

VÖLKER schlugen über ihm zusammen,
die er küren durfte und verdammen;
und erratend, daß er sich verlor,
klomm er aus dem Volksgeruch mit klammen
Händen einen Säulenschaft empor,

der noch immer stieg und nichts mehr hob,
und begann, allein auf seiner Fläche,
ganz von vorne seine eigne Schwäche
zu vergleichen mit des Herren Lob;

und da war kein Ende: er verglich;
und der Andre wurde immer größer.
Und die Hirten, Ackerbauer, Flößer
sahn ihn klein und außer sich

immer mit dem ganzen Himmel reden,
eingeregnet manchmal, manchmal licht;
und sein Heulen stürzte sich auf jeden,
so als heulte er ihm ins Gesicht.
Doch er sah seit Jahren nicht,

wie der Menge Drängen und Verlauf
unten unaufhörlich sich ergänzte,
und das Blanke an den Fürsten glänzte
lange nicht so hoch hinauf.

to the edge of earth, to upper air,
far as their imagining could roam;
and the sons would later from somewhere
bring what fathers knew was there,
sublimated and enhardened, home;

where it waxed awhile, and then would seize
chance to quit those weakened by its staying,
where it never felt at ease.
Only in the last nights (goes the saying)
will it rise and look on these.

Paris, between 22 August and 5 September 1907

Meroë (l. 8): once the capital of Ethiopia, the richest gold-producing region in the ancient world.

THE STYLITE

NATIONS all around him were contending
whom to heaven or hell he might be sending;
and, divining that he lost his pains,
numbly from the stench of men ascending,
summit of a column he attains,

one that, rising still, had ceased to raise,
and, alone upon its level bleakness,
there began comparing his own weakness
all anew with the Almighty's praise;

and there was no end: he would compare,
and the Other grew forever greater.
And the shepherding and ploughing spectator
saw him small and in despair

still conversing with the boundless sky there,
sometimes rain-enshrouded, sometimes clear;
and his howling hurtled from on high there
on to each as meant for his own ear.
He'd not marked, though, many a year

how the concourse of the multitude
down below incessantly extended,
and the princes' glitter now ascended
to far lesser altitude.

Aber wenn er oben, fast verdammt
und von ihrem Widerstand zerschunden,
einsam mit verzweifeltem Geschreie
schüttelte die täglichen Dämonen:
fielen langsam auf die erste Reihe
schwer und ungeschickt aus seinen Wunden
große Würmer in die offnen Kronen
und vermehrten sich im Samt.

DIE ÄGYPTISCHE MARIA

Seit sie damals, bettheiß, als die Hure
übern Jordan floh und, wie ein Grab
gebend, stark und unvermischt das pure
Herz der Ewigkeit zu trinken gab,

wuchs ihr frühes Hingegebensein
unaufhaltsam an zu solcher Größe,
daß sie endlich, wie die ewige Blöße
Aller, aus vergilbtem Elfenbein

dalag in der dürren Haare Schelfe.
Und ein Löwe kreiste; und ein Alter
rief ihn winkend an, daß er ihm helfe:

(und so gruben sie zu zwein).

Und der Alte neigte sie hinein.
Und der Löwe, wie ein Wappenhalter,
saß dabei und hielt den Stein.

l. 9, *Schelfe*. A more or less archaic word with a meaning similar to that of Hülse:
husk, shell, pod, etc.

When above, though, almost nullified
and beside himself with their resistance,
he would all alone, with desperate yell,
shake the daily demons from his shoulders:
down into the open crowns there fell
where the foremost stood of his beholders
from his wounds large worms with slow persistence
and in velvet multiplied.

Paris, early summer 1908

THE EGYPTIAN MARY

SINCE her fleeing, bed-hotly, as the whore,
over Jordan, when she yielded up
all her pure heart's undiluted store,
grave-like, for Eternity to sup,

former givingness had ceaselessly
grandeured into such unselfawareness,
she at last, all beings' eternal bareness,
nothing but time-yellowed ivory,

lay there in her husk of brittle hair.
And a lion circled, and there sought her
one who summoned it to help him there:

(and they dug in unison).

And the ancient laid her there alone.
And the lion, like a shield-supporter,
sat near by and held the stone.

Paris, early summer 1908

According to the *Golden Legend*, St. Mary of Egypt, having lived, from the age of
twelve, for seventeen years as a courtesan in Alexandria, went on a pilgrimage to
Jerusalem to worship the Holy Cross. After being several times invisibly prevented
from entering the church, she was seized with contrition, begged the Virgin to
intercede for her, and promised to forsake the world. She was then able to enter
the church, where a voice said to her: 'If thou wilt pass and go over the Jordan
thou shalt be safe.' So she crossed the Jordan and lived alone in the desert for
forty-seven years. Here she was discovered by an aged monk called Zosimus, whom
she begged to return a year later, bringing the Sacrament. This he did; but when,
as he had promised, he returned the next year also, he found her dead, with a
letter beside her requesting him to bury her. He was in despair, for he had nothing
to dig with, but 'anon he saw the earth dolven, and a sepulchre made by a lion
that came thither. And then Zosimus buried her, and the lion departed debonairly.'

KREUZIGUNG

LÄNGST geübt, zum kahlen Galgenplatze
irgend ein Gesindel hinzudrängen,
ließen sich die schweren Knechte hängen,
dann und wann nur eine große Fratze

kehrend nach den abgetanen Drein.
Aber oben war das schlechte Henkern
rasch getan; und nach dem Fertigsein
ließen sich die freien Männer schlenkern.

Bis der eine (fleckig wie ein Selcher)
sagte: Hauptmann, dieser hat geschrien.
Und der Hauptmann sah vom Pferde: Welcher?
und es war ihm selbst, er hätte ihn

den Elia rufen hören. Alle
waren zuzuschauen voller Lust,
und sie hielten, daß er nicht verfalle,
gierig ihm die ganze Essiggalle
an sein schwindendes Gehust.

Denn sie hofften noch ein ganzes Spiel
und vielleicht den kommenden Elia.
Aber hinten ferne schrie Maria,
und er selber brüllte und verfiel.

DER AUFERSTANDENE

ER vermochte niemals bis zuletzt
ihr zu weigern oder abzuneinen,
daß sie ihrer Liebe sich berühme;
und sie sank ans Kreuz in dem Kostüme
eines Schmerzes, welches ganz besetzt
war mit ihrer Liebe größten Steinen.

Aber da sie dann, um ihn zu salben,
an das Grab kam, Tränen im Gesicht,
war er auferstanden ihrethalben,
daß er seliger ihr sage: Nicht –

202

CRUCIFIXION

LONG-ACCUSTOMED as they were to taking
riff-raff to the treeless gallows-place,
heavy troopers hung about there, making
merely now and then a large grimace

at the thus exterminated three.
Up there, though, the clumsy operation
soon was over; and the men now free
started swinging off to relaxation.

When one (spotted as a butcher) said there:
'Captain, that one there has given a shout.'
'Which?' – the riding captain turned his head there,
and it seemed to him beyond a doubt

he had heard him call Elijah. Here
was a spectacle they all must see,
and a sponge of vinegar, for fear
he should go, they proffered on a spear
to his failing utterancy.

For they hoped that quite a play was on,
with, perhaps, Elijah's self descending.
Far behind, though, Mary gave a rending
cry, and with a bellow he was gone.

Paris, summer 1908

THE ARISEN

HE had never brought himself as yet
to forbid and chide those subtle tones
that betrayed her love as self-admired;
and she sank before the cross attired
in a sorrow that was all beset
with her love's most precious stones.

When she came, though, on her ministration,
to the sepulchre in bitter woe,
he had risen, just for her salvation,
saying with final benediction: No –

Sie begriff es erst in ihrer Höhle,
wie er ihr, gestärkt durch seinen Tod,
endlich das Erleichternde der Öle
und des Rührens Vorgefühl verbot,

um aus ihr die Liebende zu formen,
die sich nicht mehr zum Geliebten neigt,
weil sie, hingerissen von enormen
Stürmen, seine Stimme übersteigt.

MAGNIFICAT

Sie kam den Hang herauf, schon schwer, fast ohne
an Trost zu glauben, Hoffnung oder Rat;
doch da die hohe tragende Matrone
ihr ernst und stolz entgegentrat

und alles wußte ohne ihr Vertrauen,
da war sie plötzlich an ihr ausgeruht;
vorsichtig hielten sich die vollen Frauen,
bis daß die junge sprach: Mir ist zumut,

als wär ich, Liebe, von nun an für immer.
Gott schüttet in der Reichen Eitelkeit
fast ohne hinzusehen ihren Schimmer;
doch sorgsam sucht er sich ein Frauenzimmer
und füllt sie an mit seiner fernsten Zeit.

Daß er mich fand. Bedenk nur; und Befehle
um meinetwillen gab von Stern zu Stern –.

Verherrliche und hebe, meine Seele,
so hoch du kannst: den Herrn.

Only in her cave she comprehended
how at last, grown stronger through his death,
proffered oil's relief he had forfended
and presentiment of touch and breath,

that from her he might create the lover
whom a loved one can no longer bind,
since, upswept by forces far above her,
she has left his voice so far behind.

Paris, autumn 1907 or Capri, spring 1908
John, xx, 1-18.

MAGNIFICAT

SHE came, already heavy, up the hill,
unsure of hope, advice, or consolation;
when, though, with proud and earnest salutation,
the stately carrying matron crossed the sill

and knew all, without hearing it, directly,
she, leaning on her, felt her tiredness go;
the full pair held each other circumspectly,
until the younger spoke: I feel as though

from now on, dearest, I shall have no ending.
God pours into the wealthy's vanity,
with scarce a glance, the glitter thence ascending;
yet searches out with care an unpretending
female and fills her with futurity.

That he found me. Just think; and constellation
on constellation bade with me accord. –

Oh, magnify, my soul, with exaltation
as lofty as you can: the Lord.

Paris, summer 1908
Luke, i, 39-56.

ADAM

STAUNEND steht er an der Kathedrale
steilem Aufstieg, nah der Fensterrose,
wie erschreckt von der Apotheose,
welche wuchs und ihn mit einem Male

niederstellte über die und die.
Und er ragt und freut sich seiner Dauer
schlicht entschlossen; als der Ackerbauer
der begann, und der nicht wußte, wie

aus dem fertig-vollen Garten Eden
einen Ausweg in die neue Erde
finden. Gott war schwer zu überreden;

und er drohte ihm, statt zu gewähren,
immer wieder, daß er sterben werde.
Doch der Mensch bestand: sie wird gebären.

EVA

EINFACH steht sie an der Kathedrale
großem Aufstieg, nah der Fensterrose,
mit dem Apfel in der Apfelpose,
schuldlos-schuldig ein für alle Male

an dem Wachsenden, das sie gebar,
seit sie aus dem Kreis der Ewigkeiten
liebend fortging, um sich durchzustreiten
durch die Erde, wie ein junges Jahr.

Ach, sie hätte gern in jenem Land
noch ein wenig weilen mögen, achtend
auf der Tiere Eintracht und Verstand.

Doch da sie den Mann entschlossen fand,
ging sie mit ihm, nach dem Tode trachtend;
und sie hatte Gott noch kaum gekannt.

ADAM

HE, on the cathedral's steep ascent,
stands and stares near where the window-rose is,
as if awed by the apotheosis
which, when it had reached its full extent,

set him over these and these below.
And he towers and joys in his duration,
plain-resolved; who started cultivation
first of all mankind, and did not know

how he'd find a way from Eden-garden,
ready-filled with all it could supply,
to the new Earth. God would only harden,

and, instead of granting him his prayer,
kept on threatening he should surely die.
But the man persisted: She will bear.

Paris, summer 1908

EVE

SHE, on the cathedral's vast ascent,
simply stands there near the window-rose,
with the apple in the apple-pose,
ever henceforth guilty-innocent

of the growingness she brought to birth
since that time she lovingly departed
from the old eternities and started
struggling like a young year through the Earth.

Ah, she could have stayed so gladly, though,
just a little longer there, attending
to the sense and concord beasts would show.

But she found the man resolved to go,
so she went out with him, deathwards tending;
and yet God she'd scarcely got to know.

Paris, summer 1908
The two figures by Viollet-le-Duc on the façade of Notre-Dame.

IRRE IM GARTEN

DIJON

Noch schließt die aufgegebene Kartause
sich um den Hof, als würde etwas heil.
Auch die sie jetzt bewohnen, haben Pause
und nehmen nicht am Leben draußen teil.

Was irgend kommen konnte, das verlief.
Nun gehn sie gerne mit bekannten Wegen,
und trennen sich und kommen sich entgegen,
als ob sie kreisten, willig, primitiv.

Zwar manche pflegen dort die Frühlingsbeete,
demütig, dürftig, hingekniet;
aber sie haben, wenn es keiner sieht,
eine verheimlichte, verdrehte

Gebärde für das zarte frühe Gras,
ein prüfendes, verschüchtertes Liebkosen:
denn das ist freundlich, und das Rot der Rosen
wird vielleicht drohend sein und Übermaß

und wird vielleicht schon wieder übersteigen,
was ihre Seele wiederkennt und weiß.
Dies aber läßt sich noch verschweigen:
wie gut das Gras ist und wie leis.

DIE IRREN

Und sie schweigen, weil die Scheidewände
weggenommen sind aus ihrem Sinn,
und die Stunden, da man sie verstände,
heben an und gehen hin.

Nächtens oft, wenn sie ans Fenster treten:
plötzlich ist es alles gut.
Ihre Hände liegen im Konkreten,
und das Herz ist hoch und könnte beten,
und die Augen schauen ausgeruht

LUNATICS IN THE GARDEN

DIJON

THE monkless Charterhouse is still enclosing
the court, as though some wound were healing there.
Those too who now possess it are reposing
and taking in the life outside no share.

All that could come to them was fugitive.
Now gladly with familiar paths they're pacing,
and parting from each other and re-facing,
as though in orbits, willing, primitive.

By some indeed the spring flower-beds are tended
with humble, kneeling insufficiency;
they have, though, when there's none to see,
a half-concealed, convulsively extended

gesture towards the tender early grass,
a timorous, exploratory caressing:
for that is friendly, and one can't help guessing
whether the red of roses won't surpass

once more with menacing excess the measure
of what they recognise and keep in mind.
This, though, in silence they can treasure:
how quiet the grass is and how kind.

Paris, between 22 August and 5 September 1907

THE LUNATICS

AND they hold their peace, since the partitions
have been moved from their intelligence,
and the hours when one might share their visions
start to strike and vanish hence.

Often at nocturnal windows there:
suddenly it all comes right.
Such substantialness their hands can share,
and their hearts are high and fit for prayer,
and their eyes are resting on the sight

auf den unverhofften, oftentstellten
Garten im beruhigten Geviert,
der im Widerschein der fremden Welten
weiterwächst und niemals sich verliert.

AUS DEM LEBEN EINES HEILIGEN

Er kannte Ängste, deren Eingang schon
wie Sterben war und nicht zu überstehen.
Sein Herz erlernte, langsam durchzugehen;
er zog es groß wie einen Sohn.

Und namenlose Nöte kannte er,
finster und ohne Morgen wie Verschläge;
und seine Seele gab er folgsam her,
da sie erwachsen war, auf daß sie läge

bei ihrem Bräutigam und Herrn; und blieb
allein zurück an einem solchen Orte,
wo das Alleinsein alles übertrieb,
und wohnte weit und wollte niemals Worte.

Aber dafür, nach Zeit und Zeit, erfuhr
er auch das Glück, sich in die eignen Hände,
damit er eine Zärtlichkeit empfände,
zu legen wie die ganze Kreatur.

of the unhoped, often scarce-existent
garden on the peaceful court embossed,
which, illumined there from worlds so distant,
goes on growing and never getting lost.

Paris, between 22 August and 5 September 1907

FROM THE LIFE OF A SAINT

HE knew of terrors that encompassed one
swiftly and unsurvivably as death.
His heart toiled slowly through with labouring breath,
the heart he nurtured like a son.

Ineffable extremities he knew,
dawnless as dungeons hidden from the sky;
obediently he gave his soul up too,
when she reached womanhood, that she might lie

beside her bridegroom and her lord; while he
remained behind without her, in a place
where loneliness surpassed reality,
and shunned all speech and never showed his face.

But as some recompense, before the sands
had quite run out, he knew the happiness
of holding, when he yearned for tenderness,
himself, like all creation, in his hands.

Paris, 22 August - 5 September 1907

DIE BETTLER

Du wußtest nicht, was den Haufen
ausmacht. Ein Fremder fand
Bettler darin. Sie verkaufen
das Hohle aus ihrer Hand.

Sie zeigen dem Hergereisten
ihren Mund voll Mist,
und er darf (er kann es sich leisten)
sehn, wie ihr Aussatz frißt.

Es zergeht in ihren zerrührten
Augen sein fremdes Gesicht;
und sie freuen sich des Verführten
und speien, wenn er spricht.

FREMDE FAMILIE

So wie der Staub, der irgendwie beginnt
und nirgends ist, zu unerklärtem Zwecke
an einem leeren Morgen in der Ecke
in die man sieht, ganz rasch zu Grau gerinnt,

so bildeten sie sich, wer weiß aus was,
im letzten Augenblick vor deinen Schritten
und waren etwas Ungewisses mitten
im nassen Niederschlag der Gasse, das

nach dir verlangte. Oder nicht nach dir.
Denn eine Stimme, wie vom vorigen Jahr,
sang dich zwar an und blieb doch ein Geweine;
und eine Hand, die wie geliehen war,
kam zwar hervor und nahm doch nicht die deine.
Wer kommt denn noch? Wen meinen diese vier?

THE BEGGARS

It escaped you, what made that swelling
heap. One from foreign lands
found beggars in it. They're selling
the hollows out of their hands.

They're showing to the man from yonder
their mouths full of muck, and he
(who can well afford it) may wonder
at the greed of their leprosy.

In their meltingly melancholy
eyes his strange face grows weak;
and they take delight in his folly
and spit when he starts to speak.

Paris, early summer 1908

FOREIGN FAMILY

As dust, which starts collecting in some way
and nowhere is, will on some empty morning
in some inspected corner without warning
condense for unknown reasons into grey,

these had collected, who could say from where,
in the last moment left before you entered,
and formed an indetermined something, centred
in the damp débris of the street, which there

was waiting for you. Or perhaps not you.
For though a voice, as from the previous year,
was singing you, it still remained a moan there;
and though a hand, as if it held you dear,
was being outstretched, it did not take your own there.
Who's coming, then? Whom have these four in view?

Paris, summer 1908

LEICHEN-WÄSCHE

SIE hatten sich an ihn gewöhnt. Doch als
die Küchenlampe kam und unruhig brannte
im dunkeln Luftzug, war der Unbekannte
ganz unbekannt. Sie wuschen seinen Hals,

und da sie nichts von seinem Schicksal wußten,
so logen sie ein anderes zusamm,
fortwährend waschend. Eine mußte husten
und ließ solang den schweren Essigschwamm

auf dem Gesicht. Da gab es eine Pause
auch für die zweite. Aus der harten Bürste
klopften die Tropfen; während seine grause
gekrampfte Hand dem ganzen Hause
beweisen wollte, daß ihn nicht mehr dürste.

Und er bewies. Sie nahmen wie betreten
eiliger jetzt mit einem kurzen Huster
die Arbeit auf, so daß an den Tapeten
ihr krummer Schatten in dem stummen Muster

sich wand und wälzte wie in einem Netze,
bis daß die Waschenden zu Ende kamen.
Die Nacht im vorhanglosen Fensterrahmen
war rücksichtslos. Und einer ohne Namen
lag bar und reinlich da und gab Gesetze.

EINE VON DEN ALTEN

PARIS

ABENDS manchmal (weißt du, wie das tut?)
wenn sie plötzlich stehn und rückwärts nicken
und ein Lächeln, wie aus lauter Flicken,
zeigen unter ihrem halben Hut.

Neben ihnen ist dann ein Gebäude,
endlos, und sie locken dich entlang
mit dem Rätsel ihrer Räude,
mit dem Hut, dem Umhang und dem Gang.

CORPSE-WASHING

THEY'D got quite used to him by now. But when
the kitchen-lamp came and its flame was blowing
in the dark draughtiness, beyond all knowing
was the unknown. They washed his neck, and then,

knowing nothing of his history, bit by bit
they fabricated one without demur,
washing away. One had a coughing fit,
and let the heavy sponge of vinegar

lie on his face. And then a little rest
was taken by the second. Drops descended
with thuds from the hard brush, while his compressed
horrific hand was trying to manifest
to the whole house that now his thirst was ended.

And he succeeded. As though guiltily
surprised, they now with some acceleration
resumed their task, and on the tapestry
their bending shadows in the figuration

as in a net contorted and gyrated,
till with their washing to an end they came.
The night in each uncurtained window-frame
was pitiless. And one without a name
lay bare and cleanly there and legislated.

Paris, summer 1908

ONE OF THE OLD ONES

PARIS

SUDDENLY some dusk they'll stop awhile
with a backward nod they hope you're catching,
and – as though made wholly now of patching –
showing from under their half-hats a smile.

There beside extends some tall erection
which they lure you to perambulate
with the riddle of their skin-infection,
with their hats, their mantles, and their gait.

Mit der Hand, die hinten unterm Kragen
heimlich wartet und verlangt nach dir:
wie um deine Hände einzuschlagen
in ein aufgehobenes Papier.

DER BLINDE

PARIS

Sieh, er geht und unterbricht die Stadt,
die nicht ist auf seiner dunkeln Stelle,
wie ein dunkler Sprung durch eine helle
Tasse geht. Und wie auf einem Blatt

ist auf ihm der Widerschein der Dinge
aufgemalt; er nimmt ihn nicht hinein.
Nur sein Fühlen rührt sich, so als finge
es die Welt in kleinen Wellen ein:

eine Stille, einen Widerstand –,
und dann scheint er wartend wen zu wählen:
hingegeben hebt er seine Hand,
festlich fast, wie um sich zu vermählen.

EINE WELKE

Leicht, wie nach ihrem Tode
trägt sie die Handschuh, das Tuch.
Ein Duft aus ihrer Kommode
verdrängte den lieben Geruch,

an dem sie sich früher erkannte.
Jetzt fragte sie lange nicht, wer
sie sei (: eine ferne Verwandte),
und geht in Gedanken umher

und sorgt für ein ängstliches Zimmer,
das sie ordnet und schont,
weil es vielleicht noch immer
dasselbe Mädchen bewohnt.

With a hand below an overlapping
collar waiting for you to decide:
as if both your hands it would be wrapping
in some piece of paper put aside.

Paris, 21 August 1907

THE BLIND MAN

PARIS

LOOK, his progress interrupts the scene,
absent from his dark perambulation,
like a dark crack's interpenetration
of a bright cup. And, as on a screen,

all reflections things around are making
get depicted on him outwardly.
Just his feeling stirs, as if intaking
little waves of world invisibly:

here a stillness, there a counter-stand, –
as if pondering whom to choose, he'll tarry:
then surrenderingly he'll lift his hand,
almost ritually, as if to marry.

Paris, 21 August 1907

FADED

LIGHTLY as past Death's doors
she's wearing her gloves, her wraps.
A scent from her chest of drawers
supplanted the one which perhaps

gave her most self-sensation.
She long has ceased asking who
she is (: a distant relation),
and wanders the whole day through

in thought and is always arranging
an anxious room with such care
because maybe an unchanging
girl is still living there.

Paris, early summer 1908

ABENDMAHL

Ewiges will zu uns. Wer hat die Wahl
und trennt die großen und geringen Kräfte?
Erkennst du durch das Dämmern der Geschäfte
im klaren Hinterraum das Abendmahl:

wie sie sichs halten und wie sie sichs reichen
und in der Handlung schlicht und schwer beruhn.
Aus ihren Händen heben sich die Zeichen;
sie wissen nicht, daß sie sie tun

und immer neu mit irgendwelchen Worten
einsetzen, was man trinkt und was man teilt.
Denn da ist keiner, der nicht allerorten
heimlich von hinnen geht, indem er weilt.

Und sitzt nicht immer einer unter ihnen,
der seine Eltern, die ihm ängstlich dienen,
wegschenkt an ihre abgetane Zeit?
(Sie zu verkaufen, ist ihm schon zu weit.)

DIE BRANDSTÄTTE

Gemieden von dem Frühherbstmorgen, der
mißtrauisch war, lag hinter den versengten
Hauslinden, die das Heidehaus beengten,
ein Neues, Leeres. Eine Stelle mehr,

auf welcher Kinder, von Gott weiß woher,
einander zuschrien und nach Fetzen haschten.
Doch alle wurden stille, sooft er,
der Sohn von hier, aus heißen, halbveraschten

LAST SUPPER

THE eternal's trying to reach us. Who is free
to part the greater forces from the slighter?
Can't you, through glimmering shop-fronts, in the brighter
back-room, feel the Last Supper's what you see:

the way they're grasping it and circulating
it there with simple, grave acceptingness?
From those hands symbols are originating,
though this their makers do not guess,

nor that they're instituting ever-newly
with casual words what men shall drink and share.
For there's not one of them who is not truly
going off in secret to some otherwhere.

And sits there not among them always one
who gives his parents hovering round their son
away to that discarded time of theirs?
(To sell them's too remote from his affairs.)

Paris, summer 1908
In a letter to his wife of 4 October 1907 Rilke described with a certain envy the
life of the antiquarian dealers and second-hand booksellers in streets such as the
Rue de Seine, who, apparently without ever doing any business, were able to
spend the whole day peacefully reading behind their crowded shop-windows. 'I've
sometimes had a wish to buy myself such a full shop-window and set myself down
behind it with a dog for twenty years. In the evening there would be light in the
back-room, in front everything quite dark, and the three of us [himself, his wife,
and their daughter] would sit and eat our meal, behind; I've noticed how, seen
from the street, that always appears like a Last Supper, so grandly and solemnly
through the dark space.'

THE SITE OF THE FIRE

SHUNNED by the autumn morning, which had got
mistrustful, lay behind the sooty-stemmed
lime trees by which the heath-house had been hemmed
a newness, emptiness. Just one more spot

where children, whence they'd come a mystery,
snatched after rags and filled the air with screams.
But all of them grew quiet whenever he,
the son from here, out of hot, half-charred beams,

Gebälken Kessel und verbogne Tröge
an einem langen Gabelaste zog, –
um dann, mit einem Blick als ob er löge
die andern anzusehn, die er bewog

zu glauben, was an dieser Stelle stand.
Denn seit es nicht mehr war, schien es ihm so
seltsam: phantastischer als Pharao.
Und er war anders. Wie aus fernem Land.

DIE GRUPPE

PARIS

ALS pflückte einer rasch zu einem Strauß:
ordnet der Zufall hastig die Gesichter,
lockert sie auf und drückt sie wieder dichter,
ergreift zwei ferne, läßt ein nahes aus,

tauscht das mit dem, bläst irgendeines frisch,
wirft einen Hund, wie Kraut, aus dem Gemisch
und zieht, was niedrig schaut, wie durch verworrne
Stiele und Blätter, an dem Kopf nach vorne

und bindet es ganz klein am Rande ein;
und streckt sich wieder, ändert und verstellt
und hat nur eben Zeit, zum Augenschein

zurückzuspringen mitten auf die Matte,
auf der im nächsten Augenblick der glatte
Gewichteschwinger seine Schwere schwellt.

SCHLANGEN-BESCHWÖRUNG

WENN auf dem Markt, sich wiegend, der Beschwörer
die Kürbisflöte pfeift, die reizt und lullt,
so kann es sein, daß er sich einen Hörer
herüberlockt, der ganz aus dem Tumult

der Buden eintritt in den Kreis der Pfeife,
die will und will und will und die erreicht,
daß das Reptil in seinem Korb sich steife
und die das steife schmeichlerisch erweicht,

with manage of a long forked bough, was trying
to rescue kettles and bent cooking-ware, –
till, looking at them as if he were lying,
he'd bring the others to believe what there,

upon that very spot, once used to stand.
It seemed so strange now it had ceased to be:
fantasticer than Pharoah seemed. And he
was also different. As from some far land.

Paris, early summer 1908

THE GROUP

PARIS

LIKE someone gathering a quick posy: so
Chance here is hastily arranging faces,
widens and then contracts their interspaces,
seizes two distant, lets a nearer go,

drops this for that, blows weariness away,
rejects, like weed, a dog from the bouquet,
and pulls headforemost what's too low, as through
a maze of stalks and petals, into view,

and binds it in, quite small, upon the hem;
stretches once more to change and separate,
and just has time, for one last look at them,

to spring back to the middle of the mat
on which, in one split second after that,
the glistening lifter's swelling his own weight.

Paris, early summer 1908

SNAKE-CHARMING

WHEN in the market-place the charmer, swaying,
plays on his rouse-and-lulling pipe of gourd,
it may be that some hearer of it, straying
out of the tumult of the stalls, is lured

into the circling field of its effect there,
that pipe that wills and wills until it's made
the reptile in the basket stand erect there
and then has coaxed its rigidness to fade,

abwechselnd immer schwindelnder und blinder
mit dem, was schreckt und streckt, und dem, was löst –;
und dann genügt ein Blick: so hat der Inder
dir eine Fremde eingeflößt,

in der du stirbst. Es ist, als überstürze
glühender Himmel dich. Es geht ein Sprung
durch dein Gesicht. Es legen sich Gewürze
auf deine nordische Erinnerung,

die dir nichts hilft. Dich feien keine Kräfte,
die Sonne gärt, das Fieber fällt und trifft;
von böser Freude steilen sich die Schäfte,
und in den Schlangen glänzt das Gift.

SCHWARZE KATZE

EIN Gespenst ist noch wie eine Stelle,
dran dein Blick mit einem Klange stößt;
aber da an diesem schwarzen Felle
wird dein stärkstes Schauen aufgelöst:

wie ein Tobender, wenn er in vollster
Raserei ins Schwarze stampft,
jählings am benehmenden Gepolster
einer Zelle aufhört und verdampft.

Alle Blicke, die sie jemals trafen,
scheint sie also an sich zu verhehlen,
um darüber drohend und verdrossen
zuzuschauern und damit zu schlafen.
Doch auf einmal kehrt sie, wie geweckt,
ihr Gesicht und mitten in das deine:
und da triffst du deinen Blick im geelen
Amber ihrer runden Augensteine
unerwartet wieder: eingeschlossen
wie ein ausgestorbenes Insekt.

st. 3, l. 7, *geelen.* In reply to a questionnaire from his Polish translator Rilke wrote,
10 April 1924: ',,geel" alte Form für ,,gelb", besonders ein helles, ambra-farbenes
Gelb. Die Katzenaugen werden mit Amber oder gelbem Bernstein verglichen,
darin sich zuweilen Insekten eingeschlossen finden.'

what frights and stretches being alternated
more and more dizzyingly with what unchains; –
and then one look: the Indian's infiltrated
a foreigness into your veins

you die in. It's as though a fulgurating
heaven fell upon you. Through your face there springs
a crack. And spices are accumulating
on all those Nordical rememberings,

now unavailing. Not one power's propitious,
the sun ferments, the fever falls and takes;
the palm-stems steepen, gleefully malicious,
and poison glistens in the snakes.

Paris, autumn 1907 or Capri, spring 1908

BLACK CAT

GLANCES even at an apparition
still seem somehow to reverberate;
here on this black fell, though, the emission
of your strongest gaze will dissipate:

as a maniac, precipitated
into the surrounding black, will be
halted headlong and evaporated
by his padded cell's absorbency.

All the glances she was ever swept with
on herself she seems to be concealing,
where, with lowering and peevish mind, they're
being downlooked upon by her and slept with.
As if wakened, though, she turns her face
full upon your own quite suddenly,
and in the yellow amber of those sealing
eyes of hers you unexpectedly
meet the glance you've given her, enshrined there
like an insect of some vanished race.

Paris, summer 1908

VOR-OSTERN

MORGEN wird in diesen tiefgekerbten
Gassen, die sich durch getürmtes Wohnen
unten dunkel nach dem Hafen drängen,
hell das Gold der Prozessionen rollen;
statt der Fetzen werden die ererbten
Bettbezüge, welche wehen wollen,
von den immer höheren Balkonen
(wie in Fließendem gespiegelt) hängen.

Aber heute hämmert an den Klopfern
jeden Augenblick ein voll Bepackter,
und sie schleppen immer neue Käufe;
dennoch stehen strotzend noch die Stände.
An der Ecke zeigt ein aufgehackter
Ochse seine frischen Innenwände,
und in Fähnchen enden alle Läufe.
Und ein Vorrat wie von tausend Opfern

drängt auf Bänken, hängt sich rings um Pflöcke,
zwängt sich, wölbt sich, wälzt sich aus dem Dämmer
aller Türen, und vor dem Gegähne
der Melonen strecken sich die Brote.
Voller Gier und Handlung ist das Tote;
doch viel stiller sind die jungen Hähne
und die abgehängten Ziegenböcke
und am allerleisesten die Lämmer,

die die Knaben um die Schultern nehmen
und die willig von den Schritten nicken;
während in der Mauer der verglasten
spanischen Madonna die Agraffe
und das Silber in den Diademen
von dem Lichter-Vorgefühl beglänzter
schimmert. Aber drüber in dem Fenster
zeigt sich blickverschwenderisch ein Affe
und führt rasch in einer angemaßten
Haltung Gesten aus, die sich nicht schicken.

EASTER-EVE

NAPLES

HERE to-morrow in these deep-indented
streets, that press through high-piled habitation
darkly to the harbour down below,
golden-bright processions will be going;
and instead of rags the testamented
counterpanes, so eager to be blowing,
will, from ever-higher elevation,
hang, as if reflected in some flow.

But to-day there's knocking at the doors
some full-laden porter every minute,
and they keep on bearing some new buying;
stalls, though, still are bursting with their stocks.
At the corner there, displaying what's in it,
hangs a recently cut-open ox,
and a pennon on each hoof is flying.
And, as for a thousand offerings, stores

crowd on trestles, hang from peg and pillar,
squeezing, arching, rolling in a riot
from each glimmering doorway, and before
gaping melons stretch the loaves of bread.
Lust and action fill these jostling dead;
but the cockerels, and even more
those now well-hung he-goats, are far stiller,
and above all else the lambs are quiet,

which the boys bear off around their shoulders
and which nod obedience to their paces;
while within the wall the jewelled brooches
of the Spanish Virgin, glass-protected,
and the silver in her crown are gleaming
brighter with a fore-sense of reflected
torch-light. Over there, though, making faces
from a window-sill at the beholders,
sits an ape, and suddenly encroaches
with its gestures on the unbeseeming.

Paris, summer 1908

225

DER BALKON

Von der Enge, oben, des Balkones
angeordnet wie von einem Maler
und gebunden wie zu einem Strauß
alternder Gesichter und ovaler,
klar im Abend, sehn sie idealer,
rührender und wie für immer aus.

Diese aneinander angelehnten
Schwestern, die, als ob sie sich von weit
ohne Aussicht nacheinander sehnten,
lehnen, Einsamkeit an Einsamkeit;

und der Bruder mit dem feierlichen
Schweigen, zugeschlossen, voll Geschick,
doch von einem sanften Augenblick
mit der Mutter unbemerkt verglichen;

und dazwischen, abgelebt und länglich,
längst mit keinem mehr verwandt,
einer Greisin Maske, unzugänglich,
wie im Fallen von der einen Hand

aufgehalten, während eine zweite
welkere, als ob sie weitergleite,
unten vor den Kleidern hängt zur Seite

von dem Kinder-Angesicht,
das das Letzte ist, versucht, verblichen,
von den Stäben wieder durchgestrichen
wie noch unbestimmbar, wie noch nicht.

AUSWANDERER-SCHIFF

Denk: daß einer heiß und glühend flüchte,
und die Sieger wären hinterher,
und auf einmal machte der
Flüchtende kurz, unerwartet, Kehr
gegen Hunderte –: so sehr
warf sich das Erglühende der Früchte
immer wieder an das blaue Meer:

THE BALCONY

Up there, by their balcony's inhemming
caused, as by a painter, to cohere,
bound as into a bouquet, comprised
of old and youthful faces, they appear
more ideal, more touching, in the clear
evening, and as though eternalised.

Those two sisters, each on each inclining,
as if out of some great distantness
hopelessly for one another pining,
loneliness supporting loneliness;

and their gravely silence-keeping brother,
unconfiding, full of destiny,
none the less, though, all-unnoticedly
matched by one soft moment with his mother;

and between, outlived and elongated,
long now unrelated to them all,
mask of an old woman, insulated,
stayed, as in the middle of a fall,

by one hand, whose fellow, shrivelleder,
like a leaf downspinning, as it were,
hangs adheringly in front of her

by that child-face, thereinto
last inserted, contoured without shading,
quickly crossed out by the balustrading,
as if still unsettled, still to do.

Paris, 17 August 1907

EMIGRANT SHIP

NAPLES

Think: that one were fleeing, hot and glowing,
with the victors gaining rapidly,
and the fleer suddenly
turned and hurtled unexpectedly
upon hundreds: – so impetuously
did the glow of fruits there keep on throwing
its reflection at the dark blue sea:

als das langsame Orangen-Boot
sie vorübertrug bis an das große
graue Schiff, zu dem, von Stoß zu Stoße,
andre Boote Fische hoben, Brot, –
während es, voll Hohn, in seinem Schooße
Kohlen aufnahm, offen wie der Tod.

LANDSCHAFT

WIE zuletzt, in einem Augenblick
aufgehäuft aus Hängen, Häusern, Stücken
alter Himmel und zerbrochnen Brücken,
und von drüben her, wie vom Geschick,
von dem Sonnenuntergang getroffen,
angeschuldigt, aufgerissen, offen –
ginge dort die Ortschaft tragisch aus:

fiele nicht auf einmal in das Wunde,
drin zerfließend, aus der nächsten Stunde
jener Tropfen kühlen Blaus,
der die Nacht schon in den Abend mischt,
so daß das von ferne Angefachte
sachte, wie erlöst, erlischt.

Ruhig sind die Tore und die Bogen,
durchsichtige Wolken wogen
über blassen Häuserreihn
die schon Dunkel in sich eingesogen;
aber plötzlich ist vom Mond ein Schein
durchgeglitten, licht, als hätte ein
Erzengel irgendwo sein Schwert gezogen.

as the orange-boat would slowly press
over with them to the shortly-leaving
great, grey ship, where other boats were heaving
fish and bread up with such willingness,
while it, full of scorn, went on receiving
coal into its death-wide openness.

Paris, 18 August 1907

LANDSCAPE

How, at last, all instantaneously,
one piled heap of houses and of ridges,
bits of ancient sky and broken bridges,
lighted on, as though by destiny,
by the blazing sunset over there,
criminated, broken open, bare,
that small place would have a tragic ending:

fell there not into its woundedness
from the next hour's sudden presentness
that cool drop of blue which now is blending
night already with the evening,
so that what the sunset fired acquires
soft, redemption-like extinguishing.

Gate and arch in rest are now arrayed,
translucent clouds parade
above pale rows of houses, so
absorbed already into gathering shade;
yet a sudden moon-cast gleam will go
brightly gliding through it all, as though
some archangel had unsheathed his blade.

Capri, end of March, and Paris, 2 August 1907

RÖMISCHE CAMPAGNA

Aus der vollgestellten Stadt, die lieber
schliefe, träumend von den hohen Thermen,
geht der grade Gräberweg ins Fieber;
und die Fenster in den letzten Fermen

sehn ihm nach mit einem bösen Blick.
Und er hat sie immer im Genick,
wenn er hingeht, rechts und links zerstörend,
bis er draußen atemlos beschwörend

seine Leere zu den Himmeln hebt,
hastig um sich schauend, ob ihn keine
Fenster treffen. Während er den weiten

Aquädukten zuwinkt herzuschreiten,
geben ihm die Himmel für die seine
ihre Leere, die ihn überlebt.

LIED VOM MEER

CAPRI, PICCOLA MARINA

Uraltes Wehn vom Meer,
Meerwind bei Nacht:
   du kommst zu keinem her;
wenn einer wacht,
so muß er sehn, wie er
dich übersteht:
   uraltes Wehn vom Meer,
welches weht
nur wie für Ur-Gestein,
lauter Raum
reißend von weit herein...

O wie fühlt dich ein
treibender Feigenbaum
oben im Mondschein.

ROMAN CAMPAGNA

FROM the full-crammed city, happier sleeping,
dreaming there of those tall thermae's charms,
feverwards the straight grave-road is creeping,
and the windows in the final farms

gaze maliciously along its track.
And it always has them at its back
when it passes, spreading desolation,
till it lifts, with breathless invocation,

all its emptiness towards the sky,
quickly looking round lest any ranging
window see. And while it hails the far

aqueducts to come from where they are,
for that emptiness the sky's exchanging
one the road shall be outlasted by.

Paris, early summer 1908

l. 2. The ruins of the thermae, or baths, of Caracalla, originally of unparallelled
magnificence, are the last important building passed by the Appian Way before
its exit from the city.

SONG OF THE SEA

CAPRI, PICCOLA MARINA

PRIMEVAL breath from sea,
sea-wind by night;
  you come unseekingly;
one lying till light
must seek and find what he
may interpose:
  primeval breath from sea,
that only blows
as for primeval stone,
pure space
rushing from realms unknown . . .

How felt by a high-sown
fig-tree that clings for place
in the moonlight alone.

Capri, end of January 1907

NÄCHTLICHE FAHRT

SANKT PETERSBURG

Damals als wir mit den glatten Trabern
(schwarzen, aus dem Orloff'schen Gestüt) –,
während hinter hohen Kandelabern
Stadtnachtfronten lagen, angefrüht,
stumm und keiner Stunde mehr gemäß –,
fuhren, nein: vergingen oder flogen
und um lastende Paläste bogen
in das Wehn der Newa-Quais,

hingerissen durch das wache Nachten,
das nicht Himmel und nicht Erde hat, –
als das Drängende von unbewachten
Gärten gärend aus dem Ljetnij-Ssad
aufstieg, während seine Steinfiguren
schwindend mit ohnmächtigen Konturen
hinter uns vergingen, wie wir fuhren –:

damals hörte diese Stadt
auf zu sein. Auf einmal gab sie zu,
daß sie niemals war, um nichts als Ruh
flehend; wie ein Irrer, dem das Wirrn
plötzlich sich entwirrt, das ihn verriet,
und der einen jahrelangen kranken
gar nicht zu verwandelnden Gedanken,
den er nie mehr denken muß: Granit –
aus dem leeren schwankenden Gehirn
fallen fühlt, bis man ihn nicht mehr sieht.

NIGHT DRIVE

ST. PETERSBURG

When, with that black, smoothly trotting pair
(fathered by some Orloff stallion), –
while behind the lofty street-lamps there
city night-fronts lay, dawn-greyed upon,
dumb, responsive to no hour's decrees, –
we were driving – no, were flying or surging,
and round burdening palaces emerging
out into the Neva breeze,

whirled on through that wakefully extended
nightfall that has neither earth nor sky, –
as the pressure of unsuperintended
gardens mounted bubblingly on high
from the Ljetnij-Ssad, whose stone-upreared
forms with swooning contours disappeared
fadingly behind as we careered: –

then this city with a sigh
stopped existing. All at once confessed
it had never been, imploring rest:
as when suddenly one long insane
finds his twist untwisted and outgrown,
and can feel a morbid, deep-enwrought,
utterly unalterable thought
he need nevermore be thinking: Stone –
falling from his empty, reeling brain
down and down into the unbeknown.

Paris, 9-17 August 1907
st. 2, l. 5, Ljetnij-Ssad: lit. 'Summer Garden', a private domain of the Czars,
eventually opened to the public.

PAPAGEIEN-PARK

JARDIN DES PLANTES, PARIS

UNTER türkischen Linden, die blühen, an Rasenrändern,
in leise von ihrem Heimweh geschaukelten Ständern
atmen die Ara und wissen von ihren Ländern,
die sich, auch wenn sie nicht hinsehn, nicht verändern.

Fremd im beschäftigten Grünen wie eine Parade,
zieren sie sich und fühlen sich selber zu schade,
und mit den kostbaren Schnäbeln aus Jaspis und Jade
kauen sie Graues, verschleudern es, finden es fade.

Unten klauben die duffen Tauben, was sie nicht mögen,
während sich oben die höhnischen Vögel verbeugen
zwischen den beiden fast leeren vergeudeten Trögen.

Aber dann wiegen sie wieder und schläfern und äugen,
spielen mit dunkelen Zungen, die gerne lögen,
zerstreut an den Fußfesselringen. Warten auf Zeugen.

l. 9, *duffen.* In reply to a questionnaire from his Polish translator Rilke wrote,
10 April 1924: '„Duff" bedeutet: Nicht-glanzend, also dumpf, glanzlos, beschlagen,
in Bezug auf die Oberfläche irgendeiner Färbung; hier die gedämpften, verhaltenen
Töne im Gefieder der Tauben.'

DIE PARKE

I

UNAUFHALTSAM heben sich die Parke
aus dem sanft zerfallenden Vergehn;
überhäuft mit Himmeln, überstarke
Überlieferte, die überstehn,

um sich auf den klaren Rasenplänen
auszubreiten und zurückzuziehn,
immer mit demselben souveränen
Aufwand, wie beschützt durch ihn,

und den unerschöpflichen Erlös
königlicher Größe noch vermehrend,
aus sich steigend, in sich wiederkehrend:
huldvoll, prunkend, purpurn und pompös.

PARROT PARK

JARDIN DES PLANTES, PARIS

UNDER blossoming Turkish limes, at margins of mowing,
on perches their pining for home gently is to-and-froing,
breathe the aras and seem, though they can't see, to be knowing
about their native lands where no change is showing.

Foreign in this preoccupied greenness as some parade,
they put on airs and feel that they've got mislaid,
and with those beaks of precious jasper and jade
chew a grey something, find it insipid, let it cascade.

And the dullish doves below pick up what they're throwing away,
while the scornful birds above are bowing their heads between
each now almost emptiedly-squandered tray.

Then they start rocking again, though, and slumber and preen,
and with dusky tongues, that would gladly be lying, play
with the links of their fettering chains. Wait to be seen.

Paris, autumn 1907 or Capri, early 1908

THE PARKS

I

UNWITHOLDABLY the parks are flowering
from the softly decomposing past;
overheaped with heavens, overpowering
over-handings that will over-last,

and along the shining turf's diffusion
now expand and now again withdraw,
still with that same sovereign profusion
that protects them like a kind of law;

still contributing new increment
to some royal grandeur's endless earning,
rising from themselves and self-returning:
gracious, gorgeous, purple, prominent.

II

Leise von den Alleen
ergriffen, rechts und links,
folgend dem Weitergehen
irgend eines Winks,

trittst du mit einem Male
in das Beisammensein
einer schattigen Wasserschale
mit vier Bänken aus Stein;

in eine abgetrennte
Zeit, die allein vergeht.
Auf feuchte Postamente,
auf denen nichts mehr steht,

hebst du einen tiefen
erwartenden Atemzug;
während das silberne Triefen
von dem dunkeln Bug

dich schon zu den Seinen
zählt und weiterspricht.
Und du fühlst dich unter Steinen,
die hören, und rührst dich nicht.

III

Den Teichen und den eingerahmten Weihern
verheimlicht man noch immer das Verhör
der Könige. Sie warten unter Schleiern,
und jeden Augenblick kann Monseigneur

vorüberkommen; und dann wollen sie
des Königs Laune oder Trauer mildern
und von den Marmorrändern wieder die
Teppiche mit alten Spiegelbildern

hinunterhängen, wie um einen Platz:
auf grünem Grund, mit Silber, Rosa, Grau,
gewährtem Weiß und leicht gerührtem Blau
und einem Könige und einer Frau
und Blumen in dem wellenden Besatz.

II

Caught by the lightly-alluring
avenues, left and right,
following the reassuring
lead of some beckoning sight,

suddenly you've invaded
the intimacy so deep
a fountain basin, shaded,
and four stone benches keep;

all in a separated
time that goes by alone.
On long-ago vacated
bases of mossy stone

breaths from a tensely-gripping
expectancy you mount;
while the silvery dripping
from the sombre fount

talks on, already appearing
sure of your kindredness.
And you feel yourself among hearing
stones, and are motionless.

III

The lakes and framed pools one keeps hesitating
to tell that king has been by commoner
arraigned and sentenced. Under veils they're waiting,
and still at any moment Monseigneur

can pass that way, and then they will be fain
to mollify his humours or dejections
and from their marble margins once again
to let the carpets with antique reflections

hang down as from the windows round a square:
silver, rose, grey on ground of greenish hue,
with glimpse of white and lightly quivering blue
and with a monarch and a woman too
and flowers in the rippling border there.

IV

Und Natur, erlaucht und als verletze
sie nur unentschloßnes Ungefähr,
nahm von diesen Königen Gesetze,
selber selig, um den Tapis-vert

ihrer Bäume Traum und Übertreibung
aufzutürmen aus gebauschtem Grün
und die Abende nach der Beschreibung
von Verliebten in die Avenün

einzumalen mit dem weichen Pinsel,
der ein firnisklares aufgelöstes
Lächeln glänzend zu enthalten schien:

der Natur ein liebes, nicht ihr größtes,
aber eines, das sie selbst verliehn,
um auf rosenvoller Liebes-Insel
es zu einem größern aufzuziehn.

V

Götter von Alleen und Altanen,
niemals ganzgeglaubte Götter, die
altern in den gradbeschnittnen Bahnen,
höchstens angelächelte Dianen
wenn die königliche Venerie

wie ein Wind die hohen Morgen teilend
aufbrach, übereilt und übereilend –;
höchstens angelächelte, doch nie

angeflehte Götter. Elegante
Pseudonyme, unter denen man
sich verbarg und blühte oder brannte, –
leichtgeneigte, lächelnd angewandte
Götter, die noch manchmal dann und wann

Das gewähren, was sie einst gewährten,
wenn das Blühen der entzückten Gärten
ihnen ihre kalte Haltung nimmt;
wenn sie ganz von ersten Schatten beben
und Versprechen um Versprechen geben,
alle unbegrenzt und unbestimmt.

As if only vague approximation
hurt her, an ennobled Nature there
moved within those monarchs' regulation,
and to tower around the tapis-vert

their trees' visionary exaggeration
in outswollen green would take delight,
and to superadd, from the relation
of enamoured pairs, the evening light

to those avenues with brush appearing
to contain a gleaming, varnish-clear
melted smile as chief ingredient:

not her most miraculous, but dear
to her, one of hers, and one she meant
on some rose-filled love-isle to be rearing
into more unmatched development.

V

Gods of avenues and platformed stairs,
never quite believed-in gods, to-day
ageing in the straight-cut thoroughfares,
Dians deigned at most a smile of theirs
when the royal hunt's array,

lofty mornings like a wind partaking,
rode out, overtook and overtaking; –
smiled upon at most, but in no way

ever called-on gods. Just dignifying
pseudonyms beneath which now and then
one concealed one's graces or one's sighing, –
easy-going, smilingly-complying
gods, who yet at moments once again

will be granting us what once they granted,
when the blossoming of these enchanted
gardens takes away their chilliness;
when, with earliest shadows all a-quiver,
each becomes an endless promise-giver,
all so undefined and limitless.

VI

Fühlst du, wie keiner von allen
Wegen steht und stockt;
von gelassenen Treppen fallen,
durch ein Nichts von Neigung
leise weitergelockt,
über alle Terrassen
die Wege, zwischen den Massen
verlangsamt und gelenkt,
bis zu den weiten Teichen,
wo sie (wie einem Gleichen)
der reiche Park verschenkt

an den reichen Raum: den Einen,
der mit Scheinen und Widerscheinen
seinen Besitz durchdringt,
aus dem er von allen Seiten
Weiten mit sich bringt,
wenn er aus schließenden Weihern
zu wolkigen Abendfeiern
sich in die Himmel schwingt.

VII

Aber Schalen sind, drin der Najaden
Spiegelbilder, die sie nicht mehr baden,
wie ertrunken liegen, sehr verzerrt;
die Alleen sind durch Balustraden
in der Ferne wie versperrt.

Immer geht ein feuchter Blätterfall
durch die Luft hinunter wie auf Stufen,
jeder Vogelruf ist wie verrufen,
wie vergiftet jede Nachtigall.

Selbst der Frühling ist da nicht mehr gebend,
diese Büsche glauben nicht an ihn;
ungern duftet trübe, überlebend
abgestandener Jasmin

alt und mit Zerfallendem vermischt.
Mit dir weiter rückt ein Bündel Mücken,
so als würde hinter deinem Rücken
alles gleich vernichtet und verwischt.

Can you feel how none of these wending
ways stagnate and stop?
From leisurely steps descending,
lured so gently on by
merest trace of drop,
over each terrace flowing,
between steep banks of growing
guided in slowed career,
till they reach the distant lakes there,
and the rich park makes there
a present (as to its peer)

of them to that rich space, shining
over and firm-outlining
all its embosomings,
out of whose co-existence
such distances it brings,
when from the terminating
pools to the celebrating
evening clouds it wings.

VII

There are basins, though, where the reflections
of the nymphs once bathed by their ejections
lie, with much distortion, as if drowned;
and the pathways, through stone-railed erections
in the distance, seem inbound.

As on stairs, with every lightest gale
clammy leaves descend from every side there,
every bird-cry seems as though decried there,
poisoned every nightingale.

Spring itself has ceased to be reviving,
bushes there have lost belief in it;
dimly and unwillingly, surviving
jasmin yields indefinite

fragrance, stale and mingled with decay.
On with you a swarm of gnats are humming,
as if all behind you were becoming
null and non-existent straight away.

Paris, 9-17 August 1907

BILDNIS

DASS von dem verzichtenden Gesichte
keiner ihrer großen Schmerzen fiele,
trägt sie langsam durch die Trauerspiele
ihrer Züge schönen welken Strauß,
wild gebunden und schon beinah lose;
manchmal fällt, wie eine Tuberose,
ein verlornes Lächeln müd heraus.

Und sie geht gelassen drüber hin,
müde, mit den schönen blinden Händen,
welche wissen, daß sie es nicht fänden, –

und sie sagt Erdichtetes, darin
Schicksal schwankt, gewolltes, irgendeines,
und sie giebt ihm ihrer Seele Sinn,
daß es ausbricht wie ein Ungemeines:
wie das Schreien eines Steines –

und sie läßt, mit hochgehobnem Kinn,
alle diese Worte wieder fallen,
ohne bleibend; denn nicht eins von allen
ist der wehen Wirklichkeit gemäß,
ihrem einzigen Eigentum,
das sie, wie ein fußloses Gefäß,
halten muß, hoch über ihren Ruhm
und den Gang der Abende hinaus.

VENEZIANISCHER MORGEN

Richard Beer-Hofmann zugeeignet

FÜRSTLICH verwöhnte Fenster sehen immer,
was manchesmal uns zu bemühn geruht:
die Stadt, die immer wieder, wo ein Schimmer
von Himmel trifft auf ein Gefühl von Flut,

sich bildet ohne irgendwann zu sein.
Ein jeder Morgen muß ihr die Opale
erst zeigen, die sie gestern trug, und Reihn

242

PORTRAIT

Lᴇsᴛ there fall from her renouncing face
even one of those great sorrows there,
slowly through the tragedy she'll bear
all her beauty's withering bouquet,
wildly tied and almost loose already;
sometimes, like a tuberose, will eddy
some lost smile outweariedly away.

And she tiredly passes, with those thin,
beautiful blind hands that have resigned it,
hands aware that they would never find it, –

and she speaks fictitiousness, wherein
some too common lot is made to moan,
and she makes it with her soul akin,
till it sounds like something all its own:
like the crying of a stone –

and she lets those words, with high-held chin,
all those words she's given, once more fall,
doing without them; for not one of all
answers to that sad reality
which, sole thing that she can claim,
like some foot-less vessel she
has to hold out high above her fame
and the passage of her evenings.

Paris, 1-2 August 1907
The subject is Eleonora Duse.

VENETIAN MORNING

Dedicated to Richard Beer-Hofmann

Tʜᴇsᴇ princely-pampered windows see forever
what deigns to trouble us occasionally:
the city that perpetually, whenever
a glimpse of sky has met a feel of sea,

will start becoming without ever being.
Each morning must be showing her the selection
of opals she wore yesterday and freeing

vor Spiegelbildern ziehn aus dem Kanale
und sie erinnern an die andern Male:
dann giebt sie sich erst zu und fällt sich ein

wie eine Nymphe, die den Zeus empfing.
Das Ohrgehäng erklingt an ihrem Ohre;
sie aber hebt San Giorgio Maggiore
und lächelt lässig in das schöne Ding.

SPÄTHERBST IN VENEDIG

NUN treibt die Stadt schon nicht mehr wie ein Köder,
der alle aufgetauchten Tage fängt.
Die gläsernen Paläste klingen spröder
an deinen Blick. Und aus den Gärten hängt

der Sommer wie ein Haufen Marionetten
kopfüber, müde, umgebracht.
Aber vom Grund aus alten Waldskeletten
steigt Willen auf: als sollte über Nacht

der General des Meeres die Galeeren
verdoppeln in dem wachen Arsenal,
um schon die nächste Morgenluft zu teeren

mit einer Flotte, welche ruderschlagend
sich drängt und jäh, mit allen Flaggen tagend,
den großen Wind hat, strahlend und fatal.

from the canals reflection on reflection
and bringing past times to her recollection:
then only she'll comply and be agreeing

as any nymph that gave Zeus welcoming.
Her ear-rings tinkling at her ears, she raises
San Giorgio Maggiore up and gazes
with lazy smile into that lovely thing.

Paris, early summer 1908

Ruskin (*Stones of Venice*, Vol. III, Venetian Index) describes the church of San Giorgio Maggiore as 'a building which owes its interesting effect chiefly to its isolated position, being seen over a great space of lagoon'.

The Viennese poet Beer-Hofmann, to whom the poem is dedicated, had given Rilke much preliminary information about Venice before his first visit to that city in November 1907.

LATE AUTUMN IN VENICE

THE city drifts no longer like a bait now,
upcatching all the days as they emerge.
Brittlier the glassy palaces vibrate now
beneath your gaze. And from each garden verge

the summer like a bunch of puppets dangles,
headforemost, weary, made away.
Out of the ground, though, from dead forest tangles
volition mounts: as though before next day

the sea-commander must have rigged and ready
the galleys in the sleepless Arsenal,
and earliest morning air be tarred already

by an armada, oaringly outpressing,
and suddenly, with flare of flags, possessing
the great wind, radiant and invincible.

Paris, early summer 1908

SAN MARCO

VENEDIG

In diesem Innern, das wie ausgehöhlt
sich wölbt und wendet in den goldnen Smalten,
rundkantig, glatt, mit Köstlichkeit geölt,
ward dieses Staates Dunkelheit gehalten

und heimlich aufgehäuft, als Gleichgewicht
des Lichtes, das in allen seinen Dingen
sich so vermehrte, daß sie fast vergingen –.
Und plötzlich zweifelst du: vergehn sie nicht?

und drängst zurück die harte Galerie,
die, wie ein Gang im Bergwerk, nah am Glanz
der Wölbung hängt; und du erkennst die heile

Helle des Ausblicks: aber irgendwie
wehmütig messend ihre müde Weile
am nahen Überstehn des Viergespanns.

EIN DOGE

Fremde Gesandte sahen, wie sie geizten
mit ihm und allem was er tat;
während sie ihn zu seiner Größe reizten,
umstellten sie das goldene Dogat

mit Spähern und Beschränkern immer mehr,
bange, daß nicht die Macht sie überfällt,
die sie in ihm (so wie man Löwen hält)
vorsichtig nährten. Aber er,

im Schutze seiner halbverhängten Sinne,
ward dessen nicht gewahr und hielt nicht inne,
größer zu werden. Was die Signorie

in seinem Innern zu bezwingen glaubte,
bezwang er selbst. In seinem greisen Haupte
war es besiegt. Sein Antlitz zeigte wie.

SAN MARCO

VENICE

In this interior which, as excavated,
arches and twists within the golden foil,
round-cornered, glistening as with precious oil,
this city's darkness was accommodated

and secretly heaped up to balance out
that overplus of brightness, so pervading
all her possessions they were almost fading. –
And 'Aren't they fading?' comes the sudden doubt;

and, thrusting back the minish gallery
suspended near the vaulting's golden gleam,
you hail the unimpaired illumination

of that wide view; yet somehow mournfully
measuring its fatigued continuation
with that of the adjacent four-horse team.

Paris, early summer 1908

A DOGE

Ambassadors observed their intricateness
about him and his whole activity;
while they themselves were luring him to greatness,
they circumscribed the golden dogacy

with still more spies and limitations, ever
fearful that power might rend them limb from limb
which they were feeding (like a lion) in him
so circumspectly. He, though, never,

protected by his half-obscured sensation,
came to perceive this, and without cessation
kept growing greater. What the Council now

thought quelled within him by their practices,
he quelled himself. In that grey head of his
it was subdued. His countenance showed how.

Paris, between 22 August and 5 September 1907

DIE LAUTE

Ich bin die Laute. Willst du meinen Leib
beschreiben, seine schön gewölbten Streifen:
sprich so, als sprächest du von einer reifen
gewölbten Feige. Übertreib

das Dunkel, das du in mir siehst. Es war
Tullias Dunkelheit. In ihrer Scham
war nicht so viel, und ihr erhelltes Haar
war wie ein heller Saal. Zuweilen nahm

sie etwas Klang von meiner Oberfläche
in ihr Gesicht und sang zu mir.
Dann spannte ich mich gegen ihre Schwäche,
und endlich war mein Inneres in ihr.

DER ABENTEUERER

I

Wenn er unter jene, welche *waren*
trat: der Plötzliche, der *schien*,
war ein Glanz wie von Gefahren
in dem ausgesparten Raum um ihn,

den er lächelnd überschritt, um einer
Herzogin den Fächer aufzuheben:
diesen warmen Fächer, den er eben
wollte fallen sehen. Und wenn keiner

mit ihm eintrat in die Fensternische
(wo die Parke gleich ins Träumerische
stiegen, wenn er nur nach ihnen wies),
ging er lässig an die Kartentische
und gewann. Und unterließ

nicht, die Blicke alle zu behalten,
die ihn zweifelnd oder zärtlich trafen,
und auch die in Spiegel fielen, galten.
Er beschloß, auch heute nicht zu schlafen

THE LUTE

I AM the lute. To make my body rise
out of your words, its strips' fine curvature,
speak of me as you would of some mature
upcurving fig. And overemphasise

the dark you see in me. That darkness there
was Tullia's own. Not in her shyest nook
was there so much, and her illumined hair
was like a lighted hall. At times she took

a little sound from the outside of me
into her face and sang. Then I'd bestir
and stretch myself against her frailty,
till all I had within me was in her.

Paris, autumn 1907 or Capri, spring 1908
'Tullia' is probably the celebrated Roman courtesan and poetess, Tullia d'Aragona
(c. 1510-56), who is said to have been an excellent musician.

THE ADVENTURER

I

WHEN he moved among those who *existed*,
he, the instantaneous, who *appeared*,
gleams of peril still persisted
in that space wherein he was insphered,

and would smilingly outstep, to proffer
to some noble dame the fan she'd dropped:
that warm fan which he had never stopped
hoping to see fall. And should none offer

to go with him to the window-seat
(where the parks would straightaway retreat
into dreamland when he started showing),
lazily he'd stroll on to complete
some game, and win it. And, without their knowing,

every glance that met him he would keep,
whether tender-looking or suspecting,
even those the mirrors were reflecting.
He decided to dispense with sleep

wie die letzte lange Nacht, und bog
einen Blick mit seinem rücksichtslosen,
welcher war: als hätte er von Rosen
Kinder, die man irgendwo erzog.

II

In den Tagen – (nein, es waren keine),
da die Flut sein unterstes Verlies
ihm bestritt, als wär es nicht das seine,
und ihn, steigend, an die Steine
der daran gewöhnten Wölbung stieß,

fiel ihm plötzlich einer von den Namen
wieder ein, die er vor Zeiten trug.
Und er wußte wieder: Leben kamen,
wenn er lockte; wie im Flug

kamen sie: noch warme Leben Toter,
die er, ungeduldiger, bedrohter,
weiterlebte mitten drin;
oder die nicht ausgelebten Leben,
und er wußte sie hinaufzuheben,
und sie hatten wieder Sinn.

Oft war keine Stelle an ihm sicher,
und er zitterte: Ich bin – – –
doch im nächsten Augenblicke glich er
dem Geliebten einer Königin.

Immer wieder war ein Sein zu haben:
die Geschicke angefangner Knaben,
die, als hätte man sie nicht gewagt,
abgebrochen waren, abgesagt,
nahm er auf und riß sie in sich hin;
denn er mußte einmal nur die Gruft
solcher Aufgegebener durchschreiten,
und die Düfte ihrer Möglichkeiten
lagen wieder in der Luft.

as he'd done last night. And then and there
bore a glance down with his own, that gazed
as if out of roses it had raised
children being now brought up somewhere.

Paris, c. 5 September 1907 (lines 1-4) and early summer 1908

II

In those days (no, days there were unknown)
when the tide, disputing his possession
of that deepest dungeon for his own,
rose and stumbled him against the stone
of a roof inured to such aggression,

suddenly he found he'd recollected
one of his own names of long ago.
And back came the knowledge: lives collected
when he lured; would come as though

flying: the still warm lives of dead, which he,
more impatient, more imperilledly,
went on living from inside;
or those lives which had not been lived out,
which he knew the way to set about
till they once more signified.

Often, all uncertainty, to tremble
'I am —' was all he could do;
yet a moment later he'd resemble
one a queen had yielded to.

Evermore some being was to be had:
destinies of many a started lad,
which, as more than could be contemplated,
had been broken off and abdicated,
he took to him and appropriated;
for he only needed once to fare
through the crypts of such surrenderednesses
for the scents of their potentialnesses
to re-gather in the air.

Paris, between 22 August and 5 September 1907

FALKEN-BEIZE

KAISER sein heißt unverwandelt vieles
überstehen bei geheimer Tat:
wenn der Kanzler nachts den Turm betrat,
fand er *ihn*, des hohen Federspieles
kühnen fürstlichen Traktat

in den eingeneigten Schreiber sagen;
denn er hatte im entlegnen Saale
selber nächtelang und viele Male
das noch ungewohnte Tier getragen,

wenn es fremd war, neu und aufgebräut.
Und er hatte dann sich nie gescheut,
Pläne, welche in ihm aufgesprungen,
oder zärtlicher Erinnerungen
tieftiefinneres Geläut
zu verachten, um des bangen jungen

Falken willen, dessen Blut und Sorgen
zu begreifen er sich nicht erließ.
Dafür war er auch wie mitgehoben,
wenn der Vogel, den die Herren loben,
glänzend von der Hand geworfen, oben
in dem mitgefühlten Frühlingsmorgen
wie ein Engel auf den Reiher stieß.

FALCONRY

EMP'RING means unchangedly dominating
many challenges all out of sight:
when the chancellor at dead of night
climbed the tower, he found *him* there, dictating
that bold princely tract on falcon-flight

to the scribe that sat incurvatured;
for in some sequestered gallery
he himself nights long and frequently
had been carrying that still uninured

creature, strange, new-captured, and enseeled.
And then everything had had to yield:
plans which so excitingly upsprung,
chimes deep, deep within him rung
by soft memories he concealed, –
he had spurned them for that timid young

falcon's sake, to enter whose awaring
his attentiveness had never stopped.
Whence he too became a co-ascender
when the bird to which the lordliest render
homage, hoisted from his hand in splendour,
up in that spring morning they were sharing
like an angel on the heron dropped.

Paris, early summer 1908

The Emperor Frederick II (1194-1250) composed a treatise on falconry, *De arte venandi cum avibus*.

    st. 3, l. 1, *enseeled*. To enseel or seel (later form of *sile*, from O.F. *ciller*, probably connected with *cil*, eyelash) was to stitch up the eyelids of a newly-caught hawk or falcon with a thread tied behind its head. The thread was carefully removed after the bird had become accustomed to its captor and captivity.

CORRIDA

IN MEMORIAM MONTEZ, 1830

SEIT er, klein beinah, aus dem Toril
ausbrach, aufgescheuchten Augs und Ohrs,
und den Eigensinn des Picadors
und die Bänderhaken wie im Spiel

hinnahm, ist die stürmische Gestalt
angewachsen – sieh: zu welcher Masse,
aufgehäuft aus altem schwarzen Hasse,
und das Haupt zu einer Faust geballt,

nicht mehr spielend gegen irgendwen,
nein: die blutigen Nackenhaken hissend
hinter den gefällten Hörnern, wissend
und von Ewigkeit her gegen Den,

der in Gold und mauver Rosaseide
plötzlich umkehrt und, wie einen Schwarm
Bienen und als ob ers eben leide,
den Bestürzten unter seinem Arm

durchläßt, – während seine Blicke heiß
sich noch einmal heben, leichtgelenkt,
und als schlüge draußen jener Kreis
sich aus ihrem Glanz und Dunkel nieder
und aus jedem Schlagen seiner Lider,

ehe er gleichmütig, ungehässig,
an sich selbst gelehnt, gelassen, lässig
in die wiederhergerollte große
Woge über dem verlornen Stoße
seinen Degen beinah sanft versenkt.

CORRIDA

IN MEMORIAM MONTEZ, 1830

SINCE, small almost, through the opened door
with upstartled eyes and ears he came
and supposed the baiting picador
and beribboned barbs to be a game,

that wild figure seems now to consist
of an ever-concentrating weight
of accumulated old black hate,
and his head is clenched into a fist,

no more meeting any playfully:
no, but rearing bloody barbs behind
those presented horns, and in his mind
his opponent from eternity,

who, in gold and mauve-pink silk arrayed,
suddenly turns round and, like a swarm
of bees, and as if vexed but undismayed,
lets the baffled beast beneath his arm

rush by, – while his burning looks are lifting
up once more in tremulous accord,
as if all that circling throng were drifting
down from their own shine and sombering
and his eyelids' every fluttering,

till, so unexcitedly, unhating,
leaning on himself, deliberating,
into that great wave's refluctuance
over its dispersed precipitance
almost softly he insheathes his sword.

Paris, 3 August 1907

It was in 1830, as Rilke informed his wife in a letter (6 September 1907) enclosing
this and another poem, that the torero Francisco Montez first practised what
afterwards became an established technique, namely, to step aside from the path
of the charging bull and to dispatch the baffled animal when it returned. A portrait
of Montez, 'in gold and mauve-pink silk', by Eugenio Lucas the elder (1824-70)
was for many years on loan at the Kaiser Friederich Museum in Berlin, which
Rilke often visited. At the time when he wrote this poem he had never been in
Spain or seen a bull-fight (*corrida*).

DON JUANS KINDHEIT

In seiner Schlankheit war, schon fast entscheidend,
der Bogen, der an Frauen nicht zerbricht;
und manchmal, seine Stirne nicht mehr meidend,
ging eine Neigung durch sein Angesicht

zu einer, die vorüberkam, zu einer,
die ihm ein fremdes altes Bild verschloß:
er lächelte. Er war nicht mehr der Weiner,
der sich ins Dunkel trug und sich vergoß.

Und während ein ganz neues Selbstvertrauen
ihn öfter tröstete und fast verzog,
ertrug er ernst den ganzen Blick der Frauen,
der ihn bewunderte und ihn bewog.

DON JUANS AUSWAHL

Und der Engel trat ihn an: Bereite
dich mir ganz. Und da ist mein Gebot.
Denn daß einer jene überschreite,
die die Süßesten an ihrer Seite
bitter machen, tut mir not.
Zwar auch du kannst wenig besser lieben,
(unterbrich mich nicht: du irrst),
doch du glühest, und es steht geschrieben,
daß du viele führen wirst
zu der Einsamkeit, die diesen
tiefen Eingang hat. Laß ein
die, die ich dir zugewiesen,
daß sie wachsend Heloïsen
überstehn und überschrein.

DON JUAN'S CHILDHOOD

ALREADY in his slimness it was clear,
that bow which, bent on women, does not split;
and, now no longer failing to appear,
an inclination through his face would flit

to one who passed him by, to one whose deeper
secrets some ancient foreign portrait kept:
he smiled. He was no longer now the weeper,
who stole away into the dark and wept.

And while a wholly novel self-assurance
oftener consoled him almost spoilingly,
he now confronted with a grave endurance
what gazed from women so disturbingly.

Paris, autumn 1907 or Capri, spring 1908

DON JUAN'S ELECTION

AND the Angel came to him: Be given
wholly up to me. That's my behest.
For, till someone be surpassing even
those by whom the sweetest partner's driven
into bitterness, I cannot rest.
You're not much more capable of love
(do not interrupt, you're wrong),
still, you're ardent. And it's written above
that you'll lead a goodly throng
to that loneness you'll supply
entrance to. Let in thereby
those whom I into your way may
send, that Eloisa they may
overtop and overcry.

Paris, beginning of August 1908

257

SANKT GEORG

UND sie hatte ihn die ganze Nacht
angerufen, hingekniet, die schwache
wache Jungfrau: Siehe, dieser Drache,
und ich weiß es nicht, warum er wacht.

Und da brach er aus dem Morgengraun
auf dem Falben, strahlend Helm und Haubert,
und er sah sie, traurig und verzaubert
aus dem Knieen aufwärtsschaun

zu dem Glanze, der er war.
Und er sprengte glänzend längs der Länder
abwärts mit erhobnem Doppelhänder
in die offene Gefahr,

viel zu furchtbar, aber doch erfleht.
Und sie kniete knieender, die Hände
fester faltend, daß er sie bestände;
denn sie wußte nicht, daß Der besteht,

den ihr Herz, ihr reines und bereites,
aus dem Licht des göttlichen Geleites
niederreißt. Zuseiten seines Streites
stand, wie Türme stehen, ihr Gebet.

SAINT GEORGE

AND she'd called to him the whole night through,
kneeling on and on, that vigilating,
helpless virgin: Look, this dragon waiting,
and I know not what it means to do.

And he issued from the morning haze
on the dun horse, helm and hauberk blazing,
and beheld her, sad and spell-bound, gazing
up from her long kneeling in amaze

at the splendour that was he.
And he flashed along the far-extended
lands and with uplifted sword descended
to the open enmity,

far too dreadful, and yet what she would.
And she knelt more kneelingly and wed her
hands more lockedly, that he might bestead her;
for she did not know that One bestood

whom her pure and ready heart was wresting
down from those resplendent ranks investing
light divine. Alongside his contesting,
like a standing tower, her prayer stood.

Paris, between 5 and 9 August 1907

St. George was a tribune of Cappadocia under Diocletian, by whom he was
martyred, and in the *Golden Legend* and in most pictorial representations it is before
his martyrdom and in sight of King and people that he kills the dragon and rescues
the princess. Rilke, however, imagines him as descending from Heaven in response
to the lady's prayer, and, both here and in two other poems on the same subject
which he wrote in the same month (*Poems 1906 to 1926,* Hogarth Press, 1959,
pp. 91-92), as performing his act of rescue in a castle park, where he and she and
the dragon alone are present.

DAME AUF EINEM BALKON

PLÖTZLICH tritt sie, in den Wind gehüllt,
licht in Lichtes, wie herausgegriffen,
während jetzt die Stube wie geschliffen
hinter ihr die Türe füllt

dunkel wie der Grund einer Kamee,
die ein Schimmern durchläßt durch die Ränder;
und du meinst der Abend war nicht, ehe
sie heraustrat, um auf das Geländer

noch ein wenig von sich fortzulegen,
noch die Hände, – um ganz leicht zu sein:
wie dem Himmel von den Häuserreihn
hingereicht, von allem zu bewegen.

BEGEGNUNG IN DER KASTANIEN-ALLEE

IHM ward des Eingangs grüne Dunkelheit
kühl wie ein Seidenmantel umgegeben
den er noch nahm und ordnete: als eben
am andern transparenten Ende, weit,

aus grüner Sonne, wie aus grünen Scheiben,
weiß eine einzelne Gestalt
aufleuchtete, um lange fern zu bleiben
und schließlich, von dem Lichterniedertreiben
bei jedem Schritte überwallt,

ein helles Wechseln auf sich herzutragen,
das scheu im Blond nach hinten lief.
Aber auf einmal war der Schatten tief,
und nahe Augen lagen aufgeschlagen

in einem neuen deutlichen Gesicht,
das wie in einem Bildnis verweilte
in dem Moment, da man sich wieder teilte:
erst war es immer, und dann war es nicht.

LADY ON A BALCONY

Out she steps enshawled to windiness,
bright to brightness, as if extricated,
while the room, as if consolidated,
fills the door behind her, lustreless

as the background of a cameo
letting through a shimmer round its edging;
and you feel the evening failed to show
till she came to lay upon the ledging

just a little of herself away,
just her hands, – to make herself quite light:
as if holden by the house-rows right
out to heaven, for everything to sway.

Paris, 17 August 1907

MEETING IN THE CHESTNUT AVENUE

He felt the entrance's green dark descending
cool as a silken mantle he was then
only just donning and arranging, when,
there at the opposite transparent ending,

through green sunlight, as through green window-paning,
whitely a single figure showed,
far off at first, and so for long remaining,
till finally, by lashes of downraining
light at each footstep overflowed,

it bore on it a brilliant counter-dancing,
whose blond would shyly backwards leap.
All of a sudden, though, the shade was deep,
and now-near eyes wide-openedly were glancing

out of a new, distinguishable face,
which, as within a picture, had duration
within the moment of re-separation:
first always there, then gone without a trace.

Paris, summer 1908

DIE SCHWESTERN

SIEH, wie sie dieselben Möglichkeiten
anders an sich tragen und verstehn,
so als sähe man verschiedne Zeiten
durch zwei gleiche Zimmer gehn.

Jede meint die andere zu stützen,
während sie doch müde an ihr ruht;
und sie können nicht einander nützen,
denn sie legen Blut auf Blut,

wenn sie sich wie früher sanft berühren
und versuchen, die Allee entlang
sich geführt zu fühlen und zu führen:
Ach, sie haben nicht denselben Gang.

ÜBUNG AM KLAVIER

DER Sommer summt. Der Nachmittag macht müde;
sie atmete verwirrt ihr frisches Kleid
und legte in die triftige Etüde
die Ungeduld nach einer Wirklichkeit,

die kommen konnte: morgen, heute abend –,
die vielleicht da war, die man nur verbarg;
und vor den Fenstern, hoch und alles habend,
empfand sie plötzlich den verwöhnten Park.

Da brach sie ab; schaute hinaus, verschränkte
die Hände; wünschte sich ein langes Buch –
und schob auf einmal den Jasmingeruch
erzürnt zurück. Sie fand, daß er sie kränkte.

THE SISTERS

Look with what a difference each engages
in the self-same duties she assumes,
like a passing-by of different ages
through two indistinguishable rooms.

Each supposes she supports the other,
while she tiredly rests on her support;
and they can't make use of one another,
for it's blood to blood they've brought

when they softly touch as in preceding
years, and, as they circumambulate,
try to feel being led and to be leading:
ah, they haven't got the self-same gait.

Paris, early summer 1908

PIANO PRACTICE

The summer hums. The afternoon is tiring.
She breathed her fresh white dress distractedly,
and put into that piece she was acquiring
impatience after some reality

might come to-morrow, or to-night – was there,
perhaps, already, though they kept it dark;
and then she all at once became aware,
through the tall windows, of the pampered park.

Thereupon stopped her playing; gazed out, clasped her
two hands together; longed for a long book –
and in a sudden fit of anger shook
the jasmin scent away. She found it rasped her.

Paris, autumn 1907 or Capri, spring 1908

263

DIE LIEBENDE

Das ist mein Fenster. Eben
bin ich so sanft erwacht.
Ich dachte, ich würde schweben.
Bis wohin reicht mein Leben,
und wo beginnt die Nacht?

Ich könnte meinen, alles
wäre noch Ich ringsum;
durchsichtig wie eines Kristalles
Tiefe, verdunkelt, stumm.

Ich könnte auch noch die Sterne
fassen in mir; so groß
scheint mir mein Herz; so gerne
ließ es ihn wieder los

den ich vielleicht zu lieben,
vielleicht zu halten begann.
Fremd, wie niebeschrieben
sieht mich mein Schicksal an.

Was bin ich unter diese
Unendlichkeit gelegt,
duftend wie eine Wiese,
hin und her bewegt,

rufend zugleich und bange,
daß einer den Ruf vernimmt,
und zum Untergange
in einem Andern bestimmt.

DAS ROSEN-INNERE

Wo ist zu diesem Innen
ein Außen? Auf welches Weh
legt man solches Linnen?
Welche Himmel spiegeln sich drinnen
in dem Binnensee
dieser offenen Rosen,
dieser sorglosen, sieh:
wie sie lose im Losen

WOMAN IN LOVE

THAT is my window. Ending
softly the dream I was in
of being on wings ascending.
How far is my life extending,
and where does the night begin?

Everything, I'm inclining
to think, is me all round;
a crystal's deep through-shining,
dark and without a sound.

I could still let stars be filling
the spaces in me; my heart
seems so immense, so willing
to let him again depart

whom I perhaps have started
to love – to hold, maybe.
Strange and all-uncharted
seems my destiny.

What, amid this unfailing
endlessness, am I, though?
Meadowy, scent-exhaling,
swaying so to-and-fro,

calling and full of fear
lest someone should hear my call,
and fated to disappear
in another for good and all.

Paris, 5-9 August 1907

THE ROSE-INTERIOR

WHERE for this inner's waiting
an outer? What pains partake
such lawn's alleviating?
What heavens are contemplating
themselves in the inland lake
of these wide-open roses,
these all-unheeding: see,
how rootless their repose is,

liegen, als könnte nie
eine zitternde Hand sie verschütten.
Sie können sich selber kaum
halten; viele ließen
sich überfüllen und fließen
über von Innenraum
in die Tage, die immer
voller und voller sich schließen,
bis der ganze Sommer ein Zimmer
wird, ein Zimmer in einem Traum.

DAMEN-BILDNIS AUS DEN
ACHTZIGER-JAHREN

WARTEND stand sie an den schwergerafften
dunklen Atlasdraperien,
die ein Aufwand falscher Leidenschaften
über ihr zu ballen schien;

seit den noch so nahen Mädchenjahren
wie mit einer anderen vertauscht:
müde unter den getürmten Haaren,
in den Rüschen-Roben unerfahren
und von allen Falten wie belauscht

bei dem Heimweh und dem schwachen Planen,
wie das Leben weiter werden soll:
anders, wirklicher, wie in Romanen,
hingerissen und verhängnisvoll, –

daß man etwas erst in die Schatullen
legen dürfte, um sich im Geruch
von Erinnerungen einzulullen;
daß man endlich in dem Tagebuch

einen Anfang fände, der nicht schon
unterm Schreiben sinnlos wird und Lüge,
und ein Blatt von einer Rose trüge
in dem schweren leeren Medaillon,

welches liegt auf jedem Atemzug.
Daß man einmal durch das Fenster winkte;
diese schlanke Hand, die neuberingte,
hätte dran für Monate genug.

as never could possibly
some quivering hand be spilling.
Themselves their whole endeavour
scarce holds; and many are willing
to be filled to overflowing
with inner-space and stream
into the days, forever
fuller and fuller growing,
till summer has all become a
chamber within a dream.

Paris, 2 August 1907

PORTRAIT OF A LADY OF
THE EIGHTIES

WAITING there against the heavy-weighing
sombre satin drapery,
that above her seems to be displaying
shows of false intensity;

since her scarce-outdistanced girlishnesses
changed with someone else, it might appear:
weary underneath her high-heaped tresses,
inexperienced in her ruche-trimmed dresses,
and as if those folds could overhear

all her homesickness and hesitating
plans for what life now is going to be:
realer, as in novels, scintillating,
full of rapture and fatality, –

to have something safe from all detection
in one's escritoire and, when inclined,
lull oneself in fragrant recollection;
for one's diary at last to find

some beginning that no longer grows,
while one writes, mendacious and unmeaning,
and to wear a petal from a rose
in that heavy, empty locket, leaning

on each indrawn breath. To have at some
time just waved out of the window there –
that would be sufficient and to spare
for this new-ringed hand for months to come.

Paris, 22 August - 5 September 1907

DAME VOR DEM SPIEGEL

WIE in einem Schlaftrunk Spezerein
löst sie leise in dem flüssigklaren
Spiegel ihr ermüdetes Gebaren;
und sie tut ihr Lächeln ganz hinein.

Und sie wartet, daß die Flüssigkeit
davon steigt; dann gießt sie ihre Haare
in den Spiegel und, die wunderbare
Schulter hebend aus dem Abendkleid,

trinkt sie still aus ihrem Bild. Sie trinkt,
was ein Liebender im Taumel tränke,
prüfend, voller Mißtraun; und sie winkt

erst der Zofe, wenn sie auf dem Grunde
ihres Spiegels Lichter findet, Schränke
und das Trübe einer späten Stunde.

DIE GREISIN

WEISSE Freundinnen mitten im Heute
lachen und horchen und planen für morgen;
abseits erwägen gelassene Leute
langsam ihre besonderen Sorgen,

das Warum und das Wann und das Wie,
und man hört sie sagen: Ich glaube –;
aber in ihrer Spitzenhaube
ist sie sicher, als wüßte sie,

daß sie sich irren, diese und alle.
Und das Kinn, im Niederfalle,
lehnt sich an die weiße Koralle,
die den Schal zur Stirne stimmt.

Einmal aber, bei einem Gelache,
holt sie aus springenden Lidern zwei wache
Blicke und zeigt diese harte Sache,
wie man aus einem geheimen Fache
schöne ererbte Steine nimmt.

LADY BEFORE THE MIRROR

At the mirror's surface she'll begin
gently melting, like a spice-assortment
in a sleeping draught, her tired deportment;
and she'll let her smiling drop right in.

And she'll wait until the liquidness
rises from it; then she'll pour her hair
in as well, and, lifting out one bare,
marvellous shoulder from her evening-dress,

quietly drink out of her image. Drink,
what a lover would in wild caresses,
tryingly, all mistrust; and never think

of beckoning her maid until she sees
at the mirror's bottom candles, presses,
and a late hour's undissolving lees.

Paris, between 22 August and 5 September 1907

THE OLD LADY

White feminine friends in the midst of to-day
laugh, listen, and plan to-morrow's affairs;
sedater persons sequesteredly weigh
slowly their own particular cares,

the why and the when and the how to do,
and one hears them saying: I think I might;—
she in her lace cap, though, is quite
self-assured, as if she knew

these and the rest were all wrong-headed.
And her fallen chin is bedded
on that white coral through which is threaded
the shawl arranged around her head.

Sometimes, though, at a laugh's outbreaking,
she'll open the springing lids of two waking
looks and exhibit their durable making,
like one from a secret drawer taking
beautiful gems she's inherited.

Paris, summer 1908

DAS BETT

Lass sie meinen, daß sich in privater
Wehmut löst, was einer dort bestritt.
Nirgend sonst als da ist ein Theater;
reiß den hohen Vorhang fort –: da tritt

vor den Chor der Nächte, der begann
ein unendlich breites Lied zu sagen,
jene Stunde auf, bei der sie lagen,
und zerreißt ihr Kleid und klagt sich an,

um der andern, um der Stunde willen,
die sich wehrt und wälzt im Hintergrunde;
denn sie konnte sie mit sich nicht stillen.
Aber da sie zu der fremden Stunde

sich gebeugt: da war auf ihr,
was sie am Geliebten einst gefunden,
nur so drohend und so groß verbunden
und entzogen wie in einem Tier.

DER FREMDE

Ohne Sorgfalt, was die Nächsten dächten,
die er müde nichtmehr fragen hieß,
ging er wieder fort; verlor, verließ –.
Denn er hing an solchen Reisenächten
anders als an jeder Liebesnacht.
Wunderbare hatte er durchwacht,
die mit starken Sternen überzogen
enge Fernen auseinanderbogen
und sich wandelten wie eine Schlacht;

andre, die mit in den Mond gestreuten
Dörfern, wie mit hingehaltnen Beuten,
sich ergaben, oder durch geschonte
Parke graue Edelsitze zeigten,
die er gerne in dem hingeneigten
Haupte einen Augenblick bewohnte,
tiefer wissend, daß man nirgends bleibt;
und schon sah er bei dem nächsten Biegen

THE BED

LET them fancy all that one engages
there in strife with melts in private tears.
That, if anywhere, is where a stage is;
strip the lofty curtain: – straight appears,

there before the chorus of the nights
and the endless song they're now supplying,
that same hour with which the pair were lying,
and she rends her garments and indicts

her own failure with that other hour,
writhing in the background, self-defending;
for to still it she had lacked the power.
When to that strange hour, though, she was bending

gently down: on it was visible
what on the belov'd she'd contemplated:
threatening, though, and grandly integrated,
and withdrawn, as in an animal.

Paris, summer 1908

THE STRANGER

CARELESS how it struck those nearest to him,
whose inquiring he'd no longer brook,
once more he departed; lost, forsook. –
For such nights of travel always drew him
stronglier than any lover's night.
How he'd watched in slumberless delight
out beneath the shining stars all yonder
circumscribed horizons roll asunder,
ever-changing like a changing fight;

others, with their moon-bright hamlets tendered
like some booty they had seized, surrendered
peacefully, or through tall trees would shed
glimpses of far-stretching parks, containing
grey ancestral houses that with craning
head a moment he inhabited,
knowing more deeply one could never bide;
then, already round the next curve speeding,

wieder Wege, Brücken, Länder liegen
bis an Städte, die man übertreibt.

Und dies alles immer unbegehrend
hinzulassen, schien ihm mehr als seines
Lebens Lust, Besitz und Ruhm.
Doch auf fremden Plätzen war ihm eines
täglich ausgetretnen Brunnensteines
Mulde manchmal wie ein Eigentum.

DIE ANFAHRT

Wᴀʀ in des Wagens Wendung dieser Schwung?
War er im Blick, mit dem man die barocken
Engelfiguren, die bei blauen Glocken
im Felde standen voll Erinnerung,

annahm und hielt und wieder ließ, bevor
der Schloßpark schließend um die Fahrt sich drängte,
an die er streifte, die er überhängte
und plötzlich freigab: denn da war das Tor,

das nun, als hätte es sie angerufen,
die lange Front zu einer Schwenkung zwang,
nach der sie stand. Aufglänzend ging ein Gleiten

die Glastür abwärts; und ein Windhund drang
aus ihrem Aufgehn, seine nahen Seiten
heruntertragend von den flachen Stufen.

other highways, bridges, landscapes, leading
on to cities darkness magnified.

And to let all this, without all craving,
slip behind him meant beyond compare
more to him than pleasure, goods, or fame.
Though the well-steps in some foreign square,
daily hollowed by the drawers there,
seemed at times like something he could claim.

Paris, early summer 1908

On 21 October 1913, at the end of a self-reproachful letter to Lou Andreas-Salomé,
Rilke wrote: 'How often I have to recall that poem in New Poems entitled, I
think, "The Stranger" – how well I knew what was needed:
> "And to let all this, without all craving,
>   slip behind him."

And who still do nothing but crave. – Begin over again.'

THE ARRIVAL

WAS that *élan* the swerving carriage's?
Was it the glance with which those half-revealed
baroque stone angels standing in a field
among the bluebells, full of memories,

were caught, held, loosed, before the ultimate
reception of the castle park had crowded
around the ride it brushed on, overshrouded,
and suddenly set free: there stood the gate,

which now, as having shouted its intentions,
forced the long front to execute a wheeling
round to a final halt. A gleam went stealing

down the glass door, and through its opening
a greyhound forced its passage, carrying
from step to shallow step its two dimensions.

Paris, summer 1908

A letter of Rilke's to his wife on 4 November 1907 suggests that this poem may
well contain recollections of his drive from the station to Schloss Janowič in
Bohemia, on a short visit to his friends the Nadhernys.

DIE SONNENUHR

SELTEN reicht ein Schauer feuchter Fäule
aus dem Gartenschatten, wo einander
Tropfen fallen hören und ein Wander-
vogel lautet, zu der Säule,
die in Majoran und Koriander
steht und Sommerstunden zeigt;

nur sobald die Dame (der ein Diener
nachfolgt) in dem hellen Florentiner
über ihren Rand sich neigt,
wird sie schattig und verschweigt –.

Oder wenn ein sommerlicher Regen
aufkommt aus dem wogenden Bewegen
hoher Kronen, hat sie eine Pause;
denn sie weiß die Zeit nicht auszudrücken,
die dann in den Frucht- und Blumenstücken
plötzlich glüht im weißen Gartenhause.

SCHLAF-MOHN

ABSEITS im Garten blüht der böse Schlaf,
in welchem die, die heimlich eingedrungen,
die Liebe fanden junger Spiegelungen,
die willig waren, offen und konkav,

und Träume, die mit aufgeregten Masken
auftraten, riesiger durch die Kothurne –:
das alles stockt in diesen oben flasken
weichlichen Stengeln, die die Samenurne

(nachdem sie lang, die Knospe abwärts tragend,
zu welken meinten) festverschlossen heben:
gefranste Kelche auseinanderschlagend,
die fieberhaft das Mohngefäß umgeben.

st. 2, l. 3, *flasken*. An adjective coined by Rilke (presumably in order to rhyme with 'Masken') from French *flasque*, slack, limp, flabby, etc., a word derived, like Latin *flaccidus* and English *flaccid*, from Latin *flaccus*, flabby.

THE SUNDIAL

SELDOM any shower of damp putrescence
from the garden shadow, where the falling
drops can hear themselves, and there's one calling
migratory bird, can reach the presence
of that marjoram and coriander-
circled stone, with summer hours to show:

save when, soon as she, whom an attendant
always follows, in her widely pendent
bright straw hat inclines too low,
it's obscured and doesn't know;

or when, on a summer rain's emergence
from the lofty tree-top's wild insurgence,
it becomes entitled to repose;
since to tell that time exceeds its powers
which within the painted fruits and flowers
in the white pavilion then upglows.

Paris, early summer 1908

OPIUM POPPY

IN beds apart those baneful slumbers wave,
where some, contriving secret enterings,
have found the love of youthful mirrorings,
that proved most willing, open, and concave,

and dreams that in excited masks came trooping
on with a stature buskinedly imposing: —
it's all congealed within those topward drooping,
tenuous stalks, which, after long supposing,

with their bowed buds, that they were withering,
uplift the tight-shut seed-urns on their shoulders:
unfurling all the frilly petalling
that feverishly surrounds the poppy-holders.

Paris, early summer 1908

DIE FLAMINGOS

JARDIN DES PLANTES, PARIS

In Spiegelbildern wie von Fragonard
ist doch von ihrem Weiß und ihrer Röte
nicht mehr gegeben, als dir einer böte,
wenn er von seiner Freundin sagt: sie war

noch sanft von Schlaf. Denn steigen sie ins Grüne
und stehn, auf rosa Stielen leicht gedreht,
beisammen, blühend, wie in einem Beet,
verführen sie, verführender als Phryne

sich selber; bis sie ihres Auges Bleiche
hinhalsend bergen in der eignen Weiche,
in welcher Schwarz und Fruchtrot sich versteckt.

Auf einmal kreischt ein Neid durch die Volière;
sie aber haben sich erstaunt gestreckt
und schreiten einzeln ins Imaginäre.

PERSISCHES HELIOTROP

Es könnte sein, daß dir der Rose Lob
zu laut erscheint für deine Freundin: Nimm
das schön gestickte Kraut und überstimm
mit dringend flüsterndem Heliotrop

den Bülbül, der an ihren Lieblingsplätzen
sie schreiend preist und sie nicht kennt.
Denn sieh: wie süße Worte nachts in Sätzen
beisammenstehn ganz dicht, durch nichts getrennt,
aus der Vokale wachem Violett
hindüftend durch das stille Himmelbett –:

so schließen sich vor dem gesteppten Laube
deutliche Sterne zu der seidnen Traube
und mischen, daß sie fast davon verschwimmt,
die Stille mit Vanille und mit Zimmt.

THE FLAMINGOS

JARDIN DES PLANTES, PARIS

In Fragonard-like mirrorings no more
of all their white and red is proffered to you
than would have been conveyed if one who knew you
had said of her he'd chosen to adore:

'She was still soft with sleep'. For if, forsaking
pool for green grass, they stand together there,
rose-stalked, as in some blossoming parterre,
they're taken by themselves with lures more taking

than Phryne's; till they've necked that pallidness
of eye deep into their own downiness,
where black and ripe-fruit-ruddiness are hiding.

A screech of envy rends the aviary;
they, though, in stretched astonishment, are striding,
each singly, into the imaginary.

Paris, autumn 1907 or Capri, spring 1908

PERSIAN HELIOTROPE

The rose's praise might seem to you to ring
too loud for your beloved friend, so try
this herb so finely broidered and outvie
with heliotrope's insistent whispering

the bulbul, that among her favourite trees
outcries in ignorance her celebration.
For look: as sweet words, nights, in sentences
stay close together, with no separation,
from the vowels' wakeful violet fragrantly
circling beneath the silent canopy: –

in front of criss-crossed leaves these star-like lustres
conjoin thus with the silken berry-clusters
and mingle, till it almost vanishes,
vanilla and cassia with the silentness.

Paris, early summer 1908

SCHLAFLIED

EINMAL wenn ich dich verlier,
wirst du schlafen können, ohne
daß ich wie eine Lindenkrone
mich verflüstre über dir?

Ohne daß ich hier wache und
Worte, beinah wie Augenlider,
auf deine Brüste, auf deine Glieder
niederlege, auf deinen Mund.

Ohne daß ich dich verschließ
und dich allein mit Deinem lasse
wie einen Garten mit einer Masse
von Melissen und Stern-Anis.

DER PAVILLON

ABER selbst noch durch die Flügeltüren
mit dem grünen regentrüben Glas
ist ein Spiegeln lächelnder Allüren
und ein Glanz von jenem Glück zu spüren,
das sich dort, wohin sie nicht mehr führen,
einst verbarg, verklärte und vergaß.

Aber selbst noch in den Stein-Guirlanden
über der nicht mehr berührten Tür
ist ein Hang zur Heimlichkeit vorhanden
und ein stilles Mitgefühl dafür –,

und sie schauern manchmal, wie gespiegelt,
wenn ein Wind sie schattig überlief;
auch das Wappen, wie auf einem Brief
viel zu glücklich, überstürzt gesiegelt,

redet noch. Wie wenig man verscheuchte:
alles weiß noch, weint noch, tut noch weh –.
Und im Fortgehn durch die tränenfeuchte
abgelegene Allee

LULLABY

IF I lose you and your love,
will you still slumber as before
without my murmuring any more
like lofty linden leaves above?

Without my watching every sign
here beside you and reposing
on your breasts, limbs, lips, like closing
eyelids almost, words of mine?

Without my having finally
locked you with your self alone,
like a garden thickly-sown
with balm-mint and the anise tree?

Paris, early summer 1908

THE PAVILION

EVEN now, though, through that long-neglected
green-glazed pair of door-leaves dimmed with wet
smiling graciousness is still reflected
and a gleam of that delight detected
which, where they no longer lead, elected
once to hide, transfigure, and forget.

Even now, though, in the stone enwreathing
over the no longer fingered door
some incline to secrecy is breathing
and a silent sympathy therefor, –

and, as if pool-mirrored, it will shiver
when a breeze skims over, shadowingly;
even the crest, as by some hand a-quiver
sealed on missives all too happily,

still can speak. How little you've been scaring:
all still knows, still weeps, still causes pain. –
And, returning through the lonely-faring,
tear-damp avenue again,

279

fühlt man lang noch auf dem Rand des Dachs
jene Urnen stehen, kalt, zerspalten:
doch entschlossen, noch zusammzuhalten
um die Asche alter Achs.

DIE ENTFÜHRUNG

Oft war sie als Kind ihren Dienerinnen
entwichen, um die Nacht und den Wind
(weil sie drinnen so anders sind)
draußen zu sehn an ihrem Beginnen;

doch keine Sturmnacht hatte gewiß
den riesigen Park so in Stücke gerissen,
wie ihn jetzt ihr Gewissen zerriß,

da er sie nahm von der seidenen Leiter
und sie weitertrug, weiter, weiter...:

bis der Wagen alles war.

Und sie roch ihn, den schwarzen Wagen,
um den verhalten das Jagen stand
und die Gefahr.
Und sie fand ihn mit Kaltem ausgeschlagen;
und das Schwarze und Kalte war auch in ihr.
Sie kroch in ihren Mantelkragen
und befühlte ihr Haar, als bliebe es hier,
und hörte fremd einen Fremden sagen:
Ichbinbeidir.

long you feel upon the roof-ledge those
standing urns, cold, cloven by the weather:
yet determined still to hold together
round the ashes of old ohs.

Paris, 18 August 1907
In a letter to his wife of 23 August 1905, while staying with the Countess Luise
Schwerin at Schloss Friedelhausen, Rilke described how, as they were driving back
from one of their expeditions, 'Hassan' (presumably an early and unreliable motor-
car) 'went on strike again', and they had to remain until nightfall 'in "Grand-
father's Garden", in the old Londorf pavilion, where the lighted chandelier
shimmered with radiant festiveness out into the garden-paths, from which, as
from many sides, came the sound of fountains. These hours were very beautiful,
and full of memories which came and went without being ours.'

THE ABDUCTION

As a child she'd often eluded the care
of attendants to see the wind and the night
(because inside they are different quite)
at their very beginnings out there;

but no storm-night had so known how
to scatter the giant park before it
as her conscience tore it now,

when down from the silken ladder he caught her
in his arms and further and further brought her . . . :

till the carriage was everything.

And she smelt the black carriage, round which there lay
peril and hot pursuit
ready to spring.
And she found it covered with cold like spray;
and the blackness and coldness were in her too.
Into her hood she crept away
and felt her hair like a friend still true,
and heard estrangedly a stranger say:
I'mherewithyou.

Paris, summer 1908

ROSA HORTENSIE

WER nahm das Rosa an? Wer wußte auch,
daß es sich sammelte in diesen Dolden?
Wie Dinge unter Gold, die sich entgolden,
entröten sie sich sanft, wie im Gebrauch.

Daß sie für solches Rosa nichts verlangen.
Bleibt es für sie und lächelt aus der Luft?
Sind Engel da, es zärtlich zu empfangen,
wenn es vergeht, großmütig wie ein Duft?

Oder vielleicht auch geben sie es preis,
damit es nie erführe vom Verblühn.
Doch unter diesem Rosa hat ein Grün
gehorcht, das jetzt verwelkt und alles weiß.

DAS WAPPEN

WIE ein Spiegel, der, von ferne tragend,
lautlos in sich aufnahm, ist der Schild;
offen einstens, dann zusammenschlagend
über einem Spiegelbild

jener Wesen, die in des Geschlechts
Weiten wohnen, nicht mehr zu bestreiten,
seiner Dinge, seiner Wirklichkeiten
(rechte links und linke rechts),

die er eingesteht und sagt und zeigt.
Drauf, mit Ruhm und Dunkel ausgeschlagen,
ruht der Spangenhelm, verkürzt,

den das Flügelkleinod übersteigt,
während seine Decke, wie mit Klagen,
reich und aufgeregt herniederstürzt.

PINK HYDRANGEA

Who could suspect this pink? Who could deduce
that in these umbels here it was upbuilding?
Like golden-surfaced artefacts ungilding,
they're gradually unreddening, as in use.

That for such pink they should demand no pay!
Does it remain theirs, smiling from the air?
When, liberal as a scent, it melts away,
are tenderly receiving angels there?

Or they may hope, through their relinquishing,
it never shall experience brightness darkened.
Yet underneath this pink a green has hearkened,
which now is fading and knows everything.

Paris, autumn 1907 or Capri, spring 1908

THE COAT-OF-ARMS

Like a glass, once silently receiving
from afar, is the escutcheon;
first all open, then together-cleaving
over a reflection

of those beings none now can put to flight
dwelling in the family's distances,
of its things, of its realities
(right to left and left to right),

which it's indicatingly recounting.
Thereon, draped with fame and obscuration,
the foreshortened collar-helm impends,

with the wing-outspreading crest surmounting,
while its visor, as with lamentation,
richly and downrushingly descends.

Paris, 17 August 1907

DER JUNGGESELLE

LAMPE auf den verlassenen Papieren,
und ringsum Nacht bis weit hinein ins Holz
der Schränke. Und er konnte sich verlieren
an sein Geschlecht, das nun mit ihm zerschmolz;
ihm schien, je mehr er las, er hätte ihren,
sie aber hatten alle seinen Stolz.

Hochmütig steiften sich die leeren Stühle
die Wand entlang, und lauter Selbstgefühle
machten sich schläfernd in den Möbeln breit;
von oben goß sich Nacht auf die Pendüle,
und zitternd rann aus ihrer goldnen Mühle,
ganz fein gemahlen, seine Zeit.

Er nahm sie nicht. Um fiebernd unter jenen,
als zöge er die Laken ihrer Leiber,
andere Zeiten wegzuzerrn.
Bis er ins Flüstern kam; (was war ihm fern?)
Er lobte einen dieser Briefeschreiber,
als sei der Brief an ihn: Wie du mich kennst;
und klopfte lustig auf die Seitenlehnen.
Der Spiegel aber, innen unbegrenzter,
ließ leise einen Vorhang aus, ein Fenster –:
denn dorten stand, fast fertig, das Gespenst.

THE BACHELOR

THE family documents illuminated,
and night all round, extending far inside
the shelves. And he was consubstantiated
with his own kin, who now with him outdied.
He felt, the more he read, incorporated
in him their own, in all of them his pride.

The empty chairs upstiffened with hauteur
along the wall, and in the furniture
sheer self-esteems lolled drowsily around.
Down on the French clock gathered night was teeming,
and trembling from its golden mill was streaming
his own time, very finely ground.

He left it there. In order feverishly,
as though he tugged their shrouds from those inditers,
to grab times formerly existent.
Till he was whispering (What, for him, was distant?)
He'd praise some one of those old letter-writers,
as though addressed by him: 'What intuition!'
and beat his arm-chair arms delightedly.
Less inly-limited, the mirror, though,
let now a curtain, now a window go: –
for there stood, almost whole, the apparition.

Paris, summer 1908

DER EINSAME

NEIN: ein Turm soll sein aus meinem Herzen
und ich selbst an seinen Rand gestellt:
wo sonst nichts mehr ist, noch einmal Schmerzen
und Unsäglichkeit, noch einmal Welt.

Noch ein Ding allein im Übergroßen,
welches dunkel wird und wieder licht,
noch ein letztes, sehnendes Gesicht
in das Nie-zu-Stillende verstoßen,

noch ein äußerstes Gesicht aus Stein,
willig seinen inneren Gewichten,
das die Weiten, die es still vernichten,
zwingen, immer seliger zu sein.

DER LESER

WER kennt ihn, diesen, welcher sein Gesicht
wegsenkte aus dem Sein zu einem zweiten,
das nur das schnelle Wenden voller Seiten
manchmal gewaltsam unterbricht?

Selbst seine Mutter wäre nicht gewiß,
ob *er* es ist, der da mit seinem Schatten
Getränktes liest. Und wir, die Stunden hatten,
was wissen wir, wieviel ihm hinschwand, bis

er mühsam aufsah: alles auf sich hebend,
was unten in dem Buche sich verhielt,
mit Augen, welche, statt zu nehmen, gebend
anstießen an die fertig-volle Welt:
wie stille Kinder, die allein gespielt,
auf einmal das Vorhandene erfahren;
doch seine Züge, die geordnet waren,
blieben für immer umgestellt.

THE SOLITARY

No, my heart shall be a tower, and there,
beneath the topmost cornice, I'll remain:
still, where nothing else is, with a share
of world, ineffability, and pain.

Only, in the Incommensurable,
one lone thing, now glooming, now a-glance,
only one last, longing countenance
thrust into the never-silenceable.

One extreme stone face, with steadfastness
mirroring some inward equipoise;
urged by that which silently destroys
on to ever-greater blissfulness.

Paris, mid-August 1907

THE READER

Who knows him, he who's let his face descend
to where a new existency engages,
only the rapid turn of crowded pages
will sometimes violently suspend?

Even his mother could not feel quite sure
it's he, there reading something saturated
with his own shadow. And, clock-regulated,
can we know how much ebbed from him before

he labouringly uplooked: thereby upheaving
all the book's deepness to the light of day,
with eyes which, now outgiving, not receiving,
impinged upon a filled environment:
as quiet children, after lonely play,
will suddenly perceive the situation;
his features, though, in full co-ordination,
remained forever different.

Paris, summer 1908

DER APFELGARTEN

Komm gleich nach dem Sonnenuntergange,
sieh das Abendgrün des Rasengrunds;
ist es nicht, als hätten wir es lange
angesammelt und erspart in uns,

um es jetzt aus Fühlen und Erinnern,
neuer Hoffnung, halbvergeßnem Freun,
noch vermischt mit Dunkel aus dem Innern,
in Gedanken vor uns hinzustreun

unter Bäume wie von Dürer, die
das Gewicht von hundert Arbeitstagen
in den überfüllten Früchten tragen,
dienend, voll Geduld, versuchend, wie

das, was alle Maße übersteigt,
noch zu heben ist und hinzugeben,
wenn man willig, durch ein langes Leben
nur das Eine will und wächst und schweigt.

MOHAMMEDS BERUFUNG

Da aber als in sein Versteck der Hohe,
sofort Erkennbare: der Engel, trat,
aufrecht, der lautere und lichterlohe:
da tat er allen Anspruch ab und bat

bleiben zu dürfen der von seinen Reisen
innen verwirrte Kaufmann, der er war;
er hatte nie gelesen – und nun gar
ein *solches* Wort, zu viel für einen Weisen.

Der Engel aber, herrisch, wies und wies
ihm, was geschrieben stand auf seinem Blatte,
und gab nicht nach und wollte wieder: *Lies.*

Da las er: so, daß sich der Engel bog.
Und war schon einer, der gelesen *hatte*
und konnte und gehorchte und vollzog.

THE APPLE ORCHARD

COME just after sunset and inspect it,
evening greenness of the new-mown sward:
is it not like something long-collected
by ourselves and inwardly upstored,

that we now, from feeling and reviewing,
new hope, jubilation half-forgot,
mixed with inner darkness still, are strewing
out in thoughts before us on this spot,

under trees like Dürer's, that to-day
bear the weight of work-days uncomputed
in their ripe abundancy enfruited,
serving, patient, finding out the way

that which overtops all measure so
yet may be ingathered and outgiven,
when a long life willingly has striven
to will only that and quietly grow.

Paris, 2 August 1907
See note on *In a foreign Park*, p. 105.

THE CALLING OF MOHAMMED

WHEN, though, into his hiding-place the towering,
the not to be mistaken angel came,
erect, illustrious, and overpowering:
he then implored, renouncing every claim,

permission to remain that over-journeyed,
distracted merchant he was really;
he'd never been a reader – and to see
a word like that, too much for the most learned.

The angel, though, imperious, paid no heed,
but showed and kept on showing to the pleader
the writing on his scroll and willed him: *Read.*

He then so read, the angel's self saluted.
And was already one who'd *been* a reader
and could and lent his ear and executed.

Paris, 22 August - 5 September 1907

DER BERG

Sechsunddreissig Mal und hundert Mal
hat der Maler jenen Berg geschrieben,
weggerissen, wieder hingetrieben
(sechsunddreißig Mal und hundert Mal)

zu dem unbegreiflichen Vulkane,
selig, voll Versuchung, ohne Rat, –
während der mit Umriß Angetane
seiner Herrlichkeit nicht Einhalt tat:

tausendmal aus allen Tagen tauchend,
Nächte ohne gleichen von sich ab
fallen lassend, alle wie zu knapp;
jedes Bild im Augenblick verbrauchend,
von Gestalt gesteigert zu Gestalt,
teilnahmslos und weit und ohne Meinung –,
um auf einmal wissend, wie Erscheinung,
sich zu heben hinter jedem Spalt.

DER BALL

Du Runder, der das Warme aus zwei Händen
im Fliegen, oben, fortgiebt, sorglos wie
sein Eigenes; was in den Gegenständen
nicht bleiben kann, zu unbeschwert für sie,

zu wenig Ding und doch noch Ding genug,
um nicht aus allem draußen Aufgereihten
unsichtbar plötzlich in uns einzugleiten:
das glitt in dich, du zwischen Fall und Flug

noch Unentschlossener: der, wenn er steigt,
als hätte er ihn mit hinaufgehoben,
den Wurf entführt und freiläßt –, und sich neigt
und einhält und den Spielenden von oben
auf einmal eine neue Stelle zeigt,
sie ordnend wie zu einer Tanzfigur,

THE MOUNTAIN

Six-and-thirty and a hundred times
did the painter write the mountain peak,
sundered from it, driven back to seek
(six-and-thirty and a hundred times)

that incomprehensible volcano,
happy, full of trial, expedientless, –
while, forever outlined, it would lay no
bridle on its surging gloriousness:

daily in a thousand ways uprearing,
letting each incomparable night
fall away, as being all too tight;
wearing out at once each new appearing,
every shape assumed the shiningmost,
far, opinionless, unsympathising, –
to be suddenly materialising
there behind each crevice like a ghost.

Paris, 31 July 1907 (except for the first two lines, which had been drafted in July 1906)
Hokusai and his numerous paintings ('writings') of the volcano Fujiyama.

THE BALL

You roundness, letting, with no more attention
than were it yours, warmth from two hands outspread
in flight there; what in objects lacks retention,
as being for them all-too unballasted,

too little thing, though thing enough all right
not to be suddenly, without our seeing,
gliding into us from all outer being, –
that glided into you, for fall or flight

still undecider: who, when you're ascending,
as though uplifted with you through the air,
abduct and liberate the throw, – and, bending,
will pause and to the players from up there
point out a new place, as if superintending
the figure of a dance they have to do,

um dann, erwartet und erwünscht von allen,
rasch, einfach, kunstlos, ganz Natur,
dem Becher hoher Hände zuzufallen.

DAS KIND

UNWILLKÜRLICH sehn sie seinem Spiel
lange zu: zuweilen tritt das runde
seiende Gesicht aus dem Profil,
klar und ganz wie eine volle Stunde,

welche anhebt und zu Ende schlägt.
Doch die Andern zählen nicht die Schläge,
trüb von Mühsal und vom Leben träge;
und sie merken gar nicht, wie es trägt –,

wie es alles trägt, auch dann, noch immer,
wenn es müde in dem kleinen Kleid
neben ihnen wie im Wartezimmer
sitzt und warten will auf seine Zeit.

DER HUND

DA oben wird das Bild von einer Welt
aus Blicken immerfort erneut und gilt.
Nur manchmal, heimlich, kommt ein Ding und stellt
sich neben ihn, wenn er durch dieses Bild

sich drängt, ganz unten, anders, wie er ist;
nicht ausgestoßen und nicht eingereiht,
und wie im Zweifel seine Wirklichkeit
weggebend an das Bild, das er vergißt,

um dennoch immer wieder sein Gesicht
hineinzuhalten, fast mit einem Flehen,
beinah begreifend, nah am Einverstehen
und doch verzichtend: denn er wäre nicht.

and lastly, waited for and wished by all,
swift, simple, artless, Nature through and through,
into the goblet of high hands will fall.

Paris, 31 July 1907
The first poem written for the Second Part of *New Poems*. Elisabeth von Schmidt-
Pauli (*R. M. Rilke, ein Gedenkbuch*, Bâle, 1940, p. 20) reports that Rilke said of it:
'There I have expressed nothing but the near-inexpressibleness of a pure movement.'

THE CHILD

LONG they watch it playing in its place,
half-aware; at moments it's emerging
from its profile, that round, real face,
clear and whole as some full hour upsurging

into sound and striking to an end.
They, though, fail to count the strokes it's giving,
dulled with toil and indolent with living;
yet it's bearing, could they comprehend,

even now, with effort never-ending,
all things, while, as in some wearisome
waiting-room, it sits by them, intending
just to wait until its time has come.

Paris, 31 July - 1 August 1907

THE DOG

UP there's the image of a world which glances
are always re-establishing as true.
At times, though, secretly, a thing advances
and stands beside him when he's squeezing through

that image, he so different, down below;
neither excluded nor incorporate,
and squandering, as in doubt, his true estate
upon that image he forgets, although

he still keeps pushing so persistently
his face into it, almost with beseeching,
so close to comprehension, nearly reaching,
and yet renouncing: for he wouldn't *be*.

Paris, draft of lines 1-5 end of June, completed 31 July 1907

DER KÄFERSTEIN

SIND nicht Sterne fast in deiner Nähe,
und was giebt es, das du nicht umspannst,
da du dieser harten Skarabäe
Karneolkern gar nicht fassen kannst

ohne jenen Raum, der ihre Schilder
niederhält, auf deinem ganzen Blut
mitzutragen; niemals war er milder,
näher, hingegebener. Er ruht

seit Jahrtausenden auf diesen Käfern,
wo ihn keiner braucht und unterbricht;
und die Käfer schließen sich und schläfern
unter seinem wiegenden Gewicht.

BUDDHA IN DER GLORIE

MITTE aller Mitten, Kern der Kerne,
Mandel, die sich einschließt und versüßt, –
dieses Alles bis an alle Sterne
ist dein Fruchtfleisch: Sei gegrüßt.

Sieh, du fühlst, wie nichts mehr an dir hängt;
im Unendlichen ist deine Schale,
und dort steht der starke Saft und drängt.
Und von außen hilft ihm ein Gestrahle,

denn ganz oben werden deine Sonnen
voll und glühend umgedreht.
Doch in dir ist schon begonnen,
was die Sonnen übersteht.

THE BEETLE-STONE

ARE not stars almost within your grasping,
and what is there that you can't inspan,
when you can't be even just enclasping
these hard scarabees' cornelian

without bearing on your whole pulsating
blood the space that keeps their wing-shields closed?
Never was it more alleviating,
nearer, more self-given. It's reposed

on them there for aeons none can number,
space which no requirers violate;
and the beetles fold themselves and slumber
underneath its lullabying weight.

Paris, early summer 1908

'Beetle-stone' (a Rilkean coinage) = scarab or scarabee, 'a gem (of cornelian
emerald, obsidian, etc.) cut in the form of a beetle (*scarabæus*), having on the flat
underside a design in intaglio' (*O.E.D.*). The ancient Egyptians believed that
the scarabaeus, or dung-beetle, existed only in the male sex and reproduced itself
by rolling balls of ox-dung, from which, after they had been buried for twenty-
eight days and then thrown into water, new beetles emerged. It represented the
god Cheperà, father of the gods and creator of all things, and was called by his
name. Scarabs were placed upon the bodies of the dead, as symbols of reanimation,
and worn by the living as amulets and ornaments.

BUDDHA IN GLORY

CORES' core, centre of all circulations,
almond self-enclosed and sweetening,
all from here to all the constellations
is your fruit-pulp: you I sing.

How released you feel from all belonging!
In the Infinite expands your rind,
and within it your strong juice is thronging;
and a radiance from without is kind,

for those many suns of yours are spinning
full and glowingly on high.
What in you, though, 's had beginning
suns shall be outlasted by.

Paris, summer 1908

INDEX

TITLES AND FIRST LINES · GERMAN

INDEX

302